P9-DME-589

Social Relationships and Peer Support

Teachers' Guides to Inclusive Practices

Social Relationships and Peer Support

by

Martha E. Snell, Ph.D.
University of Virginia
Charlottesville

and

Rachel Janney, Ph.D.
Radford University
Radford, Virginia

with contributions from
Laura K. Vogtle, Ph.D.
Kenna M. Colley, Ed.D.
Monica Delano, M.Ed.

·P·A·U·L·H·
BROOKES
PUBLISHING CO.®

Baltimore • London • Sydney

Paul H. Brookes Publishing Co.
Post Office Box 10624
Baltimore, Maryland 21285-0624

www.brookespublishing.com

Copyright © 2000 by Paul H. Brookes Publishing Co., Inc.
All rights reserved.
"Paul H. Brookes Publishing Co." is a registered trademark of Paul H. Brookes Publishing Co., Inc.

Typeset by Barton Matheson Willse and Worthington, Baltimore, Maryland.
Manufactured in the United States of America by Versa Press, East Peoria, Illinois.

Second printing, September, 2002.

All of the vignettes in this book are composites of the authors' actual experiences. In all instances, names have been changed; in some instances, identifying details have been altered to protect confidentiality.

Purchasers of **Social Relationships and Peer Support** are granted permission to photocopy the blank forms in Appendix A for distribution for educational purposes. Although photocopying for educational purposes is unlimited, none of the forms may be reproduced to generate revenue for any program or individual. Photocopies must be made from an original book.

Permission is gratefully acknowledged to use the graphics/images appearing in this publication courtesy of ClickArt® Incredible Image Pak, © 1999 Mattel, Inc. and its licensors. All rights reserved. Used by Permission. ClickArt and Broderbund are registered trademarks of Mattel, Inc.

Library of Congress Cataloging-in-Publication Data

Snell, Martha E.
   Social relationships and peer support / by Martha E. Snell and Rachel Janney with contributions from Kenna M. Colley . . . [et al.]
      p.   cm.—(Teachers' guides to inclusive practices)
   Includes bibliographical references and index.
   ISBN 1-55766-356-4
   1. Socially handicapped children—Education—United States.   2. Social skills—Study and teaching—United States.   3. Inclusive education—United States.   I. Janney, Rachel. II. Title. III. Series.
LC4069.S54   2000
371.826'94—dc21
                                                      99-046188
                                                       CIP

British Library Cataloguing in Publication data are available from the British Library.

Contents

About the Authors

Martha E. Snell, Ph.D., is a professor in the Curry School of Education at the University of Virginia where she has taught since 1973. Her focus is special education and, specifically, the preparation of teachers of students with mental retardation and severe disabilities and young children with disabilities. Prior to completing her doctoral degree in special education at Michigan State University, she worked with children and adults with disabilities as a residential child care worker, a teacher, and a provider of technical assistance to school and residential programs. In addition to teaching coursework at the undergraduate and graduate levels, she currently coordinates the special education program, supervises teachers in training, provides in-service training to teachers and parents in schools and agencies, conducts research, serves on the boards of several community agencies serving people with disabilities, and is an active member of the American Association on Mental Retardation and TASH (formerly The Association for Persons with Severe Handicaps).

Rachel Janney, Ph.D., has worked with children and adults with disabilities in a number of capacities, including special education teacher, camp counselor, educational consultant, and researcher. She received her master's degree from Syracuse University and her doctorate from the University of Nebraska–Lincoln. Dr. Janney now teaches courses in special education, supervises student teachers, and coordinates the undergraduate program in special education at Radford University. She also serves as Co-director of the Training and Technical Assistance Center (T/TAC) for Professionals Serving Individuals with Disabilities at Radford University. The T/TAC, part of a statewide technical assistance network that is funded by the Virginia Department of Education, provides a variety of services and resources to special education teams in school divisions throughout southwest Virginia.

Dr. Snell and coauthor Dr. Janney have conducted several research projects in inclusive schools and classrooms. The focus of these projects has been on the ways that special and general education teachers work together to design and implement adaptations and accommodations for students with disabilities placed in inclusive settings. Both authors are frequent presenters of workshops on topics related to successful inclusive education.

Laura K. Vogtle, Ph.D., is an associate professor in the Department of Rehabilitation Sciences at the University of Alabama in Birmingham. Much of her professional experience is as an occupational therapist; her current focus is on educational research. She has a specific research interest in relationships that develop between children with and without disabilities.

Kenna M. Colley, Ed.D., previously an elementary school inclusion specialist, is now the lead coordinator for the T/TAC at Radford University in Radford, Virginia. Her current role involves facilitating local school systems' improvement efforts, including enhancing their use of inclusive education practices.

Monica Delano, M.Ed., is currently a doctoral student in special education in the Curry School of Education at the University of Virginia. For years, Monica has taught students of many disability categories and ages in a variety of settings and has worked toward promoting their inclusion.

Acknowledgments

Many colleagues, friends, families, and students merit recognition and deserve thanks for their contributions to our knowledge about social relationships and peer support. Some of these individuals whose work we have learned from and built on include Cap Peck, Catherine Breen, Tom Farmer, Marsha Forest, Michael F. Giangreco, Charles Greenwood, Tom Haring, Pam Hunt, Deborah Kamps, Luanna Meyer, Sam Odom, Bob Perske, Chris Salisbury, Bobbi Schnorr, Debbie Staub, and Hill Walker.

We would also like to acknowledge our editors at Brookes Publishing: Scott Beeler, who helped get the "booklet concept" off the ground, and Lisa Benson and Kristine Dorman for their excellent editing and persistence in completing this series of booklets.

To all the educators, parents, and students who are working to create and maintain inclusive school environments: places where all students have membership, enjoy social relationships with peers, and have the needed supports to learn what is important for them to be successful in life

Social Relationships
and Peer Support

Chapter 1

Building Social Relationships

This booklet has an ambitious goal: *to describe proven, practical ideas for individualizing support to students who have social limitations with their peers.* It is intended for teachers and other individuals who work in schools with students whose social relationships are lacking, nonsupportive, or troublesome. Chapters 1 and 2 lay the foundation for understanding children's social interactions and connections with their peers. Chapters 3 through 5 discuss strategies to make school environments conducive to the development of social relationships as well as strategies to assess, plan for, and teach skills that bolster positive ties among peers, particularly with students who have disabilities. Chapter 6 provides guidelines for initiating programs that encourage positive social relationships in schools and classrooms. Some students who do not have disabilities also will benefit from facilitation of social relationships. This may include teaching social skills or supporting students' membership in a classroom and among peer groups. Thus, the strategies presented in this booklet can be used to benefit students with disabilities as well as particular students without disabilities.

WHAT ARE SOCIAL RELATIONSHIPS?

Enormous variations exist in the types and intensities of social relationships that develop among people. Social relationships can be lasting or temporary, loving or hateful, mentoring or modeling, intimate or superficial, balanced or uneven; there are many ways to describe how social relationships vary. One prominent dimension along which positive social relationships can vary is the degree of closeness and intensity of caring that is maintained in the relationship. Friends, due to their close bonds and mutual alliance, are situated at one end of a closeness continuum; peer group members are located in the middle range; and acquaintances fall at the opposite end of the continuum. This book focuses on strengthening social relationships among children and adolescents, with a particular

focus on those individuals who lack close, positive peer associations.

Friendship has been defined in many ways, most likely because of its importance in our lives. A frequently cited characteristic of a "friend" is *someone who is socially important to and particularly liked by a person* (Figure 1.1). Friendships develop when several ongoing conditions or processes are present:

1. Opportunities to be together

2. Desire to interact with another person

3. Basic social interaction and communication abilities

4. Organizational, emotional, and social supports to help maintain the relationship as it develops

Friendships that are not entirely mutual or reciprocal may still be supportive and valued by one or both of the individuals; however, *social reciprocity,* or the balanced exchange of interactions between two people, is a characteristic of close relationships and differentiates mutual relationships from "helping" relationships, in which one person mainly serves as teacher, helper, or assistant to the other person (Haring, 1992; Odom, McConnell, & McEvoy, 1992).

Social networks refer to a student's reliable patterns of interaction and friendship with others as well as to the individuals that a person identifies as being socially important (e.g., kids I like to play with, those who are my friends, kids I would invite to a party).

Social support behaviors are behaviors in which a person engages to aid another person, either socially or emotionally. Social support can occur among friends, social network members, and acquaintances. Within friendships, social support is two-way and often reciprocal; however, support also can be one-way, as in a helping or teaching relationship.

Social support seems to vary both in its form (what it looks like) and its function (its purpose), depending on the supported person's age, gender, and cultural group. For example, older female friends lend emotional

Friend:	Someone socially important to an individual; someone whom a person particularly likes (Fryxell & Kennedy, 1995)
Social interaction skills:	Includes an array of interpersonal behaviors such as greeting others, approaching an individual or a group, listening to others, commenting/acting on others' requests or remarks, initiating an exchange, asking others to respond to or engage in an activity, entering into an ongoing social dyad or group, taking turns, taking actions intended to maintain an exchange or social activity, and terminating an interaction
Social competence:	Encompasses both an individual's effectiveness in influencing the behavior of a peer and the appropriateness of the behavior (given the setting, culture, and context) (Odom, McConnell, & McEvoy, 1992, p. 7)
Social networks:	The individuals identified as being socially important to a person; the patterns of interaction, acquaintance, and friendship an individual has with others, usually peers (e.g., Who do you like to play with? Who are your friends? Who would you invite to a party?)
Social reciprocity:	The interdependent exchange of interactions between two individuals that reflects balanced turn-taking.
Development of friendships:	A growth process that leads to close human relationships between two individuals and reflects several ongoing processes such as creating opportunities for interaction; learning social skills that facilitate interactions; and generating organizational, emotional, and social supports to maintain relationships. The outcome of development is a relationship between two individuals that is characterized by social reciprocity or the mutual exchange of interactions (Haring, 1992, p. 314; Odom et al., 1992, p. 8)
Peer support:	Actions taken by individuals of the same age that involve lending emotional and social sustenance or assistance to each other in a reciprocal unidirectional manner. The form of these supports may vary according to the age, gender, and cultural group of the individuals involved and also according to the manner in which the individuals communicate. The function of the support may also vary in that it can be directed toward physical care, entertainment, learning or tutoring, emotional comfort, and so forth.

Figure 1.1.   A glossary of terms.

support to each other in ways that appear different from the support that teen-age boys give to each other, but the function of giving consolation is the same. Fryxell and Kennedy (1995) identified, by their function, five peer support behaviors that were used by 6- to 12-year-olds and that were relevant both to children with severe disabilities and to their peers without disabilities:

1. Providing information about daily events

2. Lending emotional support (consoling another during a crisis or sharing during a happy event)

3. Giving access to others (introductions to new people)

4. Giving material assistance (physical help, lending needed items)

5. Assisting with daily choices (making decisions)

For most of us, social relationships give life meaning. Relationships are usually a motivating force of children's school attendance; adults' relationships at work usually make the week more interesting, if not actually pleasant. Relationships provide opportunities to give support to others, both socially and emotionally, and to receive support in return. Our ability to build and keep relationships goes hand in hand with our social skills. We call on these skills repeatedly throughout a given day; when we forget to do so, disharmony and conflict with others can result. Over the long term, our relationships have a strong impact on our general outlook on life and on our self-concept.

VALUING SOCIAL SKILLS AS AN EDUCATIONAL DOMAIN

Social skills and peer support are not tested by state assessments, and their impact on student learning is not measured on typical achievement tests. Most school curricula do not place the achievement of stable, positive social networks on par with reading, math, and geography; yet, we know that young adults who are lacking in social skills and who have minimal social supports are far more at risk for job loss than are those lacking in basic academic and production skills (Chadsey-Rusch, 1992). Many professionals view childhood social status as being a reliable predictor of mental health in adolescence and adulthood (Parker & Asher, 1987). *Children who exhibit poor relationships with their peers during childhood are at risk for an array of social adjustment problems later in life.*

These theories about social relationships are even stronger with regard to students with disabilities. Literature on social relationships suggests that students with disabilities encounter a number of social difficulties:

- The social opportunities of students with disabilities are often more limited than those of their typical peers (Farmer, Pearl, & Van Acker, 1996).

- Students who participate in general education classes and are currently eligible (or likely candidates) for special education, but who are not yet receiving special education services, are perceived negatively by their typical peers (Sale & Carey, 1995).

- Eight- to thirteen-year-old boys with mental retardation requiring intermittent support experience significantly more loneliness than their peers without mental retardation (Williams & Asher, 1992).

- Students with disabilities often are vulnerable to social networks that support or maintain their problematic social behaviors (Farmer, Pearl, & Van Acker, 1996).

It is important for those who work in schools to examine their beliefs regarding teaching social skills and supporting social relationships among students; if these skills are not valued in a school, it is doubtful that improvements can be made beyond each individual classroom. Strong justifications exist for including the development of social skills and relationships in the school curriculum; some of these justifications are listed in Figure 1.2. Schools have taken an important first step in the process of making a difference when they recognize the value of positive social relationships among students.

Why are social relationships important for *all* students?

1. Social relationships add substantial quality to our lives.
2. Social interaction skills are needed in many daily routines.
3. Social relationships are often a prime motivation for attending school, holding jobs, and making positive contributions in life.
4. A positive relationship exists between social competence and an absence of problem behavior.
5. The presence of relationships between people with disabilities and those without disabilities in a given community can serve as an indicator that disability is more an attitude than a defining human characteristic.

Figure 1.2.   Rationale for social skills and relationships. (Source: Haring, 1991.)

UNDERSTANDING DIFFERENCES IN SOCIAL RELATIONSHIPS

The nature of social relationships changes as individuals mature. Research on children's expectations of friendships states that younger children report that "a friend is someone you play with"; older children more often mention qualities such as loyalty, trust, and intimacy (Williams & Asher, 1992). Adolescent boys often interact in large groups, whereas girls spend more time in dyads. Consequently, having one good friend may prevent feelings of loneliness in girls but not in boys. The group membership of one's friends can further complicate relationships, especially for children with disabilities who are part of a special education classroom. If, for example, a boy wants to participate in a large-group activity, such as basketball, but is not accepted into the group, his friend from the special education class may be inadequate to buffer the boy from feelings of loneliness (Walker, Colvin, & Ramsey, 1995). Some of the difficulties that inhibit successful social exchanges and gatherings between students with disabilities and their typical peers are not unique to individuals with disabilities. There is, however, ample evidence to indicate that these behavior difficulties are more prevalent among children with disabilities, particularly when there is no focus on social skills intervention and when achievement in school has been poor. The major categories of behavior difficulties include the following:

1. Aggression (both physical and verbal)

2. Withdrawal from or avoidance of interactions with others during structured times (class) and unstructured times (recess)

3. Nonresponsiveness to peers or inappropriate responses to peers

4. Interactions with peers that are of poor quality or immature

5. A failure to generalize or transfer social skills across situations and people (Brady & McEvoy, 1989, pp. 214–215)

The range of possibilities for support is broad when teachers match feasible social support plans to specific students of different ages, cultures, gender, and abilities. A social support plan is an individualized set of goals and strategies that will involve peers in the promotion of a student's membership and social acceptance; the plan may include instruction in social skills and communication as well as modification of classroom practices. Some support approaches apply to rather narrow groups of students with disabilities; therefore, their widespread application is inappropriate. The process of designing support plans for individual students must be collaborative and should involve the focus student, peers, family members, educators, and other school staff. The collaborative teaming process to design social support plans for individual students should be guided by the following core principle: *The individual student (and often the family) should be given opportunities to select, to shape, and to reject social supports and to determine the kinds of supports and the location and manner in which those supports are given.*

ESTABLISHING THE CONDITIONS FOR SOCIAL RELATIONSHIPS

Because the traditional business of schools is to teach academics, not to build social relationships, many barriers to social interaction may exist within schools. These barriers can be traced to different sources: school buildings and grounds; school buses and transportation policies; teachers, staff, and administrators; schedules and student groupings; and the students themselves (Figure 1.3). These barriers can hinder teachers from creating conditions that are favorable to social relationships.

There are six major factors that influence students' social participation: 1) opportunities, 2) atmosphere, 3) social support and motivation, 4) social competence and interaction skills, 5) academic achievement, and 6) maintenance generalization of relationships (Breen, Haring, Weiner, Laitinen, & Berstein, 1991).

Physical and contextual barriers to social interaction: Building, scheduling, and staff issues that prevent opportunities for interacting with peers	Student barriers to social interactions: Student characteristics that get in the way of learning social skills or attaining social acceptance

• Students with disabilities are separated from peers (e.g., bus, classroom, daily schedule)
• Few opportunities exist for social interactions
• Architectural barriers are present (e.g., building, grounds, transportation)
• Adults encourage helping or teaching interactions rather than social interactions
• Inappropriate contexts and activities exist:
    Socially unacceptable (culture, age, or group standards)
    Stigmatizing
    Not amusing or interesting
    Nonreciprocal
• Adults interfere with interaction:
    Hovering
    Interrupting interactions
    Suggesting activities that are not "cool"
• Staff fear or misunderstand disabilities
• Staff do not value interactions between students with and without disabilities
• Staff models for positive interactions with students who have disabilities are lacking
• The school atmosphere is competitive or uncooperative; most students with disabilities never "make the grade"
	Students who are isolated socially may exhibit:
	• Antisocial behaviors: Aggression, withdrawal, nonresponsiveness
	• Age-inappropriate interests and behavior
	• Grooming problems
	• Communication difficulties
	• Challenging learning characteristics:
	    Few learned skills
	    Poor retention of learned skills
	    Poor generalization of skills
	Students who are not socially isolated may exhibit:
	• Negative attitudes (e.g., pity, fear, aversion) toward human differences in ability, culture, and beliefs
	• Inexperience with others who have disabilities or differences
	• An inability to model positive interactions with students who have disabilities

Figure 1.3.   Barriers to social relationships.

Teachers should determine whether their schools, classrooms, and individual students have shortcomings in any of these six areas. In order to build supportive social relationships between students with disabilities and their peers, teachers need to work collaboratively among themselves and with others (i.e., administrators, other school staff, students) and set goals and take actions regarding one or more of these six influencing factors.

Opportunity

Often, interactions between students with disabilities and their peers are limited by using separate classrooms, frequent "pull-out" sessions for special services, special education "wings," short lunch periods, separate buses, different arrival and departure times and bus locations, cafeteria seating arranged by classroom, and rules to reduce talking in the halls or classrooms. Some of these practices are a result of special education's being "a location that one goes to" rather than "a portable set of supports." The other practices are meant to diminish peer interaction in general; these practices are based on the philosophy that schools are for learning and that socializing "gets in the way." History, however, has taught us that if students with and without disabilities do not spend time together during their school years, they will not develop meaningful relationships. Some administrative actions, such as the elimination of separate bus schedules for students with disabilities, the use of lift-equipped buses for all students, and the replacement of pull-out special education with classroom-based support, abolish the isolation that many children with disabilities experience during their school years.

As students are brought together and opportunities for social interaction increase, other factors that influence a student's social development become more visible and may require attention. Teachers may discover a need to

- Facilitate social skills development

- Provide motivating and age-appropriate activities

- Plan individualized support for students

- Eliminate staff and student prejudices and ignorance about disabilities

Atmosphere

We all have been in schools that feel welcoming, that take pride in having a diverse student body, and that value all students as part of their community. Positive school atmospheres often are a product of the leadership of certain teachers and school administrators; however, sometimes individual students with disabilities are largely responsible for transforming attitudes (Giangreco, Dennis, Cloninger, Edelman, & Schattman, 1993). A number of specific staff and student characteristics contribute to an atmosphere in which disabilities and other human differences (e.g., racial, ethnic, cultural, ability) are less visible. These characteristics are interrelated and include one's personal attitudes toward human differences, one's prejudices, and one's knowledge of and experience with people and cultures different from one's own.

Student Snapshot

Daniel is a second grader who has multiple disabilities: He has cerebral palsy and a visual impairment, as well as a seizure disorder. Daniel uses a wheelchair and needs to be fed and dressed. To communicate with others, Daniel is learning to use a communication device that speaks for him. When Daniel first attended the preschool special education program at age 3, several staff members who did not work with Daniel wondered why he was in school. Older pupils attending the school stared at Daniel while he was being fed in the lunchroom and even imitated the way food dribbled from his mouth. Now, in a school that values diversity and practices inclusion, Daniel is an appreciated member of Ms. Kilmer's second-grade class. Students in Daniel's school have learned to look beyond Daniel's differences and instead focus on his similarities to them.

Social Support and Motivation

Although proximity and attitude strongly promote the development of peer relationships, they may not be sufficient to create supportive relationships between students with disabilities and their typical classmates or even to lead to successful, positive interactions. It may be appropriate to organize social support groups or friendship pairs to encourage the focus student's typical classmates to involve themselves as models, social partners, and problem solvers in the focus student's school routines. Adults should initiate these support groups until the focus student's peers take over and the focus student becomes comfortable with them.

The *motivational* factor concerns all of the reasons why students seek to interact socially or to avoid interaction. These motivational factors affect not only students who exhibit interaction difficulties but also students without disabilities who may be skilled at social interaction. Usually, within groups of peers who know one another, no coaxing is needed to initiate social interaction. Sometimes, however, adults discourage social interaction simply by being insensitive to peer preferences. For example, *depending on the age of the students,* if one or more of the following circumstances is added to a social situation, the motivation for interaction may be reduced or threatened:

- Students do not know one another.
- Students are of different ages.
- Students are of different genders.
- Students have few common interests.
- One or more of the students cannot be understood or cannot understand others.
- Students are fearful of an individual in the group.
- Students are not given a choice about whether they want to be in the group.

When students lack experience with interacting with their peers, they and their peers have little motivation for socializing. Their interaction rates are low, their initiations and responses to peers are inconsistent, and their social skills, in general, are deficient. The motivation factor includes strategies that teachers can use to teach and encourage positive social interactions among peers when one or more peers in the group exhibit social difficulties.

Academic Achievement

Poor academic achievement can contribute to a student's lack of social relationships. Although these students may be fairly skilled socially, they may lack the confidence that arises from having and using skills in academic areas such as reading, writing, math, science, and social studies. More often, however, antisocial behavior contributes to the student's lack of friends and companions and to the student's poor academic record.

Rick is a ninth grader who attends general education classes and also receives individualized support from special education staff in a resource room. Although he is highly articulate, Rick has been diagnosed with obsessive-compulsive disorder and Tourette syndrome; he requires extensive behavioral support throughout the day, and his social skills are immature. When Rick's academic engagement is low (e.g., when he is upset, needs to leave class, worries about mistakes), his learning is poor.

Frustration that arises from a student's inability to meet academic demands can spiral quickly into out-of-control behavior. "Very strong links exist between antisocial behavior patterns and school academic failure" (Walker, Colvin, & Ramsey, 1995, p. 63). Underachieving students' reactions to failure in school can change their existing reputation with peers and threaten their social relationships. In schools where the atmosphere is highly competitive and there are few nonacademic outlets for achievement (e.g., chorus, band, art, volunteering groups, auto or shop clubs, theater, computer clubs), only the top percentage of students will feel successful. In schools such as these, conditions fostering the development of antisocial behavior exist for a large number of students (Walker, Colvin, & Ramsey, 1995).

Because academic achievement can have a positive influence on a student's self-concept, his or her acceptance by others, and his or her success in forming social relationships, individualized educational supports may be one component of a program that is designed to build social relationships. Individualized academic support may require skill assessment, focused and effective instruction, modifications in schoolwork, and the identification and use of specific accommodations for some students. Some students need a combination of individualized academic instruction and social skills training.

Social Competence
and Interaction Skills

Many researchers who have studied peer support methods have found that the incidental modeling and teaching of social skills during school routines such as lunch, between-class breaks, and in-class cooperative groups is effective enough for students with disabilities to better their social interaction skills. For some students, however, these naturalistic opportunities may be inadequate; these students may require more structured development of their social skills. The social skills that a student needs can vary widely and are related in part to the student's cognitive ability, the amount and type of the student's communication, and the student's disability. Some students need instruction in the basics: initiating interactions with peers, responding to peers' initiations, and elaborating on the initiations or responses of peers in an appropriate manner. For other students, teams need to address reliable communication methods that the student can use with his or her peers at typical rates. Some students need to learn methods to control their anger, to monitor interfering behavior, and to self-prompt an alternate and appropriate way to react to peers.

For Rick, the ninth grader with a history of acting-out behavior, the transitions between classes and activities are particularly challenging, and Rick often reacts with confusion, anger, and aggression. At times, Rick makes comments about his own and others' biological functions, which often make peers laugh but decrease their regard for him. Both of these difficulties in social competence have motivated his team to develop teaching plans to build appropriate skills.

Age-appropriate social skills are essential to an individual's social acceptance; however, whether these skills are acquired naturalistically, through intentional, structured teaching by adults and/or peers, or through some combination of these means varies from student to student.

Maintenance and Generalization

Some children have trouble keeping and extending their social relationships; other students, especially those with cognitive disabilities, may find it hard to remember and to carry their known social skills across different people and environments. For many students, teachers need to be alert to the frequently

documented learning difficulties of skill maintenance and generalization.

Rick, who has learned to control his angry outbursts at school through a combination of self-management methods, is still verbally aggressive on the bus and at home; consequently, Rick's teachers are working with the bus driver and with Rick's family members to adjust the methods that work for Rick at school so that they are successful on the bus and at home.

Although instruction often focuses on the initial development of a socially relevant skill, it is sometimes necessary to plan ways to teach the student to use the skill in varied situations.

BUILDING SOCIAL RELATIONSHIPS

Several steps are involved in building the social relationships of students. These steps include setting goals, collaborative teaming, and, finally, developing strategies to enhance students' social relationships.

Setting Goals

When a student with disabilities is included in a general education classroom after being a member of a self-contained classroom or a resource room, both the student and his or her general education classmates experience an abrupt change. Students who have been included without adequate support experience various challenges to improving their social relationships. These students may have social skills to learn and negative reputations with their classmates to overcome and their teachers may need to modify classwork so that these students can learn and to conquer their own lowered expectations for these students' academic achievement and behavior.

How do teachers assess a student's social relationships to determine whether supports are necessary, and, if so, what form these supports should take? A variety of approaches can help the team determine this need:

- Informal conversations with those who know the focus student, including the student's peers (Figure 1.4)

- Observations gathered by team members of a particular student

- Use of various rating scales and checklists to judge the adequacy of inclusion efforts and to pinpoint any difficulties that a student may be experiencing with social relationships

For example, Meyer, Minondo, and their colleagues (1998) found that the answers to six key questions about a particular student's relationships in school could be used both to target needed improvements and to informally evaluate outcomes. These questions address the ways in which staff, classmates, and the focus student behave (a rating scale based on these questions is included in Figure 1.5):

1. *Ghost/Guest:* Does the focus child frequently get "passed over" as if he or she were not there (ghost)? Do staff members talk about another placement as soon as there is a problem (guest)?

2. *Inclusion child:* Does the teacher say, "I have 27 students plus 2 included students"?

3. *I'll help:* Do classmates use the words "work with" or "help" whenever they refer to times spent with the focus child?

4. *Just another child:* Is the child expected to participate in class activities along with everyone else?

5. *Regular friend:* Has the child ever been invited to a party by a classmate?

6. *Best friend:* Does the focus child have one or more friends who call him or her on the telephone at home and/or who visit him or her after school or on weekends? (Meyer et al., 1998, p. 216)

The last chapter of this book discusses a rating scale for individual students designed around the six previously discussed factors that influence social relationships at school: opportunities, atmosphere, social support and motivation, social competence and interaction skills, academic achievement, and maintenance and generalization of relationships. Other checklists that focus on the adequacy of inclusion can be used by team members to target ways that inclusion efforts can be im-

---

What the Research Says

Several researchers asked more than 1,000 middle school and high school students from three states about their friendships with students who have extensive disabilities. The majority of students interviewed agreed on the following:

- These friendships were not only possible but also yielded benefits for both the student with disabilities and themselves.

- Adolescents should try to make friends with peers who have disabilities.

- Relationships were more likely to develop if students with disabilities were placed in general classes for part or all of the day; they thought that placements in special classes in a general school were less facilitative, but that placements in special classes in a special school were least likely to facilitate such friendships.

- The most effective strategies teachers and schools might use to facilitate friendships are, in order of importance: (1) Use teaching approaches that allow students to work together, (2) present information on disabilities to students, teachers, and parents, (3) arrange social activities for all students, (4) teach students without disabilities to be tutors, and (5) organize a "circle of friends" around the student.

- The primary responsibility for facilitating such friendships should be on the students themselves; however, the students also listed others who should promote these relationships, including special education teachers; youth clubs and organizations; parents of students with disabilities; and guidance counselors, school psychologists, and social workers.

Figure 1.4.   Strategies adolescents think facilitate social relationships. (Source: Hendrickson, Shokoohi-Yakta, Hamre-Nietupski, & Gable, 1996.)

Assessment Question	Rating	Ideas for improvement
Ghost/Guest: Does the focus child frequently get "passed over" as if he or she were not there (ghost)? Do staff members talk about another placement as soon as there is a problem (guest)?	Frequently Sometimes Never NO	
Inclusion child: Does the teacher say "I have 27 students plus 2 included students"?	Frequently Sometimes Never NO	
I'll help: Do classmates use the words "work with" or "help" whenever they refer to times spent with the focus child?	Frequently Sometimes Never NO	
Just another child: Is the child expected to participate in class activities along with everyone else?	Frequently Sometimes Never NO	
Regular friend: Has the child ever been invited to a party by a classmate?	Frequently Sometimes Never NO	
Best friend: Does the focus child have one or more friends who call him or her on the telephone at home and/or who visit him or her after school or on weekends?	Frequently Sometimes Never NO	

School: _____   **Date:** _____
Classroom: _____   **Focus Student(s):** _____
Ratings: Frequently   Sometimes   Never   No Opportunity to Observe (NO)

Figure 1.5.   A rating scale to assess a student's social relationships. (From Meyer, L.H., Minondo, S., Fisher, M., Larson, M.J., Dunmore, S., Black, J.W., & D'Aquanni, M. [1998]. Frames of friendship: Social relationships among adolescents with diverse abilities. In L.H. Meyer, H. Park, M. Grenot-Scheyer, I.S. Schwartz, & B. Harry [Eds.], *Making friends: The influences of culture and development* [pp. 189–218]. Baltimore: Paul H. Brookes Publishing Co.; adapted by permission.)

proved in a classroom or a school. These improvements can directly or indirectly affect the conditions for social interactions among peers. One such checklist, the Integration Checklist (1989), lists both general schoolwide practices (e.g., movement around the school and scheduling) and the characteristics of students who have been included (e.g., their involvement, communication patterns, and appearance) (Figure 1.6). Other teams may find

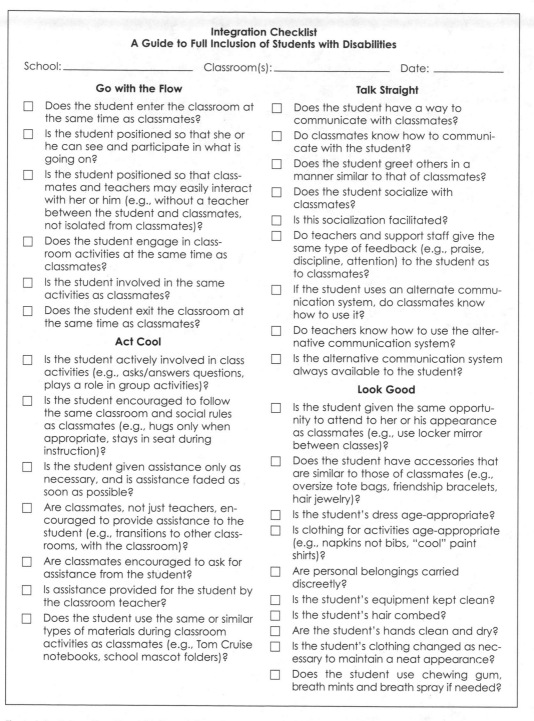

Integration Checklist
A Guide to Full Inclusion of Students with Disabilities

School: _____ Classroom(s): _____ Date: _____

Go with the Flow

☐ Does the student enter the classroom at the same time as classmates?

☐ Is the student positioned so that she or he can see and participate in what is going on?

☐ Is the student positioned so that classmates and teachers may easily interact with her or him (e.g., without a teacher between the student and classmates, not isolated from classmates)?

☐ Does the student engage in classroom activities at the same time as classmates?

☐ Is the student involved in the same activities as classmates?

☐ Does the student exit the classroom at the same time as classmates?

Act Cool

☐ Is the student actively involved in class activities (e.g., asks/answers questions, plays a role in group activities)?

☐ Is the student encouraged to follow the same classroom and social rules as classmates (e.g., hugs only when appropriate, stays in seat during instruction)?

☐ Is the student given assistance only as necessary, and is assistance faded as soon as possible?

☐ Are classmates, not just teachers, encouraged to provide assistance to the student (e.g., transitions to other classrooms, with the classroom)?

☐ Are classmates encouraged to ask for assistance from the student?

☐ Is assistance provided for the student by the classroom teacher?

☐ Does the student use the same or similar types of materials during classroom activities as classmates (e.g., Tom Cruise notebooks, school mascot folders)?

Talk Straight

☐ Does the student have a way to communicate with classmates?

☐ Do classmates know how to communicate with the student?

☐ Does the student greet others in a manner similar to that of classmates?

☐ Does the student socialize with classmates?

☐ Is this socialization facilitated?

☐ Do teachers and support staff give the same type of feedback (e.g., praise, discipline, attention) to the student as to classmates?

☐ If the student uses an alternate communication system, do classmates know how to use it?

☐ Do teachers know how to use the alternative communication system?

☐ Is the alternative communication system always available to the student?

Look Good

☐ Is the student given the same opportunity to attend to her or his appearance as classmates (e.g., use locker mirror between classes)?

☐ Does the student have accessories that are similar to those of classmates (e.g., oversize tote bags, friendship bracelets, hair jewelry)?

☐ Is the student's dress age-appropriate?

☐ Is clothing for activities age-appropriate (e.g., napkins not bibs, "cool" paint shirts)?

☐ Are personal belongings carried discreetly?

☐ Is the student's equipment kept clean?

☐ Is the student's hair combed?

☐ Are the student's hands clean and dry?

☐ Is the student's clothing changed as necessary to maintain a neat appearance?

☐ Does the student use chewing gum, breath mints and breath spray if needed?

Figure 1.6.   Integration Checklist. (From *Integration Checklist: A Guide to Full Inclusion of Students with Disabilities.* (1989). Minneapolis: University of Minnesota, Institute on Community Integration; reprinted by permission.)

that comparing their school practices to a list of social relationships barriers (see Figure 1.3) will assist them in targeting areas for improvement. Goals can be set to make general improvements in schools and classrooms so that they are conducive to the development of social relationships, but goals also may be targeted for developing and improving programs (strengthening cooperative learning groups, building a cross-age tutoring program, or organizing a Best Buddies high school chapter), staff development, peer support skills, and individual students' needs.

Making Accommodations in the IEP Educators are responsible for making academic accommodations for students in order to assist the student's educational progression. For many students, these accommodations must include some kind of social support plan suited to the student's age and social needs. For example, peer support strategies such as friendship groups or classwide peer planning (both explained in Chapter 3) may be written into the accommodation section of a student's IEP. Related instruction in social skills and communication with peers may also be listed and will appear as objectives in other sections of the IEP. Writing social skills objectives into a student's IEP ensures that students with disabilities are not just physically placed alongside their peers without disabilities in classrooms but that efforts will be made to assist them in building peer relationships.

Paul is a sixth grader with a seizure disorder, learning disabilities, and a history of exclusion by peers. The following accommodations were written into Paul's IEP:

1. *Peer planning sessions will be conducted with Paul's classmates to brainstorm issues and to provide Paul with needed support. With some assistance from the special education teacher, Paul's peers also will learn to conduct their own planning sessions for Paul.*

2. *Peers will be taught how to increase Paul's conversational skills in planned lessons and during informal conversations with him.*

3. *Paul will learn to self-manage (i.e., identify, keep track of, control) the behaviors that are annoying to his peers (repeating topics, touching others).*

Students who are exceptions to formalized peer support are

1. Students whose differences are not noticeable to peers or are ignored by peers

2. Students who have suitable social skills

3. Students who already have meaningful connections to peers or to a peer network

These students do not need planned support to establish social relationships with their peers. Other students with disabilities may choose not to have formalized peer social support, even though they may benefit from it. These exceptions more often occur with students in secondary schools who have mild disabilities and/or take an active part in their own IEP development.

Setting Goals for Social Skills and Academic Achievement Occasionally, an intervention that focuses on improving a student's academic achievement can have a positive effect on the student's social relationships. Students are more likely to be referred for special education services *before or during, rather than after, third grade,* and the referral is usually for academic rather than social-behavioral problems (Walker, Colvin, & Ramsey, 1995). Researchers studying teacher referrals to special education learned that 69% of referrals were for boys, 67% were during the early grades (kindergarten through third grade), and the seven most frequent problems that caused teachers to refer children to special education services were various academic difficulties, not antisocial behavior. Aggressive and disruptive behaviors were tenth on the list of cited reasons (Lloyd, Kauffman, Landrum, & Roe, 1991). Therefore, students who fall behind academically after the early grades are less likely to receive remedial assistance or special education during middle school and high school, even though such assistance might have positive benefits for the student both socially and academically. Research also indicates that teachers tend to target special education supports when students exhibit academic problems, but less so when students display antisocial, particularly withdrawn, behavior.

Measuring the Social Indicators   As part of the IEP process, teachers need to assess a student's progress on stated objectives. The primary yardstick that should be used to measure the effectiveness of efforts to build a student's social relationships should be the student's actual social relationships: Has the student built successful relationships with his or her neighbors; with peers at school; and, later in the student's life, with co-workers on the job or with fellow college students (Meyer, Park, Grenot-Scheyer, Schwartz, & Harry, 1998)?

Evaluation should focus on indicators such as social contacts, demonstrated support behaviors, and classroom social networks:

- *Social contacts:* The number of different peers with whom the student has positive contact, the number of activities in which the student engages, and the environments where the contacts take place

- *Demonstrated social support behaviors:* Providing emotional support, giving access to others or to information, providing material aid, and helping with decisions

- *Classroom social networks:* Numbers and size of networks, types of individuals, and positive and negative characteristics of the networks

Alternately, the six questions listed previously in Figure 1.5 can provide an informal means of assessing growth and change in students' social relationships.

As adults work to 1) understand the social limitations that a focus student experiences, 2) set goals, and 3) draw up support plans, it is important that they do the following:

1. Listen to the student's own expectations and hopes.

2. Recruit the viewpoints and ideas of the student's peers (using the guidelines that are established in Chapter 3).

3. Familiarize themselves with the developmental and group expectations for students of different genders, chronological ages, and cultures.

Collaborative Teaming

By its nature, inclusion obligates teachers to collaborate as a team. This means that the core team (general and special education teachers along with the student and the student's family) plans, selects, and implements various actions to improve the student's social relationships and peer supports. Members of the focus student's extended team may also be involved. These members may include additional teachers, therapists and other specialists, administrators, and peers. Collaborative teams are necessary: Working alone will not do the trick! Ideas that are generated individually may be off-base or incomplete in some way, especially if two or more teachers share responsibility for students with disabilities. The implementation tasks are too taxing for one person to undertake and oversee. (For more information, refer to *Collaborative Teaming* [Snell & Janney, 2000], a companion book in this series.)

The following guidelines, which are discussed in more depth in the upcoming chapters, address ways in which teams should work together to plan, select, and implement actions that have been designed to improve a student's social relationships:

1. Use collaborative teams to make decisions and to implement actions.

2. Examine the student's social relationships as the "yardstick" for measuring the need for or success of a social support plan.

3. Involve the focus student and his or her peers in the process: All can contribute to

planning, problem solving, implementing a plan, and evaluating the focus student's progress.

4. Seek team consensus about what is the simplest, yet most effective, initial action to take: This often translates into increasing the student's social opportunities before undertaking more complex actions.

5. Contextualize instruction: Embed teaching in daily routines and in natural social contexts.

6. Don't let the implemented supports become barriers to social interaction: Hovering adults, overzealous "helpers," stigmatizing support or instruction, and a failure to fade assistance hinder natural peer-to-peer contact.

Strategies to Enhance Relationships

The following five strategies are developed in detail in later chapters and are applied to case studies of students of varying ages, needs, and disabilities.

Adult Facilitation Teachers are critical in promoting the development of social relationships among children in their own classrooms. One primary method teachers use to build camaraderie among their students is to *model their acceptance of each student in a classroom by demonstrating their approval and recognition of each individual student in age- and culture-appropriate ways* (e.g., standing nearby and smiling at the student, using the student's preferred name, interacting with the student in natural ways, "pulling students into" ongoing activities unobtrusively). Teachers also can *demonstrate how to interact with an individual who may have unique ways of communicating* (e.g., use the student's picture communication board, speak slowly, wait for the person to look up first, use manual signs while speaking). Other methods that teachers report using are

- Actively promoting interactions between focus students and peers, followed by "backing off" and allowing the interaction to proceed without adult interference

- Similar treatment of each individual student

- Teaching peers to lend support to classmates who might need it without hindering the student's independence (Janney & Snell, 1996; Salisbury, Gallucci, Palombaro, & Peck, 1995; Snell et al., 1995)

Improvement of the School Environment Strategies for improving the school environment as a whole address the school's attitudes, its atmosphere, and its understanding and appreciation of human differences. Many researchers and practitioners have found that indirect strategies strengthen the school's attitudinal base to allow peer support and positive social relationships to flourish. For example, ability (or disability) awareness programs can help people without disabilities understand how particular disabilities affect learning, perception, or communication, thereby increasing their sensitivity toward and appreciation of a student with a disability. Other strategies are geared toward

1. Increasing acceptance (training in conflict resolution methods, use of classroom community groups to discuss and resolve interaction problems)

2. Accommodating human differences (learning about other cultures through social studies and reading projects, inviting speakers from other countries and cultures to address the class, teaching units on different cultures)

3. Creating cooperative and safe school environments (student problem-solving concerning schoolwide problems, use of students as conflict mediators)

4. Teaching active participation and responsibility in society (school cleanup and recycling projects, community volunteering and sharing programs, school citizenship and Key Club groups) (Salisbury, Evans, & Palombaro, 1997)

Support Through Peer Groups and Pairs Social support methods were developed in the 1980s and 1990s that encourage peers to foster social relationships and membership within stable social groups. These methods may include the following tactics:

- Promote planned peer support programs such as peer planning, friendship pairs or groups, and lunch partners.

- Focus on typical environments and activities in addition to natural strategies kids use to "get connected" to social groups. At the same time, provide "access and support to ensure that students with disabilities can participate in similar ways" (Schnorr, 1997, p. 1).

Peer support approaches generally involve answering students' questions about disability while teaching them to problem-solve ways to get along and interact with others in school who may be different from them, such as students with a disability.

Social Skills Instruction Researchers, working in tandem with teachers, have learned much about intervention approaches that can be successful with social skills difficulties such as aggression, withdrawal, nonresponsiveness, poor quality of interactions, and a failure to generalize social skills across daily routines. Frequently, a combination of proven techniques rather than a single, narrow approach are used in intervention. The combination depends on the student, his or her particular behavior difficulty, and the circumstances. The teaching emphasis has shifted from eliminating undesirable behavior to building appropriate replacement skills, or *positive behavioral support*. Most successful approaches used in schools include the teaching of alternate, appropriate behavior as a means for reducing problem behavior. Often, these alternate behaviors include social, communication, or academic skills.

Functional assessment plays an important role in the design of social skills programs. This method involves studying the "triggers" for a particular behavior difficulty and the purpose the behavior seems to serve for the student. This information is a necessary component of many combined approaches, regardless of the social skill difficulty (Horner & Carr, 1997). Functional assessment, which is recognized in special education law as a valuable teaching tool, is discussed briefly in Chapter 4 and more thoroughly in the booklet *Behavioral Support* (Janney & Snell, 2000).

Instructional Peer Supports Student-to-student teaching can be beneficial in tutoring programs and cooperative learning groups; both strategies can produce gains in academic, language, or social skills. Several tutoring models exist. In *peer tutoring*, teaching is one-way and students are the same age. Peer-mediated strategies, frequently used during play times with preschoolers, are an example of peer-to-peer teaching with a social focus: Typical youngsters are taught to initiate interactions with their classmates who have disabilities and to prompt their responses. *Cross-age tutoring* involves an older student teaching, interacting with, or reading to a younger student. Another approach is *classwide tutoring*, which incorporates *reciprocal peer tutoring*, during which each student alternates between the tutor and tutee roles; this classwide tutoring can lead to academic improvements and can also teach cooperative interdependence among students of the same age but differing abilities.

Cooperative learning entails restructuring learning and leisure activities to promote interdependence among students. Group members learn several messages:

- "We sink or swim together."

- "Do your work—we're counting on you."

- "How can I help you to do better?" (Nevin, Thousand, & Villa, 1994, p. 145)

Cooperative groups are not ability groups; group members have multiple talents and a variety of abilities and needs. The group's work tasks, activities, or games are planned to achieve academic and/or social objectives, which may vary for different group members. Students assume different responsibilities, but they problem-solve and make decisions as a group in order to achieve the stated group objective. For example, groups of fifth and sixth graders might be given math story problems that require reasoning and basic computational math skills and can be solved in several ways. Group tasks might be to build structures from toothpicks and marshmallows or to create a videotape clip or poster that illustrates the group's solution. Teachers provide the structure, monitor in ways that encourage learning and group interdependence, and evaluate academic and social learning.

Tutoring and cooperative groups promote peer support during instruction and can lead to cooperative behaviors, social skills, and academic improvements. Depending on the approach used, peers with and without disabilities may fill equitable roles in cooperative learning groups and in reciprocal peer tutoring.

The following chapters elaborate on the strategies just reviewed and set forth some guidelines for using these strategies in schools with students of different ages and disabilities.

Chapter 2

Social Relationships of Children with Disabilities

Laura K. Vogtle

This chapter highlights what is known about the social lives of children: the development of social awareness and social competence, the role of social relationships and social supports, how children form friendships, and the role that the environment plays in enhancing or limiting social outcomes. Although this booklet focuses on developing and improving the social world of children with disabilities, a review of how social relationships develop in typical children can aid in understanding the social relationships of children with disabilities. In order to build the social competence of children with special needs and expand their social world to include children without disabilities, it is important to understand how social relationships form, change, grow, and end.

Social behavior occurs when two or more people interact. The social behaviors that we use in our lives encompass everything from making requests of people whom we do not know, as when ordering in a restaurant, to interacting with friends and family. In order to successfully negotiate social interactions with others, one needs to have a basic understanding of social norms or rules. One must be able to determine the appropriate times and places to use the rules and to modify one's responses and behavior according to what others do or say (social integration). Social expectations vary across social groups: People behave differently with their families, for instance, than they do with their friends. Expectations also vary depending on the occasion and the environment where the interactions take place. For example, attending a school honors assembly requires very different behavior than participating in a class Halloween party.

Researchers agree that children need to learn the following skills and abilities in order to become socially integrated:

- Enter a group
- Take turns
- Take part in a conversation in which there is mutual input from each participant in the conversation
- Manage conflicts
- Cooperate with and support others (Rubin, 1980; Youniss & Smoller, 1985)

How do children learn these behaviors? The acquisition of social skills requires extensive experience through a succession of interactions over time and is influenced by family, environment, and individual capabilities.

SOCIAL RELATIONSHIPS

Children's first social relationships are typically formed within their immediate and extended family. Familial interactions usually encourage the development of basic skills such as reciprocal speech, the use of eye contact and smiles, and so forth; this reciprocal interaction contributes to the affective growth of the child. Researchers have even found that positive social relationships contribute to increased self-esteem and cognitive growth (Furman & Robbins, 1985; Rubin, 1980) (Figure 2.1). Parents' relationships with their children commonly provide nurturance, affection, and instrumental aid, whereas siblings may offer companionship. Family contributions to a

---

Benefits of Social Engagements

Affection	Companionship
Intimacy	Reliable support
Nurturance	Sense of being included
Source of material aid	Enhancement of self-esteem
Promotion of sensitivity to other's feelings	Endorsement of opinions and beliefs

Figure 2.1.   Benefits of social engagements. (Source: Furman & Robbins, 1985.)

child's social development may fluctuate as the child's social horizons expand, especially as the child's peer engagements receive increasing focus. For example, in a study of how children perceived their social support networks, fourth graders indicated fewer conflicts and more support from their parents than did seventh and tenth graders (Furman & Buhrmester, 1992).

By the time children are 2 years old, they demonstrate preferences for certain playmates and seek them out (Howes, 1988). Children begin to practice the social skills they have learned at the family level with their peers and to refine those skills into strategies that can be used in group engagements. These strategies include cooperating in play and joining existing playgroups, which requires a child to learn how to ask to join a group and to develop a new plan if a negative answer is received (Corsaro, 1985). Resolving disagreements is another important skill in social integration. Researchers distinguish between *conflict* (difference of opinion) and *aggression* (intent to harm verbally or physically). These are important distinctions; children who are aggressive are less accepted by their classmates than children who are able to settle conflicts skillfully (Shantz & Hobart, 1989). Rubin (1980) analyzed the conflict management stages that develop during early childhood, between about 4 and 8 years of age (Figure 2.2). This sequence can be helpful in assessing the difficulty that some children have in managing conflicts and can be used to improve their skills.

By the time that the typically developing child enters preschool, rudimentary social behaviors for exchanges between partners and for group engagement have been established (Corsaro, 1985; Rubin, 1980). It is at this time that most children begin to establish closer relationships and to make friends.

At age 2, Peter and Christopher met each other as a result of their mothers' friendship. Both of their fathers were serving in the military at the time, and the boys lived on the same air force base. Peter has cerebral palsy; Christopher does not. Peter's mother gives the following report of the boys' association:

"It was as if they had known each other in a previous life. We lived near Christopher's family for 3 years. An event for one of the boys was not complete unless the other boy was present. I am convinced that this is a relationship for life. We moved away when the boys were 6 years old. That was 4 years ago, and Peter and Chris still call each other at least once a month and often more. They see each other once or twice a year; Chris's mother and I arrange weeklong visits during the summer and Christmas. Even if they didn't see each other then, I think that they would still communicate."

Early friendships among children are based on the sharing of common activities and interests and on mutual affection (Hartup, 1996; Rizzo, 1989). This basis for friendship appears to predominate throughout elementary school. Most children show a preference for acquaintances and friends who are of the same gender and race and similar with regard to socioeconomic and ethnic status (Epstein, 1986; Hartup, 1996; Rizzo, 1989). Neighbor-

---

Stages of conflict management strategies in early childhood

1. Expressing opinions openly and honestly
2. Maintaining sensitivity to opposing views
3. Suggesting and accepting reasonable compromises
4. Standing up to unreasonable demands

Figure 2.2. Stages of conflict management strategies in early childhood. (From Rubin, Z. [1980]. *Children's friendships*. Cambridge, MA: Harvard University Press.)

hood and school locations, as well as family preferences, may influence children to select partners who are like themselves.

In middle school, children's relationships begin to focus on sharing secrets, gossip, mutual admiration, and support (Parker & Gottman, 1989; Rizzo, 1989). Friends in this age group tend to have different expectations of one another, and they are better at cooperating, communicating, exploring, and resolving disagreements than younger friends (Hartup, 1996; Hartup & Laursen, 1993; Ladd & Emerson, 1984).

In high school, young people begin to focus more on ideas and beliefs rather than on appearances (Hartup, 1996; Inderbitzen-Pisaruk, & Foster, 1990). Kinney (1993) found increasing diversity in peer cultures among high school students compared with peer cultures in junior high. Young people in high school appear less concerned with what other adolescents think and say about them; this creates freedom for young people to develop friendships with peers who are dissimilar in a number of arenas rather than attempt to maintain group identity. Interest in the opposite sex results in cross-gender engagements becoming the norm rather than a rarity, further increasing the diversity found in social environments. Relationships show increasing intimacy, loyalty, and trust. There is a difference in peer group size as well. Girls tend to focus more on intimate friendships with two or three friends; boys have more casual exchanges within larger groups (Maccoby, 1990).

Acquaintances

Acquaintances provide children with some measure of reliable relationship; however, the role of an acquaintance is less defined than that of a friend. Children confide much more in peers who are friends than they do in their acquaintances. They have more arguments and cooperate less with acquaintances (Hartup, 1996). The line between friendship and acquaintance is fluid. Some children who know each other become friends, whereas established friendships may fade and the partners become acquaintances. Researchers believe that *acquaintances* are the backbone of

social networks and social support, and *friends* teach the commitment, intimacy, and loyalty necessary to sustain adult relationships. The majority of peers in any given classroom are more likely to be acquaintances than friends, which gives some indication of the size of acquaintance pools.

Social Support Networks

Children's social networks are sources of reliable interaction within a child's world; social networks are made up of people who are important to the child, including individuals from the child's family, church, school, and neighborhood. These networks begin to form at a very young age (family) and expand quickly through toddler ages (playgroups, church, neighbors) to preschool then kindergarten. The effect of such networks on the child's developing sense of self begins at a very young age and cannot be minimized over the child's life span.

Family Influence Reflect on your parents' influence on your social life. Did they lend support to you by hosting birthday parties and sleep-overs that were attended by your classmates? If you wanted to invite a friend over for dinner or to attend a movie with you, did your parents provide transportation or even pay for your friend to go to the movie with you? These are examples of *direct support*, in which parents promote their children's social relationships by suggesting and hosting events, providing transportation, and including the child's close friends in family rituals or celebrations. Not all parents or families provide the same degree of social management. Families living in safer areas tend to do less social organizing (Rubin & Sloman, 1984), and mothers appear to be more involved than fathers in their children's social activities (Ladd & Golter, 1988).

Another aspect of direct parental influence on children's social networks includes parental coaching or modeling behaviors for social interactions. Parents coach their children, both globally and specifically, on strategies for enlarging and enhancing their social relationships. As children mature, coaching becomes less directive and intentional, and social skills are communicated more by modeling (Parke,

MacDonald, Beitel, & Bhavnagri, 1988; Rubin & Sloman, 1984).

Indirect family effects on children's social networks include such factors as the impact of neighborhoods and socioeconomic status on children's overall social exposure. Mothers who are not employed outside the home or who work part time have more time for their children's social affairs, whereas single mothers appear to have fewer social contacts, thereby limiting the social networks of their children. Children who live in unsafe or rural neighborhoods have fewer social opportunities and, consequently, smaller social networks (Cochran & Riley, 1988; Lewis, Fiering, & Kotsonis, 1984).

An indirect effect of families' neighborhood choices that is seen in children who were bused for the sake of integration mirrors the situation that many children with disabilities experience. African American children who were located so far from their neighborhood schools that they needed to be bused to school had little opportunity to reap the benefits of after-school social opportunities at the integrated schools or in their own neighborhoods (Cochran & Riley, 1988). This is similar to the dilemma that is faced by children who are bused to special education classes.

Peer Supports The opportunity to meet other children is a critical part of building social networks. Children's and adolescents' social networks can and often do overlap across various environments. For instance, children who live across the street from each other may also go to the same church and attend the same school. Activity groups, such as bands or sports teams, can originate in schools, or they may be part of an organized community or neighborhood effort. Children often develop relationships with other children who are in the same activities or environments. Peers in these environments can and usually do provide a support system to one another, either as friends or acquaintances. In childhood, these groups function under the close supervision of parents; however, as children grow into early adolescence, parental supervision subsides as peer groups shift their base from neighborhood to school and adolescents spend more time with their peers than with their families (Brown, 1990).

Cliques and crowds (Figure 2.3) are descriptive terms that help to identify the social networks of preteens and adolescents in Western countries. Other cultures may have different social trends, an important fact to remember when children from other countries enter local middle and high schools. Different social expectations can make the transition for foreign children difficult.

The passage from elementary age to junior high school age is a difficult time for many children. Prepubescent physical changes are beginning to occur, and familiar schools and teachers are often lost in the transition to a new school building. Rather than hold class in a central classroom environment with one teacher, most middle schools and high schools rotate children through classes in larger buildings with new and various teachers. Such transitions affect social networks and interactions (Evans & Eder, 1993; Hirsche & Rapkin, 1987; Kinney, 1993). Middle school students

---

Subgroups within the peer system	
Peer groups:	Any formal or informal grouping of peers.
Cliques:	Small, intimate groups of peers who "hang around" together and develop close relationships within the group.
Crowds:	Large, reputation-based collectives of similarly stereotyped people who may or may not spend much time together (e.g., jocks, brains, loners).
Peer cultures:	A set of shared attitudes, beliefs, and values held by a collective of young people.

Figure 2.3.   Subgroups within the peer system. (From Brown, B.B. [1990]. Peer groups and peer cultures. In S.S. Feldman & G.R. Elliott [Eds.], *At the threshold: The developing adolescent* [pp. 171–196]. Cambridge, MA: Harvard University Press.)

do not usually have much self-esteem, and they look to their peer group to validate their beliefs and feelings (Evans & Eder, 1993).

An important feature of social networks and social groups is the sense of inclusion and self-esteem that they can instill in children (Berndt, 1989). Unfortunately, as children grow up, social networks can provide a sense of inclusion while also having a negative influence on self-esteem. Brown and Lohr (1987) found that adolescents who valued crowd membership demonstrated a strong relationship between self-esteem and perceived crowd status. The ranking of the various crowds by the overall peer group appears to have an effect on how children view themselves. Those adolescents who were members of "high status" crowds, such as the athletes, typically had high self-esteem. Adolescents who were viewed as part of "low status" crowds, such as nerds or geeks, typically had low self-esteem despite their inclusion in an established social network. Although members of a crowd are included in an established social network, the perceived rank of that network by others appears to influence each individual member's self-esteem.

Although social support networks are generally considered to be positive influences, this may not always be the case (Hartup, 1996). Participation in a crowd can result in negative behaviors that would not generally be seen in the individual. Evans and Eder (1993) described a scene where a crowd of about 50 middle school students took turns sneaking up behind a peer and kicking her in the backside during recess. Likewise, peers can pretend an individual is a member of their "group" and then direct misbehavior as part of group participation.

Student Snapshot

*Ten-year-old Cara, placed in a self-contained classroom for children with mental retardation, was "included" in a general education sixth-grade class for 2 hours each day as part of the school system's decision to move to an inclusive educa-*tion model. The classroom teacher was given no instruction or support as to how to manage Cara and consequently left her without assignments or direction at the back of the room. A group of boys quickly realized they could steer Cara into mischief by pretending to accept her, then telling her to misbehave. She was in trouble constantly. Cara was delighted to be a part of this group and would proudly point out her "friends" to others. Cara is vulnerable to the misdirection of classmates and needs some individualized supports planned collaboratively by her teachers and other team members. Cara's classmates would benefit from learning more about Cara (her challenges, her needs for friendships, and her skills) and how they can support her.*

Children Who Are Not Popular

Not all children are well liked by their classmates. Investigations that use sociometric procedures (i.e., a process in which individuals are asked to identify preferred children within a peer group) suggest that a hierarchy of peer acceptance exists within peer groups. Coie, Dodge, and Coppotelli (1982) described a classification that includes the following categories:

1. *Popular:* Children who receive large numbers of positive nominations from their peers

2. *Average:* Children who receive an average numbers of positive nominations from their peers

3. *Neglected:* Children who do not receive either positive or negative nominations from their peers

4. *Rejected:* Children who receive large numbers of negative nominations from their peers

5. *Controversial:* Children who receive equal numbers of positive and negative nominations from their peers.

Follow-up studies suggest that children tend to stay in the same social groupings over time (Bukowski & Newcomb, 1984; Newcomb &

Bukowski, 1983; Taylor, 1989). These findings do not indicate that children who are neglected or average have no friends, but are indicative of crowd attitudes' toward individuals.

Do unpopular children have friends? There are indications that they do (Parker & Asher, 1993; Vandell & Hembree, 1994). If so, then what are the potential problems associated with being unpopular? It is possible to make the argument that children who are not popular have smaller peer support networks; that is, if a boy's classmates do not care for him, they will be less available to loan him books, give him information, cheer him on, or come to his assistance when he is in need. Recall that social networks are a source of self-esteem and that they provide a sense of inclusion. Although these same two benefits may result from friendship, one unanswered question is whether friendships between unpopular children can make up for the sense of rejection that these children feel from their acquaintances, the peer group, or the "crowd" at large.

Outcomes for Children with Poor Peer Status   Problems with peer acceptance appear to predict or contribute to academic and social difficulties during a child's school years as well as later in life. Children who are not accepted by their peers often do not like school, do not succeed as well academically, and are more prone to emotional disorders than their accepted peers (Hymel, Rubin, Rowden, & LeMare, 1990; Ladd, 1990; Parker & Asher, 1987, 1993; Vandell & Hembree, 1994). In a review of the literature associating social problems with long-term outcomes, Parker and Asher (1987) found a high incidence of high school dropout rates in adolescents and criminal acts in adults who had a history of being unpopular. Alcoholism, drug addiction, and adult psychopathology are also more common among adults who were unpopular as children than they are among adults who were accepted by their peer groups. Parker and Asher (1987) concluded that children who are unpopular are at risk for a range of problems as adults. This same concern exists for children with disabilities who do not have social networks or friends.

SOCIAL INFLUENCES ON CHILDREN AND ADOLESCENTS WITH DISABILITIES

Information from studies regarding the social relationships of children with disabilities tends to sound discouraging. Bear in mind that many of the inquiries on which these studies were based included children who were educated in segregated classrooms and even in segregated schools. Currently, there is greater awareness than there was a decade ago regarding social acceptance and prosocial environments for children with disabilities. Practices such as inclusion and family-centered care are helping to change the educational and social outlook for children with disabilities and their families. Social and life satisfaction outcomes for people with special needs are improving, which is starting to be reflected in research. This trend should continue in future investigations because of shifts in societal attitudes and supportive practices.

Family Influences

Families of children with disabilities have stresses that often affect their ability to provide social opportunities to their children. These stresses may include ongoing medical procedures for the child with disabilities, financial pressures, limited support systems, sibling needs, marital issues, and lack of time for pleasurable family experiences (Brotherson & Goldstein, 1992). There is evidence that parents of children with physical disabilities may be reluctant to ask parents of peers to invite their child to social gatherings such as birthday and slumber parties because of the care their child requires. Some parents of typical peers are equally reluctant to accept the extra responsibilities of taking care of a child with special needs at social events that are held in their homes (Vogtle, 1996). Families of children who have disabilities tend to

- Participate in more limited family and friendship networks themselves (Kazak, 1987; Kazak & Marvin, 1984)

- Live in poorer, less accessible neighbor-hoods (Parke & Bhavnagri, 1989)
- Have fewer financial and time resources with which to provide social outings (Broth-erson & Goldstein, 1992)

These issues may further isolate children with disabilities.

Children who have ongoing health condi-tions may have frequent medical appoint-ments, may be sick and in the hospital more often than their peers, and may be less likely to participate in physical activities with their typical peers (Graetz & Shute, 1995). The so-cial network of children with physical disabil-ities is more likely to be provided by the adults who tend to their physical needs than it is to be provided by their peers (Wallender & Hu-bert, 1987).

A lack of curb cuts and the high cost of vans with lifts can create barriers for children with severe or multiple disabilities who use wheelchairs when they enter adolescence or adulthood. Young children with disabilities who need wheelchairs can be maneuvered up and down hills and steps and over curbs with relative ease. As these children grow older, however, the change in their body size makes lifting and pushing them increasingly difficult. Peers' vehicles are rarely modified for wheel-chairs, and public transportation for wheel-chairs is scarce and costly. The telephone may become the chief social agent for people with physical limitations (J. Pugliese, personal com-munication, November 13, 1996).

Young people with mental retardation face somewhat different constraints than those with physical disabilities. Adolescents with cognitive impairments are often restricted from attend-ing impromptu gatherings of their peers after school or on the weekends (Luftig, 1989). Such social restrictions often result from parents' concerns that their children will be made fun of, exploited, or talked into participating in ac-tivities that they do not understand, such as engaging in sexual encounters or drinking (Tharinger, Horton, & Millea, 1990).

Social Problems of Children with Disabilities

There is much documentation of the various social shortcomings seen in children with dis-abilities. Although past research in this area has not always considered environmental and peer influences, it nonetheless focuses on im-portant concerns. This section reviews the common social skill difficulties of children with disabilities.

Self-Management of Behavior   The abil-ity to regulate behavior and emotion is im-portant in social engagements (Hubbard & Coie, 1994). Emotional regulation and atten-tion are examples of behaviors that affect so-cial engagements.

Regulating emotions is difficult for many peo-ple, including children with disabilities. Some children with disabilities may change their emotional states quickly, accelerating from one mood to another with startling speed. Once feelings have escalated, children with disabilities often have problems "letting go" or calming down, creating problems for their peer group and their social network. Typical peers in these situations may become frus-trated, not only because of the emotionally charged situation but also because of their in-ability to calm the person.

Other examples of difficulties with emo-tional regulation that affect some students with disabilities include a low tolerance for frustration and irrational fears. Unless they are brought under self-control, these emotional regulation problems also may affect social in-teractions (Lazzari & Wood, 1997; O'Neill, 1997).

Attention, the ability to focus on a task or an activity and to stay focused over time, is an-other problem area for many children with disabilities. Lack of attention and persevera-tion represent both ends of the attention spectrum. Both behaviors can cause disrup-tion in social interaction. For example, play scenarios are central themes around which the "rules" for imaginative roles, dialogue, and actions are organized during play. Cor-saro (1985) found that typical preschool children developed play scenarios over periods of time. Children who have short attention spans or who cannot shift attention will experience difficulties being attentive to the cues of the other group members. For example, the child who is constantly distracted by other engagements in the classroom cannot follow the train of thought that his or her peers are demonstrating during the creation of a grocery store game. Similarly, the child who becomes so focused on a particular item that he or she cannot share it with fellow playmates is less able to participate with the group appropriately.

Prosocial Skills in Children with Disabilities   Behaviors that benefit others are termed *prosocial skills* (Barton, 1986). Some examples of prosocial skills include altruism, cooperation, sharing, and sympathizing. There is considerable evidence that these behaviors develop through interaction with one's peers (Odom, McConnell, & McEvoy, 1992; Vygotsky, 1978). Specific *social strategies,* such as how to initiate interactions, enter a group, and respond and reciprocate during conversation and play, are also necessary for acceptance into peer groups in which social interaction occurs. Children with disabilities appear to have difficulty learning social strategies and prosocial skills that are acceptable to their peer group. The strategies that children with disabilities use often differ in frequency and method from those strategies that their typical peers use (Odom, McConnell, & McEvoy, 1992). Without the opportunity to interact with groups of peers, social behaviors will be less likely to develop.

Children with disabilities usually make fewer attempts to initiate social exchanges with their peers, and they often respond to social initiations in a manner that their typical peers do not understand (Beckman & Kohl, 1987; Guralnick & Groom, 1987; Ridlehoover, 1996). Poor communication skills can limit social exchanges (Guralnick, 1990), as can restricted awareness of other children's feelings. The inability to "read" emotional responses is a serious obstacle in the social engagements of children with disabilities that

has received considerable attention by researchers, particularly in children who have autism (O'Neill, 1997). Similarly, understanding the appropriate time for showing emotions by peer group standards is a skill that is necessary for successful group membership (Hubbard & Coie, 1994). Even if joining a group is successfully negotiated, a child can be excluded quickly if he or she demonstrates inappropriate laughter or aggression or cries without apparent cause.

Strategies that children with disabilities use to effect group entry may not meet accepted subgroup norms (Siperstein & Leffert, 1997). "Crashing" into a group of classmates and demanding toys or giving a poke to a classmate's ribs to gain attention are examples of how children may attempt group entry using unacceptable methods. The experience of a number of inappropriate efforts over time can make typical children leery of accepting any bids for entry into the group, even if the bids are appropriate. Hubbard and Coie (1994) cited previous study findings that linked group entry skills to peer status and popularity; that is, those children who were able to analyze peer groups accurately and join them successfully were more popular.

Children with disabilities have been observed to practice social behaviors in a different manner than their peers. For instance, Luftig (1989) found that teenagers with mental retardation often told "secrets" to the peer group at large rather than limiting their confidences, thus demonstrating a different understanding of confidentiality between friends than their typical classmates. As young children enter their preteen years and adolescence, social behaviors become particularly important. Friendships and group memberships are based on one's ability to exchange confidences, demonstrate trust and loyalty, and act in the same manner as the group at large. Preteens and young adolescents are quick to penalize classmates who behave or look different than themselves (Evans & Eder, 1993).

Peer Attitudes   When children are taught in segregated classrooms, children without disabilities lack the opportunity to get to know their peers with special needs and, therefore, view their classmates in self-contained classrooms as less capable than themselves (Bak, Cooper, Dobroth, & Siperstein, 1987). Although the practice of mainstreaming is an improvement over segregated classrooms, children with disabilities still are not necessarily viewed as part of the mainstreamed class.

Additional factors that affect the attitudes of typical children toward their peers with special needs include perceptions of physical attractiveness, athletic ability, and ability to engage in the same play activities as others (Guralnick, 1986; Strain, 1985; Zetlin & Murtaugh, 1988). Typical children recognize as early as 4 years of age the constraints that a wheelchair imposes on play and prefer to play with partners who are not restricted by a disability (Weinberg, 1978). Young children and females tend to be more tolerant of differences in their peers, although this frequently changes with age and shifts in peer group norms.

Studies of children's beliefs and attitudes toward people with mental retardation reveal that children often have negative attitudes toward mental retardation that appear to increase as they grow older (Bromfield, Weisz, & Messer, 1986; Elam & Sigelman, 1983; Furnham & Gibbs, 1984; Goodman, 1989). Goodman (1989) found that children viewed mental retardation as unchangeable and as something with which people were born, a response similar to adult beliefs. Appearance of atypical facial features, such as those features seen in children with Down syndrome, caused children to label individuals as retarded, even when this was not the case (Goodman, 1989; Graffi & Minnes, 1988).

Social perceptions, as discussed in the preceding paragraphs, may also increase the perceived risk of knowing a child who has a disability (Buysse & Bailey, 1993; Hymel, Wagner, & Butler, 1990; Weiserbs & Gottlieb, 1992). By associating with children who have disabilities, typical peers fear that they may endanger their own social status. One particular theory, *reputational bias*, addresses how people unconsciously try to maintain existing

beliefs or attitudes in the face of contradictory evidence (Hymel, Wagner, & Butler, 1990). This theory suggests that refusing to change our perceptions about others allows us to maintain our own positive social identity by negative comparison to people whom we believe to be inferior.

Reputational bias can exist in people with disabilities as well as in those without disabilities (Zola, 1982). People with milder disabilities tend to have negative biases toward those who have more severe impairments. Zola (1982) described social "ranking" among adults with disabilities living in a Dutch community for people with special needs; for example, those adults who had acquired disabilities refused to associate with adults who had congenital disabilities. Siperstein and Bak (1989) found similar ranking behaviors when they studied adolescents in self-contained classrooms for students with mental retardation. Some individuals with disabilities may compare themselves to those with more severe disabilities to highlight their own abilities.

In spite of the early development of negative attitudes in typical children, those typical children who have been exposed to peers with mental retardation in a positive group format seem to have more positive attitudes toward disabilities than those children who have not had this exposure (Furnham & Gibbs, 1984). Rosenbaum, Armstrong, and King (1986) compared methods for changing attitudes in typically developing children. They found that interventions that were designed to alter typical children's attitudes toward classmates with disabilities were more likely to have lasting results if the classmates with disabilities were included in the approach. Siperstein and Leffert (1997) studied middle school children with mental retardation and found that a number of them were socially accepted by their typically developing peers. Those who were socially accepted exhibited more of the social behaviors deemed appropriate by the peer group.

Although past research on social relationships has depicted less than positive peer attitudes toward children with disabilities, current literature on inclusive environments is demonstrating that negative attitudes can be changed, resulting in improved social networks and friendships (Meyer et al., 1998).

SUCCESSFUL SOCIAL INTEGRATION IN SCHOOL

Social perceptions of people with disabilities are changing; this change is evidenced by laws, such as the Americans with Disabilities Act (ADA) of 1990 (PL 101-336) and the Individuals with Disabilities Education Act (IDEA) Amendments of 1997 (PL 105-17); increasing visibility of people with disabilities; and a movement to educate children with disabilities in classrooms alongside their typically developing peers. Due to the large amount of time that students spend in school, educators need to be concerned with students' social skills.

One reason for focusing on children's social acceptance and friendships at school is that social acceptance strongly relates to children's self-esteem. Though it seems obvious, we all have a need for regular social contact with people to whom we feel connected. Life happiness is highly correlated to the presence of close relationships (Baumeister & Leary, 1995). People with and without disabilities who have a history of social problems during childhood have a higher incidence of both internalizing and externalizing mental health problems as adults (Clegg & Standen, 1991).

A second reason for attending to children's social relationships in school is that a child's social status affects his or her performance across a variety of environments. Social acceptance is related to a child's ability to work in groups and to attain assistance from his or her peers when it is needed. In academic environments, those children who are not accepted by their peers often do not like school as well and do not experience as much academic success as their accepted peers (Hymel, Rubin, Rowden, & LeMare, 1990; Ladd, 1990; Parker & Asher, 1987, 1993; Vandell & Hembree, 1994). Social difficulties are often one of the primary rea-

sons for being unsuccessful in employment after high school (Rusch, Chadsey-Rusch, & Johnson, 1990). The skills that are necessary to build and call on a positive social support network become critical to success. Schools, where groups of peers already exist, provide a natural environment in which to develop social skills and relationships.

Elementary and Preschool Environments

The social effects of integrating children with and without disabilities has been the focus of a lot of research during the late 1980s and the 1990s. Some, though not all, of the older studies that investigated the social benefits of integrated classrooms found an increase in the number of social initiations made by children with disabilities, an increase in the social bids from typical peers, an improvement in social competence, and a decline in the amount of time spent with adults (Beckman & Kohl, 1987; Cole & Meyer, 1991; Jenkins, Odom & Speltz, 1989). Cole and Meyer (1991) highlighted improvements in children's social regulation, ability to follow the rules, tendency to offer assistance to peers, and ability to cope with negative feedback; other researchers have focused more on improvements in children's social initiation and communication skills.

Other research has examined the social changes that occur in inclusive classrooms. Rather than just examine skill changes, these studies have also investigated alterations in children's social networks as well as their social acceptance and friendships. The findings from this research have demonstrated some intriguing results. Evans, Salisbury, Palombaro, Berryman, and Hollowood (1992) followed eight elementary-age children throughout a school year. They found that the number of social interactions for some of the children actually declined during the year. The study's most interesting finding was that, in this sample, social acceptance was not related to social competence. The authors postulated that this outcome challenges the social skills training approach because the children with the highest social acceptance in the study had the most limited social competence and skill.

Staub, Schwartz, Gallucci, and Peck (1994) studied four friendships between children with and without disabilities in an inclusive classroom. All four friendships grew out of participation in the same classes but not out of tutoring roles or other helping activities. The research revealed that the students' friendships were built on some similarities in the children's personalities (e.g., sense of humor, shyness), despite their very different ability levels. Some of the relationships were initiated with a typical peer playing a helping role but evolved into balanced relationships. Typical peers knew their friends with disabilities well enough to "read" their feelings and to understand their often unique ways of communicating. In turn, the children with disabilities shared qualities with their typical friends that the typical friends valued (e.g., sense of humor, comfort). Thus, the relationships were not one-way but had some reciprocal characteristics of shared enjoyment.

Fryxell and Kennedy (1995) compared social standards across students with disabilities in both inclusive and segregated environments. In contrast to similar children in segregated environments, students with disabilities in inclusive environments had higher levels of social contacts with peers without disabilities, received and provided more social support, and had larger friendship networks that included more typical peers.

Two related studies that assessed teacher practices and strategies in inclusive environments noted a focus on building community within the inclusive classrooms (Salisbury, Gallucci, Palombaro, & Peck, 1995; Salisbury, Palombaro, & Hollowood, 1993). All members of these classrooms were valued, no matter what their abilities were. By using an approach that stresses community values at an early age, social networks are built without resorting to direct methods such as peer tutoring and friendship groups.

Middle School and High School Students

Schnorr (1997) documented some of the social struggles of typical middle school and secondary school students who were attempting to become members of existing subgroups in new school environments. The students in the study made recommendations for gaining membership:

- Class membership depends on belonging to a class subgroup.
- Broad class participation is not enough to ensure subgroup membership.
- New students need to make conscious efforts to be accepted into a subgroup.

Once a student becomes part of a subgroup, continuing membership needs to be pursued, not just assumed. Further observations by Schnorr (1997) indicated that some of these same strategies were used by the more popular students with multiple disabilities, though not by the less accepted students with disabilities.

Approximately 2% of middle school and high school students are socially isolated with "high negative visibility" to their peers (Evans & Eder, 1993, p. 164). A vicious cycle often develops in middle schools:

1. Students don't understand or have support for their own social insecurities.
2. Students easily fall into the trap of labeling those who are socially isolated as "nerds," "stupid," or "ugly."
3. Students distance themselves from the traits and behaviors associated with the isolated students. The labeling and distancing pattern isolates these students even further.

Some middle schools anticipate the developmental challenges of adolescence and try to involve students in generating solutions to their own school difficulties. These schools offer student forums on social concerns such as being teased or ridiculed, disability/ability awareness, and racism. Other middle schools purposefully seek to expand the typically narrow extracurricular offerings (e.g., sports, cheerleading) to allow more students opportunities for participation and achievement. These schools offer a diverse range of extracurricular opportunities in which many students of varying abilities can be active (e.g., jazz band, choral groups, art studio, computer clubs, a television station, theater and acting opportunities, service groups). Middle school is a critical time for students to develop their unique talents, experience success, and improve their peer status (Evans & Elder, 1993).

As Kennedy, Shukla, and Fryxell (1997) pointed out, the central arrangement of elementary school classrooms facilitates social engagements. By contrast, middle and high school classes are usually in multiple rooms with different teachers rather than in one classroom with a single primary teacher as is typically the case in elementary schools. Middle school and high school students are expected to be able to negotiate social issues on their own, with limited help from teachers. Functional and social integration is more challenging with this age group than with younger children, especially with the greater differences in academic achievement that exist between adolescents with and without disabilities.

In spite of such challenges, a group of studies focusing on middle and high school students with disabilities who are included in general education environments suggest that some positive shift in overall support networks can occur. Special education students who were placed in inclusive classrooms demonstrated consistent, positive social gains (Fryxell & Kennedy, 1995; Kennedy, Cushing, & Itkonen, 1997; Kennedy, Shukla, & Fryxell, 1997). Results indicated that students in inclusive classrooms

- Have more frequent interactions with their typically developing classmates

- Have social contacts that occur across a broader range of environments and that consist of various types of engagements

- Receive and give more social support to others

- Have larger friendship networks composed largely of students without disabilities

- Have more durable relationships

Effects of Social Contact on Children without Disabilities

The literature in this area is sparse, yet promising. Kishi and Meyer (1994) interviewed a population of typically developing children who participated in a nonstructured social interaction program with children who have severe disabilities (contact group). The social interaction program took place while the typically developing students were in elementary school. The students' impressions were compared with those of others who had been exposed to but had no regular social contact with children with disabilities (exposure group) and to a third group who had attended schools where there were no children with disabilities (control group):

- Girls who participated in the study scored significantly higher than boys on acceptance of children with disabilities.

- The contact group and the exposure group (especially girls) scored higher on acceptance than the control group.

- All students in the contact group scored significantly higher in self-assertion than students in the control and exposure groups.

- Boys in the contact group scored significantly higher in their own security than the boys in the other two groups.

Several qualitative studies have been carried out to investigate how students without disabilities feel about their interactions with people who have special needs (Biklan, Corrigan, & Quick, 1989; Helmstetter, Peck, & Giangreco, 1994; Murray-Seegert, 1989; Peck, Donaldson, & Pezzoli, 1990; Vogtle, 1996). The results of these studies suggest that students who spend quality time with classmates who have disabilities often develop their own personal understanding and tolerance of individual differences. Findings have shown that peers

- Increased their tolerance of other people
- Learned not to "feel sorry" for students with disabilities
- Improved their self-concept
- Became more aware of other people's prejudices
- Developed new personal principles
- Experienced relaxed friendships
- Learned to care about other people who were different
- Satisfied their altruistic intentions
- Improved their self-reflection—students saw their own actions in a different light

In addition to the preceding benefits, these studies also documented some difficulties that typical peers experience in their relationships with children who have disabilities. In some cases, it was hard for peers to give clear feedback to students with disabilities regarding behaviors they perceived as negative. There were other times when the typical students were uncomfortable in school or social environments because of something that their partner with a disability said or did. Despite these kinds of problems, typical children were able to persist and maintain the relationships. Clearly, the benefits outweighed the occasional problems that the typical children encountered. The presence of sensitive adult facilitators to lend support is important in such programs.

The outcomes of studies of the relationships between students with and without disabilities are encouraging; however, one issue remains unresolved. People who participate in programs that encourage social interactions with people who have disabilities are likely to be flexible and responsive to differences. There is some suggestion that children who interact well with other children who have disabilities have similar traits: They are nurturing children who are not class leaders but are known for taking care of others

(Staub, Schwartz, Gallucci, & Peck, 1994; Vogtle, 1996). The students who do not readily participate in such peer support programs are likely to be resistant to changing their attitudes regarding disability. We need to learn more about these students and how to affect their attitudes.

Parental Concerns

It is clear that parents of children with and without disabilities want their children to have friends and to participate in social activities throughout their lives. Important benefits of inclusive education include social integration, larger social networks, increased sensitivity to diversity, and the opportunity for increased friendships. How do parents, both those of children with disabilities and of typical children, feel about their children attending an inclusive school?

Parents of Children with Disabilities Parents of children with disabilities who attend inclusive schools reported that they looked forward to their children's having increased opportunities for academic achievement as well increased opportunities to learn social skills and make friends. Some parents stated that social relationships were not seen as goals in segregated classrooms (Hanline & Halvorsen, 1989). Other parents, however, voiced concerns about possible social rejection from teachers and peers, diminished school facilities and services, and transportation issues (Green & Shinn, 1994; Guralnick, Connor, & Hammond, 1995). Some parents believed that their children's self-esteem would improve in inclusive classrooms, whereas other parents believed it would not. Some parents believed that their children would be more socially accepted by other children who had the same problems than they would be by typical classmates.

The few studies to date have shown that most parents' fears about inclusive schools have not been realized. Parents of children with disabilities in inclusive schools believe that their children have more friends, have higher self-esteem, and engage in more social interactions with typical children (Green & Shinn, 1994; Guralnick et al., 1995; Reichart et al., 1989). A benefit that parents of children with disabilities see for their children's typical peers is the opportunity for the typical peers to learn tolerance and understanding of those students who have different abilities.

Parents of Typically Developing Children
Though even fewer studies have been conducted on the perceptions of typical children's parents regarding their children's attendance of inclusive schools, the information is generally positive. Reichart et al. (1989) sent surveys to parents of preschool-age children with and without disabilities to study their views on inclusive environments. Parents of typical chil-dren did not see an increase in behavior problems as a result of their children's participation in inclusive classrooms and believed that inclusive environments promoted positive social contact. In a similar survey, Lowenbraum, Madge, and Affleck (1990) found that about one-third of the parents of typical children actually had requested that their children be placed in inclusive classrooms. A large majority of parents with typical children were very satisfied with their children's social and academic progress and indicated that they would choose an inclusive environment for their children's education in the future.

Chapter 3

Approaches for Facilitating
Positive Social Relationships

with Kenna M. Colley

Think back to when you attended school: What do you think of first? Many of your memories are probably of your friends and of the special relationships that you had with your classmates. Friendships are what many children, both with and without disabilities, love most about school.

Many levels of supportive relationships develop among children and adolescents. Particularly when children are young, their relationships will change from year to year and even within a given school year. Some children may have acquaintances to whom they speak on the bus and in passing but do not play with or seek out for other social occasions. Other children may have friends from other grade levels, especially if they live in the same neighborhood or if their parents are friends.

Social relationships among school-age children typically develop and grow with little facilitation from adults, parents, and teachers; however, when a child has difficulty establishing positive social relationships, parents and teachers may need to become more involved in the relationship-building process, even if only during the initial stages. Although adults cannot manufacture or mandate friendships, they can assist in the creation of a variety of positive relationships among children with diverse abilities. This chapter describes some proven strategies for facilitating social relationships between students who have disabilities and their typically developing peers.

CONFIDENTIALITY AND SELF-DISCLOSURE OF DISABILITY

Many of the structured approaches for building social relationships that are described in this chapter involve a carefully planned, age-appropriate disclosure of the student's disability to the student's classmates. An individual's disability is private information that must be handled with care. As with any other confidential student information, staff must be certain about the wishes of students and their families regarding the sharing of such information. Even though some physical and cognitive disabilities are highly visible, staff must not assume that explanations about the disability (e.g., labels, history, medical information) are public information. It is always the individual student's choice (or for younger students, his or her family's choice) to reveal or disclose information about his or her disability.

TYPE OF DISABILITY AND PEER SUPPORT STRATEGY

Many methods of peer support have been applied to students who have complex support needs as a result of their disabilities, including cognitive disabilities such as mental retardation, physical disabilities such as cerebral palsy, and developmental and behavioral disabilities such as autism. For students with less visible or noncognitive disabilities, it seems most appropriate to use more naturalistic and less structured approaches for building social relationships. Students with less visible and/or noncognitive disabilities may also be involved in efforts to improve their social skills and to self-manage any inappropriate behaviors (see Chapter 4). Some students with disabilities can be excellent *providers of support* in structured peer support groups organized around other students with disabilities. Some of these same students assist in disability awareness activities by sharing aspects of their own disability. Selecting students for peer support, identifying objectives, and planning the approach is a team process that involves both the general and special educators, family members, the student, and often the student's peers.

ADULT FACILITATION

One key to building positive peer relationships in schools for students with and without disabilities is *facilitation by adults*. Adult facilitators include teachers, paraprofessionals, parents, related services personnel, other school staff, and volunteers. Adults can choose between an indirect and preparatory approach to facilitating social relationships (e.g., improving the school atmosphere and student/staff attitudes) or a direct approach to building positive relationships between students (e.g., building peer support). Typically, both a preparatory and a direct approach are used in concert, with environmental improvements strengthening the groundwork so that schools are more receptive to efforts to build peer support.

Real friendships between children can usually be attributed to shared mutual interests, similarities in life, and positive reciprocity; however, whether the focus is on improving the environment or on building peer support, adults still play a crucial, facilitative role in nurturing relationships between children. In this section, adult facilitation is described and applied to school environments.

Structure, Effort, and Extent of Adult Facilitation

Adults' roles vary depending on the approach used and the specific strategy selected. Table 3.1 gives a "feel" for two approaches— improving the school environment and building peer support—by listing several common strategies. The amount of *structure and effort* required from adults and/or peers to use these strategies varies widely. *Structure and effort* encompass the degree of organization, the amount of planning time and teaming, whether a naturally occurring or a new peer activity is used, and the amount and type of

adult involvement (e.g., presence, prompting, feedback, data collection). For example, some strategies for building peer support build on existing scheduled school activities, such as lunch, and other strategies require the creation of activities, such as Best Buddy events. Similarly, "ability awareness" activities to improve the school environment could be planned for an entire school and could extend across several weeks; however, this strategy requires a major time commitment by a planning group in contrast to a classroom unit on abilities and disabilities.

Building social relationships in a classroom or school requires teachers and administrators to employ a variety of strategies. The process is not a "one-shot approach" but an evolving one. Many schools apply *environmental strategies* on an ongoing basis to build and periodically update students' understanding of and appreciation for diversity. Such environmental strategies might include sharing children's and young adults' literature about differences and similarities, demonstrating ways to interact with someone who uses pictures to communicate instead of words, or providing explanations to peers about classmates with disabilities in respectful, student-oriented language. These same environmental improvement strategies also are valuable at the middle and secondary school levels but must be matched to adolescents' ages, inter-

Table 3.1. Approaches for facilitating positive social relationships

Improving the school environment (atmosphere and attitudes)	Building peer support
• Ongoing staff in-services on disability • Understanding diversity: Information infused into class content and reading • Ability/disability awareness: Sensitive simulations of disability, guests with disabilities, age-appropriate literature, and videotapes • Adults modeling appropriate interactions and expressing positive attitudes • Circle of Friends exercise	• Students meet regularly with an adult • Start with facts about a focus student • Add, as appropriate, information on the student's personality, history, disability, communication, and any required equipment or procedures • Develop guidelines for lending support and for social interaction • Teach or shape problem-solving skills • Problem-solve difficulties that arise • Implement and improve solutions

ests, and increased awareness about life. It is also effective to have all students participate in an awareness day during which they

- Experience simulations of physical, sensory, or learning disabilities
- Learn about different disabilities and facilitative technology by using electronic communication boards and braille
- Talk to productive adults who have a disability
- Use wheelchairs and evaluate the accessibility of a school building or part of the surrounding community

When teachers and administrators first work to improve the atmosphere of the school and the attitudes of its students by extending knowledge about disability and challenging students' prejudices or negative attitudes, the second approach—creating mechanisms for peer support (e.g., recruit students, explain the rationale, maintain the strategy)—becomes easier.

Modeling

Modeling is a key element adults use in most approaches that are designed to promote social relationships. Modeling involves incidental (and sometimes explicit) teaching of appropriate ways to assist, relate to, and interact with students who have disabilities. Modeling can be used by adults (and by peers) and includes one's actions as well as one's attitudes as expressed in conversations and nonverbal remarks made about students who have disabilities. When students with disabilities are new to a school or a classroom, typical students, who may feel uneasy, often look to their teachers for guidance on how to interact with the new students. The special education teacher, in cooperation with the student's family members, may be the best initial model for other staff and students. However, when other school staff members such as librarians, guidance counselors, principals, paraprofessionals, therapists, school nurses, secretaries, cafeteria staff, bus drivers, and custodians are comfort-

able and appropriate in their interactions with students who have disabilities and are familiar with the child and his or her capabilities and needs, positive modeling permeates the school. Two important functions these adults can serve are to 1) model appropriate interactions by using age-appropriate language, voice tone, and interaction style and adjusting the complexity and modality to suit the student's communication methods, and 2) answer peers' questions in an honest but sensitive manner without providing more information than necessary and using explanations suited to the students' level of understanding.

Modeling includes both actions and words. Students often learn from watching the manner in which adults *talk about* students with disabilities. Adults' words and gestures can communicate respect and comfort or avoidance and uncertainty. Adults' comments about students with disabilities may be fair or unfair and may focus on positive or negative aspects of the students' abilities and personalities. Despite the fact that modeling, whether positive or negative, is a subtle strategy, it can be powerful to students of all ages. Students also learn from *watching the way in which others react to their ways of interacting* with students who have disabilities and from *the reaction of the individual with disabilities.* Do teachers (or students' peers) approve or disapprove? Are students successful in their efforts to assist and communicate with their classmate or to defuse potentially disruptive behavior?

To be effective models, adults should have positive attitudes about human diversity and some awareness of the focus students' abilities (e.g., mode of communication, knowledge level, visual and auditory capabilities, mobility) and personalities. If teachers and staff are uncomfortable around students with disabilities and show outward signs of uneasiness or fear, other students usually detect their discomfort and feel uncomfortable themselves.

Another powerful philosophy is the belief that the included student is "just another student" and is generally expected to follow the same school rules as others for lining up, taking turns, listening, being in his or her place on time, and putting his or her head down when it gets noisy (Janney & Snell, 1996). Teachers who do this teach their students to treat their classmate with a disability as they would treat each other—not to coddle, patronize, treat as if much younger, or address using "baby talk."

When a particular student with a disability enters a new school or a class, it is appropriate to share helpful information with the staff who will be involved with the student. Early in-service sessions organized by the school's special education teachers should be held to address the general areas of knowledge about students' ability and disability that influence

adult modeling. For typical students to be accepting of students with diverse learning styles and needs, teachers must teach through their actions, not merely by instructing and advising (Goodman, 1994).

Before Daniel arrived for second grade at Mountain Ridge Elementary, his special education teacher organized a team planning session and shared his Program at-a-Glance (Figure 3.1). Daniel, who was new to the school district, had multiple disabilities (cerebral palsy, vision impairments, and a seizure disorder) and, therefore, a large edu-

Program-at-a-Glance

Student: _Daniel_   **Date:** _1998–1999_   **School:** _Mountain View Elem._   **Grade:** _2nd_

IEP Objectives (briefly)	Accommodations
• Play with peers—structured turn taking • Maintain ROM in upper extremities through daily activity & stretching • Improve visual gaze & attention • Partial participation—grade-level lessons—motor, communicative intent, & alertness • Recognize visual, tactile, & auditory cues to assist in anticipating events • Initiate, respond, make choices, reject, & show displeasure using recognizable communication cues (yes = head moved up; no = head dropped and to the side; reject/displeasure = makes a sad face) • Reactions to daily object schedule	• Educational team instructed in positioning equipment, feeding & drinking techniques, toileting, dispensing medication, lifting & positioning in/out of wheelchair & other personal care needs • Separate changing area provided • PT, OT, speech-language therapist consult with team regarding issues/techniques • Special education teacher provides direct/consultative services for general ecucation teacher & teaching assistant • Peer support program • Computer/assistive technology explored by educational team
Academic/ Social management needs	**Comments/Special needs**
• Partial participation to greatest extent possible with peers • Peers included in therapies as much as possible	• New staff trained by experienced staff or parents in specialized routines (e.g., feeding, g-tube, toileting, handling, positioning) • Communication log between home and school

Figure 3.1.   Daniel's Program-at-a-Glance.

cational team. Along with Daniel's mom and brother, the special education teacher and Daniel's therapists (speech-language, vision, physical, and occupational) organized two short in-service sessions for Daniel's second-grade teacher; several paraprofessionals; the principal; the guidance counselor; and the music, P.E., and library teachers. Daniel arrived for the last part of both sessions to meet everyone. Before he arrived, those attendees who knew Daniel well gave the group some general guidelines about how to interact with him (e.g., look at Daniel when you talk, not at his teacher or mother; use a normal voice as his hearing is normal; talk to him as a second grader but use simpler vocabulary—he understands a lot; know that Daniel indicates "yes" by lifting his head). By discussing these guidelines before he arrived, the group did not have to talk about Daniel in front of him. During Daniel's visit, teachers had an opportunity to see Daniel interact with his mom, his brother, and the special education teacher, who knew him well already. The guidelines and models gave Daniel's teachers confidence to try interacting with Daniel during his visits.

Role Playing

When teachers use role playing to promote social relationships, they are simply increasing the structure or intensity of modeling. For example, some role playing within peer support groups has been used to let classmates practice ways that they might 1) prompt a classmate who pushes and grabs instead of using words to ask for something, 2) act when a classmate starts to get angry or has a tantrum, and 3) pose a question to a student who uses a yes/no system of communicating. Often it is helpful to accompany a demonstration with a simple explanation for the actions that are being role played. When students understand the general rationale for what they are learning, they are more likely to generalize it to other situations.

Using Person-First Language

Emphasizing the person, not the disability, is one way adults can communicate respect for students with disabilities. *"Person-first" language does not equate people with their condition ("the disabled"); it simply means that you put the person, not the disability, first.* Therefore, you name the person first, and then, if necessary, name the disability: a teenager who is blind, an infant with Down syndrome, a boy who has autism. Although this way of speaking and writing about disability is not new, it is not consistently practiced in the media and is often absent from most individuals' everyday language. The accusation of being "too politically correct" has led to some mockery of this practice; however, person-first language communicates respect for the individual human being while de-emphasizing the disability. When adults consistently model person-first language and include it in their guidelines of proper ways to write and converse, children will adopt person-first language and teach it to others outside the school.

There are numerous other commonly used words and phrases that refer to disabilities that are inaccurate, patronizing, pity-evoking, or simply negative. For example, to say that a person is "wheelchair-bound" is inaccurate. People who use a wheelchair are not actually bound to that chair; they *use* it; therefore, "wheelchair user" is a more appropriate term. Likewise, the term "mongoloid" has long since been replaced by "Down syndrome." Teach students to use emotionally neutral expressions:

She has cerebral palsy.
NOT
She suffers from cerebral palsy.

He had a brain injury.
NOT
He is a brain injury victim.

Acronyms such as CP, LD, BD, MR, and TMR are also not necessary in our discussions about students with disabilities with their typical peers. ("She's BD and ADHD").

At times, it might be necessary to use and explain the actual term (e.g., cerebral palsy, learning disabilities) to typical students; however, once the term has been explained, it can simply be omitted and the child can be referred to by name alone! (See Figure 3.2 for more examples.) Particularly with older students (beyond second grade) and adults, it is valuable to teach the rules and the rationale behind person-first language.

Amount of Adult Involvement

As discussed in Chapter 2, children and adolescents value the similarities they have with certain peers, and it is often these similarities that bring peers together into social networks and that launch friendships. Thus, teachers often will work to identify and build on the commonalities that exist among all students. An accepting atmosphere that provides information on differences while also emphasizing similarities makes it easier to build tolerance, trust, mutual support, and respect. From these interpersonal characteristics, individuals develop a sense of belonging; and, from this base, positive social relationships often result.

In addition to the philosophy of initiating social contact between peers and then backing off to promote peer interactions, there are many ways in which educators can counter the "velcro-aides" or "hovering adult" phenomenon.

> *Sometimes I think it inhibits her relationship with her peers because a lot is done for Holly and Holly doesn't have the opportunity to interact with her peers because there is always somebody hovering over her, showing her what to do or doing things for her. I'd like to get the instructional assistant away from Holly a little bit more so that peers will have a chance to get in there and work with Holly. (Giangreco, Edelman, Luiselli, & MacFarland, 1997, p. 13)*

First, staff can learn effective ways to teach pairs or small groups of students rather than just the child with disabilities. Adopting more effective methods involves an awareness of

- The extent to which some adults control or dominate the interactions between a student with disabilities and his or her peers (Do staff members physically assist a response, hold materials, speak for the student?)

- The inhibiting effects these practices have on all students

- What can be done to enable rather than prevent peer interaction

Videotaping peer interactions and small-group instruction can facilitate this learning process, and, if many segments involving various staff members are taped, teachers can more easily be self-critical. Research in the area of adult involvement has shown that typical peers, when given a choice, often left groups involving a student with support needs that was supervised by a paraprofessional. Peers left because their offers of assistance were refused by the adult, they were "rebuffed by" the adult, or their initiations were interrupted by the adult (Giangreco et al., 1997). Some adults (paraprofessionals, as well as teachers, related services staff, and administrators) may need focused direction on how to teach groups without dominating the group's interactions. At times, paraprofessional staff assigned to students with disabilities may feel their role of "helper" is threatened by or even belittled by peers who want to fill that same role and who could do so competently! Therefore, general and special educators should direct their attention to redefining teaching assistants' roles so they know that they are expected to teach mixed groups of students and to facilitate peer interactions and so they know how to do so.

The use of cooperative group activities may also be advantageous because teachers and assistants are not physically involved in the groups themselves. Instead, the teachers plan ahead for groups of three to six students of varied ability to participate in a learning

It's the 'Person First'—Then the Disability

What do you see first?

- *The wheelchair?*
- *The physical problem?*
- *The person?*

If you saw a person in a wheelchair unable to get up the stairs into a building, would you say "there is a handicapped person unable to find a ramp"? Or would you say "there is a person with a disability who is handicapped by an inaccessible building"?

What is the proper way to speak to or about someone who has a disability?

Consider how you would introduce someone—Jane Doe—who doesn't have a disability. You would give her name, where she lives, what she does or what she is interested in—she likes swimming, or eating Mexican food, or watching Robert Redford movies.

Why say it differently for a person with disabilities? Every person is made up of many characteristics—mental as well as physical—and few want to be identified only by their ability to play tennis or by their love for fried onions or by the mole that's on their face. Those are just parts of us.

In speaking or writing, remember that children or adults with disabilities are like everyone else—except they happen to have a disability. Therefore, here are a few tips for improving your language related to disabilities and handicaps.

1. Speak of the person first, then the disability.
2. Emphasize abilities, not limitations.
3. Do not label people as part of a disability group—don't say "the disabled"; say "people with disabilities."
4. Don't give excessive praise or attention to a person with a disability; don't patronize them.
5. Choice and independence are important; let the person do or speak for him/herself as much as possible; if addressing an adult, say "Bill" instead of "Billy."
6. A **disability** is a functional limitation that interferes with a person's ability to walk, hear, talk, learn, etc.; use **handicap** to describe a situation or barrier imposed by society, the environment or oneself.

Say . . .	Instead of . . .
child with a disability	disabled or handicapped child
person with cerebral palsy	palsied, or C.P., or spastic
person who is deaf or hard of hearing	deaf and dumb
person with retardation	retarded
person with epilepsy or person with seizure disorder	epileptic
person who has . . .	afflicted, suffers from, victim
without speech, nonverbal	mute, or dumb
developmental delay	slow
emotional disorder, or mental illness	crazy or insane
uses a wheelchair	confined to a wheelchair
with Down syndrome	mongoloid
has a learning disability	is learning disabled
nondisabled	normal, healthy
has a physical disability	crippled
congenital disability	birth defect
condition	disease (unless it is a disease)
seizures	fits
cleft lip	hare lip
mobility impaired	lame
medically involved, or has chronic illness	sickly
paralyzed	invalid or paralytic
has hemoplegia (paralysis of one side of the body)	hemiplegic
has quadriplegia (paralysis of both arms and legs)	quadriplegic
has paraplegia (loss of function in lower body only)	paraplegic
of short stature	dwarf or midget
accessible parking	handicapped parking

Figure 3.2.   People first guidelines. (From PACER Center [September, 1989]. "It's the 'person first'—then the disability." *Pacesetter*, Minneapolis, MN: The PACER Center; reprinted by permission from PACER Center, [612]827-2966.)

activity that requires each student to play a meaningful role. The adult observes from outside the group and lends direct support or prompts peers to provide assistance as needed. In order to avoid too much child–adult dependency from developing, some schools assign two paraprofessionals rather than just one to students who require extensive support; these staff members alternate part way through the day and follow the practice of assisting all students, not simply the student with disabilities. Figure 3.3 provides several "pull-back" guidelines that work across age groups to help adults gauge and limit their assistance in promoting peer interaction.

IMPROVING THE SOCIAL ENVIRONMENT AND ATTITUDES OF TEACHERS, ADMINISTRATORS, AND STAFF

In most school districts, meaningful inclusion of students with disabilities is very limited. Although a majority of students who have speech-language disabilities spend their school day in the mainstream, those with other disabilities—particularly behavior disorders, cognitive disabilities, and multiple disabilities—are not as likely to be enrolled in general education classrooms or to find individualized special education supports that allow them to learn in the mainstream. In many states, teachers and administrators are required to complete an introductory course in special education and to learn about various disabling conditions; however, many school professionals have not had even a single course. Most school staff members and students could benefit from learning some basic information about disabilities and from some firsthand, positive experience with individuals who have disabilities.

Before a school can become more inclusive, its staff members often need assistance in examining their own values and mission regarding teaching and learning and also in acquiring information and guidance about 1) children with disabilities, 2) collaborative teaming as a means of planning and problem-solving, and 3) curriculum modification to individualize learning experiences. As plans to include students with disabilities are being designed and implemented, staff members will continue to need regular in-service sessions and updates on topics related to inclusion. Guidelines for early steps in a system's change to inclusion are addressed in two of the other booklets in this series—*Modifying Schoolwork* and *Collaborative Teaming*—(Janney & Snell,

---

1. An adult should set up lessons and interactions with clear explanations to all students regarding what their roles and responsibilities are for that particular lesson.
2. After instructions have been provided, the adult should physically pull back from the lesson and move on to another task while closely observing the group's progress from a distance.
3. If the adult observes that students' interactions appear to be "falling apart" or are at a standstill, the adult should reenter the group and provide some direct assistance in the form of questions or statements (e.g., "Emma, are you losing interest in this game?" "What can we do to get Emma more involved?").
4. Once the adult gets the students "back on track," he or she should retreat again. This is called the "set up and withdraw" method of providing support for ongoing peer interactions with students who require large intitial amounts of supervision. When adults continue to "set up and withdraw," they offer the students' peers the opportunity to keep interactions going without stifling their spontaneity.
5. The keys to pulling back successfully are visual supervision from a distance, the ability to recognize when students are "floundering" and need some guidance, and the confidence to allow students to take risks and try out their skills without too much adult intervention.
6. These guidelines work with students of all ages and grade levels.

Figure 3.3. Pull-back guidelines for adults providing assistance to interactions between peers.

2000b, Snell & Janney, 2000) and in several other helpful references (e.g., Davern, Ford, Erwin, Schnorr, & Rogan, 1993; McGregor & Vogelsberg, 1998; Roach, 1995; Schaffner, Buswell, Summerfield, & Kovar, 1988; Wilcox & Nicholson, 1990; Wilcox, Nicholson, & Farlow, 1990; York-Barr, 1996). Teachers and others who work in schools need to be exposed to this basic information in ways that are suited to their existing knowledge and roles. Teaching staff should become involved in the planning and provision of information and experiences to their students only after this exposure.

Students' Perceptions of Fairness

Issues of fairness are commonly addressed in most schools and homes as children are growing up and may also influence a child's social environment. Both adults and students have their own perceptions of fairness. Although teachers adjust some standards for behavior, they should expect students with disabilities to follow classroom rules as much as possible. Generally, teachers should encourage typical peers to view their classmates with disabilities as class members who are to be "treated the same," regardless of whether the supports they require are extensive or minimal:

> *Tony goes to the office every afternoon to take medication for his hyperactivity. Usually, before lunch, it is harder for Tony to sit and work at his desk. At these times, he might be given responsibilities that let him move around, he might move his work to the floor, or he may just take a break from sitting. Do peers notice or care that he goes to the office every lunch period? Will peers think his "activity breaks" are unfair?*

> *Sylvia has myeloemingocele (spina bifida), which for her means that she uses a walker; is a grade level behind in academics, along with some other students in her class; and uses the private bathroom, where she is able to catheterize herself, only infrequently needing help. Will Sylvia's peers wonder why she takes so long on bathroom breaks or why she uses the private bathroom?*

> *Bethany's reading has always been exceptional. In eighth grade, she reads high school– and college-level materials. For special projects, her teachers provide her with books from the nearby high school and college libraries on interlibrary loan. Lately, Bethany has received permission to use the school's connection to the Internet to seek information for school assignments. While peers know she is a "super reader," will they view Bethany's book and computer privileges as "unfair"?*

Fairness issues often are raised by students, sometimes in the context of a class discussion during which issues of concern are discussed and problem-solved (later described as peer planning sessions). Students might comment about things they believe to be unfair. *"How come Tony can stop his work and we can't?" "Why does Sylvia get to use the teacher's bathroom?" "I want the good books like Bethany gets."* Try to address these questions directly with students but with great care. Many times, our answers address the issues of a reasonable accommodation. *"Because that is how Tony learns best." "Because that bathroom works best for Sylvia." "Because these books are ones that Bethany understands."* When such questions repeatedly arise, the student's educational team needs to discuss student concerns about fairness and to subsequently search for solutions. The solutions may involve improvements in the accommodation itself, in the workloads and activities of students who do not have accommodations, or in the ways that teachers treat students' differences in learning and accomplishment.

It seems easier for peers to understand treatment differences as being fair accommodations under certain classroom and school conditions:

1. The student's disability is reasonably understood by classmates. However, for less visible disabilities or when students choose not to disclose their disabilities, this understanding may not be directly associated with the student who has the disability.

2. Peers are accustomed to having their teachers treat differences in student ability

as ordinary and are taught to applaud individual accomplishments, even when a classmate's disabilities are subtle and not recognizable by typical peers.

3. The student's accommodations or modifications are appropriate, "match" his or her needs, and are nonstigmatizing.

4. Teachers and classmates routinely share, discuss, and problem-solve classroom concerns such as fairness.

5. Teachers place more emphasis on students' similarities than on their differences.

6. The classroom culture is cooperative, and competition is applied only by students to themselves: "Improving my own performance" or "Improving our team's record."

To the extent that accommodations are appropriate and fit students' needs and that class members are used to being in heterogeneous groups and working together cooperatively, students will be more accepting of differences in ability, workload, ways of responding, and accomplishments.

Teaching in ways that enable students to accept differences among classmates is rather different from teaching by the proclaimed standard of "We are all the same," particularly when it is obvious that we are not! Students in inclusive classrooms often recognize differences among themselves; denial of these differences may only further emphasize them for some students.

Staff Perceptions of Fairness

Fairness is not just an issue for students; sometimes staff members are critical of the differences certain students have in their daily school routines, treatment, and educational services. Criticism often occurs when 1) the services provided to the students are extensive in contrast to those provided to other students who may need similar services but do not qualify, and 2) the service provision itself upsets classroom rules and privileges.

Staff concerns about fairness must also be aired with the team of staff involved. Each staff member needs to raise and elaborate on his or her separate concerns; these concerns need to be discussed by the team with the intent of discovering solutions together. Because student and staff perceptions of fair treatment of students with disabilities have a strong impact on the atmosphere of a classroom, concerns need to be aired within the team or the classroom.

Information and Simulations to Increase Student Understanding and Appreciation

For elementary and middle school students, it is useful to plan *initial* activities on diversity and disability awareness on a more widespread basis, with some schoolwide activities, some activities for multiple grade clusters (fourth- and fifth-grade classrooms), and others for single grade levels (all eighth graders). *Later* in the process, when inclusion has become more systematized, activities can be organized and implemented for individual classrooms or for classrooms at a single grade level. In high schools, the coverage of information on diversity, disability, and prejudice is often more naturally integrated into classes on health, family life, history, and social studies. These topics might also be addressed for some through an after-school volunteer service requirement (Hamre-Nietupski, Ayres, Nietupski, Savage, Mitchell, & Bramman, 1989). Sometimes, middle and high school service clubs or Key Clubs may sponsor a day, or several days, of activities during which they promote understanding of differences, diversity, and positive attitudes. Planning groups should attempt to involve many different people: student leaders and representatives from all age groups, special educators, adults with disabilities from the community, staff with inclusion experience, teachers who have seniority and respect, parents of children with and without disabilities, some nonteaching and nonprofessional staff, and the principal or a key administrator.

Smaller-Scale Simulations Teaching children about disabilities through respectful classroom simulations allows students to "try out" being in the shoes of their classmate with a disability. Simulations should also be suited to the typical classmates' ability to understand.

On a day when Nate was absent, kindergartners in Ms. Hill's classroom spent their free time "being Nate." After a discussion about how Nate talks and moves about (i.e., in his wheelchair, with his walker, on the floor), the teachers and assistants helped the students figure out ways to express themselves without words, to move around the room, and to use a drinking fountain without standing upright. Nate's classmates limited their communication to several vocalizations and facial expressions, and, instead of walking, they moved about on their knees and pulled themselves partially up with the support of a table. They talked and moved in these ways as they used the centers, interacted with each other, and engaged in play activities. Teachers were surprised by the students' familiarity with Nate's ways of doing things. The class discussion that followed allowed the children to vent their own frustration. They said things such as, "It's hard to be Nate," and "I like to say words." One perceptive student asked, "Is this why Nate yells a lot?" Following this activity, the kindergarten students generated a list of ways in which they might get Nate to interact and play with them during class choice time and at recess. Over the next few weeks, the students' ideas were tried, revised, and expanded; and Nate's involvement with class activities and interaction with his classmates increased (Figure 3.4).

Another way to provide simulations is to allow typical classmates to try using some of the adapted equipment that their peer with a disability uses (but *only* with student, parental, and therapist approval). If this is not feasible, adults should try to address students' natural curiosity by providing simple explanations for

- Equipment used for mobility (e.g., wheelchairs, walkers, canes, plastic splints) and positioning (e.g., standing tables, prone boards, floor sitters, side lyers)
- Equipment, materials, and methods used for communication (e.g., electronic systems, picture communication books, signing, picture exchange systems)

Nate is 5 years old and a member of Ms. Miller's kindergarten; he has cerebral palsy and uses a walker and a wheelchair and scoots around on his knees. Nate makes some loud and soft sounds, uses some gestures, and speaks a few words to communicate. One day in October when Nate was absent, his teacher asked his classmates to think about how they could get Nate to play more with them more during center time. As they sat on the blue rug and shared their ideas, she wrote them on a big piece of paper and drew small pictures by each idea. The following are some of the creative ideas they brainstormed:

1. Build things that are OK to knock down.
2. Use small blocks to make towers.
3. Help with pictures.
4. Read him a story.
5. Invite him to play in the house.
6. Help him build something with soft blocks.
7. Play ball with him.
8. Help him climb.
9. Sing him a song.
10. Encourage him to come with you.
11. Tell him what you are doing.
12. Use the WOLF (his talking communication device) to pick songs.

Ms. Miller and Nate's other teachers helped his classmates implement these ideas during the weeks that followed.

Figure 3.4.   Kindergarten peers' ideas for getting Nate to play with them.

- Special procedures that might be observed (e.g., eating with specialized equipment, suctioning, tube feeding, grinding food, breathing through a tracheostomy)

- Adapted or specialized learning materials (e.g., Braille books, calculators, adapted writing implements, prostheses to use to make purchases)

Regardless of whether there are students with IEPs in a classroom, it is meaningful for educators to address the issue of respecting diversity and celebrating similarities and differences between students. Figure 3.5 provides suggestions for several activities that can assist students' in understanding that, although they are not all alike, each student has unique gifts and skills.

Grade Level or Schoolwide Ability/Disability Awareness Programs

The general purposes of ability/disability awareness programs often are broad. For example, one or more of the following purposes might be targeted:

- To educate a group of students about people with disabilities

- To replace stereotyped and negative views with accurate information

- To answer students' questions

- To emphasize ability and similarities between people with disabilities and those without disabilities

- To provide a combination of experiences by using carefully planned simulations of one or several disabilities and inviting guest speakers who have disabilities to speak to the students

- To promote positive attitudes toward individuals with disabilities

Ultimately, the school planning group must identify its own purposes for awareness activities and design them to match the school's specific needs and age range. The group will plan the activities to be carried out within or across classrooms and often will spread them out across a period of time. Devoting a small period of time each day to different activities during a disability awareness week (or two), while also following the typical school schedule and routine, allows for better learning than does replacing an entire day's schedule with activities devoted entirely to disability awareness. Activities must be interesting to the age group as well as informative and accurate; they should be neither condescending nor pitying but should emphasize ability and the tenet that "people with disabilities are people (first) who have a disability (second)." Examples of strategies to support this tenet include 1) studying famous people with disabilities in music, sports, writing, politics, or other careers that the students admire and 2) interacting with people who have disabilities and who fill roles that the students respect. Planning teams should determine a set of "do's" and "don'ts" to follow when simulating disabilities with typical students (Figure 3.6).

Even simple activities will require careful planning (e.g., teachers will need to preview books, stories, or films, locate or construct simulation materials, and identify appropriate guests). It also is important to hold brief *discussions after each activity* in order to answer students' questions and assess their understanding and attitudes.

Parents of children with disabilities are often the best assistants for implementing disability awareness activities and discussions. Commercially prepared materials and the use of other schools' programs as models can also save time. Classroom teachers often seek the support and assistance of the special education teacher, school counselor, or a particular therapist who knows more about certain disabilities.

A Middle School Example

Several years ago, Kim Farrington, a graduate student at the time, planned a disability awareness week at a nearby middle school. Although the week was planned by teachers, the general design actually mirrored an extensive awareness program conducted the year before

Voices from the Classroom

There are many commercially made lesson formats that address diversity, tolerance, and human similarities and differences. School guidance counselors can often help to locate such materials. A few examples that have been used successfully include the following:

- Make a large classroom grid with all names listed vertically and photos of each student portrayed across the top. In the boxes created by the intersection of two different names, have student pairs meet and discuss what they both like (e.g., to eat as a main course or dessert, to play outdoors in the summer, to read, to watch on TV) or what they like and don't like in one or more categories. Use words or pictures to show the similarities or the similarities and the differences.

- Have students choose two dissimilar items, compare them (as to function, physical characteristics, and so forth) and complete two lists on the items: How are the items similar? How are they different? Then, use the lists to discuss the similarities and differences between objects and why some of these differences are important (e.g., a cup is hollow because it has to hold water, a tree is solid because it has to support its branches).

- Describe the manner in which people perform everyday tasks. For some tasks, list adaptations that people with disabilities use to perform that particular task (e.g., walking versus using a wheelchair; writing with a pen or pencil versus typing on a computer). For other tasks, list adaptations that many people typically use to perform the task more efficiently (e.g., glasses, ladders, power rider mowers).

- Make a list of various differences among students, and add statements about why these differences are positive attributes of the student.

- Discuss people-first language and why it is used when referring to people with disabilities. Address the question "Don't all people have differences from each other based on where we were born, how we were raised, and where we currently live, not just people with disabilities?"

- Address cultural diversity through classroom units (e.g., social studies, literature) and school-wide activities (e.g., assemblies, poster displays, souvenir collections, foreign foods) that teach the richness and overlapping variations that exist across cultures in regard to languages, foods, holidays, dress, geography and products, traditions, religions, and practices around birth, marriage, and death.

Figure 3.5. Activities to teach appreciation of similarities and differences. (Contributed by Kenna Colley.)

by the student council at the University of Virginia. In the middle school version of this program, students learned about the planned activities ahead of time in their homerooms (Farrington, 1992). They then signed up to experience simulating a disability. In order to share limited equipment (e.g., wheelchairs, walkers, crutches, eye covers, handmade leg braces) and spread out the experience, the week was divided so students could experience physical disabilities and invisible disabilities. Each participant who chose an invisible disability wore a button that said, "I have an invisible disability. Ask me about it."

The physical disabilities that affected students' actions included limited mobility (students used a wheelchair or wore a leg brace made from

posterboard or newspaper rolls and duct tape), visual impairment (students wore eye covers made from felt), and limited flexibility of fingers (students wore a sock or mitten over one or both of their hands).

Invisible disabilities did not always affect the students' actions but allowed participants to give information to others. The invisible disabilities included hearing loss (students wore ear plugs), dyslexia/dysgraphia (students were instructed to write at times during the day by looking in a small mirror and not directly at the paper), illiteracy (students were instructed to act as if they could not read the blackboard or their texts by saying, "I can't quite figure this out. Can you explain it to me?"), speech-language impairment (students were asked to gesture to

Educational teams should apply several rules of caution when planning for the use of simulations in inclusive classrooms or on a larger scale:

1. Simulations should be planned by the educational team, including students' parents; the right to veto any ideas should always exist.
2. Simulations should always focus on the positive and unique characteristics of the student or disability; they should never take on a pitying or superhuman tone and should address strategies used to cope rather than focus on frustration.
3. Simulations should be used only to help students understand an aspect of a person or a disability that is difficult to explain.
4. Simulations should always be preceded with an explanation of why they are occurring and followed by a discussion.
5. Simulations should never depict a student with a disability as the class "mascot" or pet. They should always aim to explain differences by emphasizing unique characteristics or similarities.

Figure 3.6. Rules of caution with disability simulations.

indicate what they wanted), malfunctioning organs such as kidneys or heart (students gave out information), asthma (students gave out information), mental retardation (students gave out information), learning disabilities (students gave out information), and seizure disorders/epilepsy (students only gave out information, as many seizure disorders can be controlled by medication).

Rules and schedules were designed and implemented by the teachers and the organizing graduate student to be sure that 1) the experience was not disruptive, disrespectful, or destructive to the equipment and 2) the program's goals were realized (i.e., to learn about disabilities, to focus on what people with disabilities can do rather than on their limitations, to experience the challenges posed by certain disabilities, and to create the opportunity for open communication between people with disabilities and their peers). Therefore, students were given not only descriptions about the disability in which they participated, but also some general instructions (Figure 3.7). Stu-

- Take the disability seriously; this is not a game but a learning experience.
- Wheelchairs are borrowed and cost a lot of money. You will sign out the equipment and sign it back in when finished. Report any damage to your coordinator and explain how it happened.
- People using wheelchairs and eye covers will have partners to help them.
- Partners must take their job seriously so no one gets hurt.
- Someone will be by the elevator on each floor to open it up for you, so everyone does not need a key.
- If you need to use the bathroom, first tell the teacher. Those using wheelchairs are expected to make an attempt to use the handicapped stall.
- If at any point you feel it is too difficult to continue, you may opt out by returning the equipment.
- Although you still will be responsible for knowing what is covered in your classes, you can leave a minute early and may arrive a little late if necessary; however, try to get to your classes as quickly as possible.
- You will be given a rating scale of how easy or hard it was for you to get around the school with your disability. Please complete this rating scale and turn it in.

Figure 3.7. Instructions for students participating in simulations. (From Farrington, K. [1992, May]. *Practicum improvement plan: Disability awareness week at a middle school*. Unpublished paper, University of Virginia, Department of Curriculum, Instruction, and Special Education, Charlottesville; reprinted by permission.)

dents who had mobility limitations and visual impairments were assigned partners to assist them during the experience. Equipment sign-out and use was organized during homeroom so multiple students could gain access to the equipment without difficulty.

The experience was rated very positively by both students and teachers. Students took the exercises seriously; minimal violations occurred in the schedule, the equipment use, or the rules. Teachers reported that typical students helped those students with simulated disabilities by following the guidelines that had been covered earlier in the week (e.g., students read to those with the disability of illiteracy; partners explained the barriers that their partners whose eyes were covered faced). Class discussions were lively: They provided opportunities for students to share and reflect and for teachers to expand on previous information. Students who experienced a physical disability completed the *School Accessibility Rating Scale* (Figure 3.8)—information that can sensitize students to architectural barriers and the need for laws such as the Americans with Disabilities Act (ADA) of 1990, PL 101-336, which requires accessibility. Later in the year, an opportunity was given to students in this same middle school to volunteer for a peer support program designed around several students in the school who had extensive support needs and few friends. Many more students volunteered to participate in the peer support networks than had volunteered the year before, when there had been no disability awareness opportunities. The culminating planned activity was a basketball game held at the middle school between two regional teams of players

---

School Accessibility Rating Scale

Directions: After each period, put a check (✔) in the box that describes the student's ease or difficulty in getting to or using any of the following areas in the school.

	1 Very hard	2 Somewhat hard	3 Not too hard or too easy	4 Somewhat easy	5 Very easy
1st Period					
2nd Period					
3rd Period					
4th Period					
5th Period					
6th Period					
7th Period					
Bathroom					
Locker					
Water Fountain					
Outside					
Gym					

Do you have any comments you would like to make? ——————————————————

Figure 3.8.　School Accessibility Rating Scale. (From Farrington, K. [1992, May]. *Practicum improvement plan: Disability awareness week at a middle school.* Unpublished paper, University of Virginia, Department of Curriculum, Instruction, and Special Education, Charlottesville; reprinted by permission).

who used wheelchairs and a postgame opportunity to visit with the local team players.

The remainder of this chapter introduces strategies teachers can use in schools to build peer support for students who need it.

APPROACHES FOR BUILDING PEER SUPPORT

The variety of strategies used to build peer support vary in their degree of structure, as shown in Figure 3.9. Highly structured approaches include peer problem-solving groups organized and facilitated by adults; groups of peers learn to identify, discuss, and resolve issues that arise concerning the student with disabilities, with the primary strategy being peer support during the school day and, potentially, after school and on weekends. Another, less structured, type of peer support strategy involves friendship pairs or small groups (i.e., one or several students without disabilities and a peer with disabilities) organized around a leisure activity. The primary characteristic of these less structured approaches is regular, scheduled times in an enjoyable and supervised context. The least structured activities are those in which students with disabilities are

simply scheduled to be in the same activities as their peers with varied amounts and types of adult facilitation. The success of any of these approaches can be improved when conducted in a favorable school environment that fosters awareness, understanding, and appreciation of human differences.

The term *support* is not synonymous with *helping*; it is a much broader term that includes befriending, serving as a companion, teaching, mentoring, assisting, peacefully co-existing, and even tolerating. Support relationships are positive and varied in nature, but they are not always reciprocal or balanced.

Nonreciprocal Relationships

Reciprocity is a dynamic that is influenced by the activity, the partner(s), the context, the exchange, and the success of each partner's involvement in the activity. An interaction is reciprocal when turns are balanced, partners understand one another, each member is actively involved, and the involvement of each member influences the other. Many people identify reciprocity as a defining feature of friendships. In fact, it may simply be one of many possible features and one that is characteristic of *most* close friendships involving

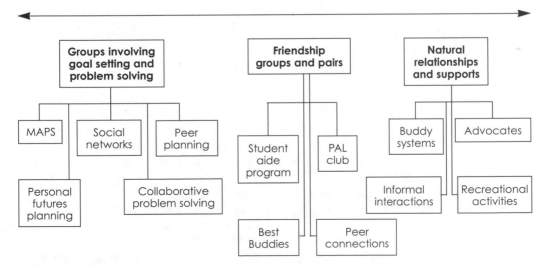

Figure 3.9. Approaches for building peer support.

children of the same age. When friends are compared with nonfriends, there is more intense social activity, more frequent resolution of conflicts, more effective task performance, and reciprocal and intimate characteristics (Newcomb & Bagwell, 1995).

Staub and her colleagues (1994) described four friendships between elementary school peers in which one member of each pair had a severe disability. Some of the friendships began as helping relationships but evolved into balanced relationships. Peers without disabilities knew their friends with disabilities well enough to "read" their feelings and understand their often unique ways of communicating. In turn, the children with disabilities also knew how to "give" something to their friends that was valued by the friend (e.g., humor, comfort). Therefore, the relationships were not one-way but had reciprocal characteristics of shared enjoyment.

In a study of pairs of acquaintances and friends, in which some pairs were mixed (one friend with learning disabilities and the other without) and some pairs were not, Siperstein, Leffert, and Wenz-Gross (1997) found some differences. The friendship pairs in which one of the friends had a disability were quite different from those in which both children had no disabilities: The interactions between the friends when one of the friends had a disability were often "out of balance" or asymmetrical because the typically developing child consistently took the leader role, and there was less cooperative play. Yet, the child with disabilities gave more verbal commands to the typical partner. These findings can be interpreted in a number of ways: 1) Children with and without disabilities may benefit from more cooperative activities and from learning to take (or share) the lead and to alternate turns, 2) symmetrical relationships between children with disabilities and typical peers may be less prevalent, and 3) children can benefit from positive social relationships, even if they are not symmetrical or reciprocal.

One conclusion of this study was that "a child's 'circle of friends' can include relationships that involve varied levels and types of interactions" (Siperstein et al., 1997, p. 121), in-

cluding best friends and other friends. Other friendships include relationships with children or adolescents who are *not the same age* and may be unrelated to the child or may be the child's siblings and relationships involving *peers,* or children of the same age. Some of these "other" friendships may involve a symmetrical distribution of leader and follower roles and a balance between interactions, whereas others may be less symmetrical. Certainly, it is not necessary that all friendships be best friendships, nor that all friendships be symmetrical. In many cases the disability—physical, cognitive, and communicative—prevents, or works against, a balanced exchange.

Helping Relationships

Many fear that when relationships are limited to one-way helping, the quality of the relationship between the partners is lessened. One-way helping relationships are the opposite of reciprocal relationships. Often educators encourage helping relationships between students in classrooms as a means of both promoting social interaction and reducing the work load. Helping may take the form of providing assistance during transitions, initiating an activity, peer tutoring, or caregiving. The rules against students helping one another in competitive classrooms are often lifted in inclusive classrooms; peers are allowed to help the classmate with disabilities (Janney & Snell, 1996). When a child's disability is extensive, the temptation to involve peers as helpers is even greater than usual.

Some argue that help-giving contact between peers "can reduce an initial sense of strangeness or fear and can, if carefully done, lay the groundwork for friendship" (Van der Klift & Kunc, 1994, p. 393). These same individuals hold that *nonreciprocal* helping can never be the basis of a friendship. A discussion of the "politics of helping" is pertinent here because helping is often an issue in inclusive classrooms. In Table 3.2, Van der Klift and Kunc (1994) contrast helping another (helper) with being helped (helpee). The data remind us of familiar feelings we have experienced as both the helper and the helpee. When the helping role in a relationship al-

Table 3.2.   Contrast between helping another and being helped

Personal dimension	Why we like offering help	Why we dislike receiving help
Ability	Affirms capacity	Implies deficiency
Value	Affirms worth	Implies burden
Position	Affirms superiority	Implies inferiority
Obligation	One is owed	One is obligated
Vulnerability	Masks our vulnerability	Reminds us of our vulnerability

(From Van der Klift, E., & Kunc, N. [1994]. Beyond benevolence: Friendship and the politics of help. In J.S. Thousand, R.A. Villa, & A.I. Nevin [Eds.], *Creativity and collaborative learning: A practical guide to empowering students and teachers* [pp. 391–401]. Baltimore: Paul H. Brookes Publishing Co.; reprinted by permission.)

ways seems to swing in one direction, we have different feelings depending on which role we have assumed: helper or helpee. If we are being helped and the helper is paid, there is no sense of obligation. However, if the helper is a peer and if the need for assistance is extensive or repeated, a feeling of lingering obligation (and gratitude) remains until the opportunity to return assistance arises. If we are always the helper, we may experience a sense of superiority; however, we also may harbor some feelings not listed in the table, such as resentment, a violation of fairness, and a threat to the relationship.

Sometimes, teachers' needs for classroom support seem to influence the kinds of peer-to-peer relationships they encourage. Staub and her colleagues (1994) found that teachers relied heavily on the friends of children with extensive support needs to assist in classroom management and to serve as instructional resources. In several cases, this reliance appeared to change the nature of the relationship from a friendship that was more balanced to one in which the peer without disabilities took on a caregiving role. Several obvious solutions to this dilemma exist:

1. Teams define guidelines for peers who help and teach other peers.

2. Teams work hard to limit their reliance on peers for providing care to classmates with disabilities.

3. Teams look to themselves and to their supervisors for the needed classroom supports.

The ideal that teachers and other school staff members should aim for is to even the score: *No students (with or without disabilities) should always be the recipients of help or always be the givers of help. Instead, students should experience getting and giving help, with help based on need.* Cooperative interactions and interdependence should replace one-way helping. Also, help should be provided on an as-needed basis: "The roles of helper and helpee are defined situationally, rather than being based on the immutable definitions of ability and disability" (Janney & Snell, 1996, p. 79).

GOAL-SETTING AND PROBLEM-SOLVING APPROACHES OF PEER SUPPORT

Peer support groups involving goal-setting and problem-solving constitute ongoing peer support systems that operate under the direction of a teacher or other adult to provide ongoing support and relationships to an individual with disabilities (Figure 3.9). Specific variations of these more structured groups include

• Peer planning

• Peer-mediated social networks (Haring & Breen, 1992)

• MAPS (also called Making Action Plans, Forest & Lusthaus, 1989; Vandercook, York, & Forest, 1989)

• Personal Futures Planning (also called person-centered planning; Browder, Bambara, & Belifore, 1997; Kincaid, 1996; Mount & Zwernick, 1988; O'Brien, 1987)

Positive social relationships and increased understanding of diversity among peers can result from each of these more structured peer support approaches (Fisher & Snell, 1999; Haring & Breen, 1992; Peck, Donaldson, & Pezzoli, 1990).

These approaches for lending peer support have several common elements:

1. An early phase that involves teachers (and, in some cases, family members or friends) providing information about a classmate who has a disability using sensitive and nonstigmatizing words suited to the typical peers' level of understanding

2. Ongoing, active group problem-solving around issues related to the classmate with disabilities

3. Identification of informal goals for group actions that have been planned to resolve identified difficulties and to support the classmate

4. Regular, informal discussion of the progress and outcomes of peer support and with revision of group goals

The unique strategies used by peer problem-solving groups involve students' meeting together with an adult on a regular basis to learn more about the individual or classmate, to discuss issues around interaction, to problem-solve difficulties that arise and ways to lend support, and to assess the group's progress on resolving difficulties and lending support. The person with disabilities may *sometimes* be a part of this group (especially during early phases when facts about the student's life are shared) or may *usually* be a part of the group. However, when the focus student is a part of the group, he or she is not "talked about" as if not present but is drawn into the discussion as much as possible and involved in any decision-making. Whether the individual is part of the group depends on the student, the topics being discussed, and the peers who are involved.

Peer Planning

Peer planning is an ongoing peer support system that operates under the direction of a teacher or another school staff member; it utilizes same-age peers or the classmates of a child with a disability to provide ongoing support and relationships for the child. Typically, the entire class, rather than a select group of peers, is involved in peer planning. Because peer planning involves whole-class brainstorming sessions, somewhat like class meetings (Nelson, 1987), it can be used to share and to air classroom or school concerns that may not relate specifically to the class member with disabilities (Figure 3.10). Peer planning can be instrumental in creating a feeling of community within a classroom and can supplement more formalized peer support groups.

Peer planning is a highly successful strategy for students from second grade to middle school; simplified variations can be used with younger children. The amount and ways in which peers are involved, as well as the ways in which adults facilitate peer planning groups, will be heavily dependent on the focus child's age, disability, communicative abilities, behavioral challenges, and personal preferences.

Peer planning works well in elementary classrooms. First, by involving all students in a classroom, there will be more consistency across classmates' interactions with the focus student and more success experienced as students relate to the student with disabilities in their classroom. Second, class time can be taken to problem-solve and practice; no special meeting time is needed.

The support that comes from peer planning must be individualized and will change over time. Some students will need peer support only temporarily, but others will benefit from support throughout their school careers.

Sherica, a preschooler in a Head Start class who has limited communication and movement, may need an adult to facilitate "playing" with her fellow students and to explain why her arms, legs, and mouth don't work like theirs do. Peer planning might involve having the preschoolers think up ways to include Sherica while they engage in sandbox play, play at the table, or sit in a circle for weather and music.

When Allen, a second grader with autism, became a member of Ms. Carey's class, the students quickly formed a peer planning group. After an informational session that taught the students more about Allen and autism, the class discussed Allen's tantrums, which the students had seen many times during the first few weeks of classes. Discussion questions included, "Why does he do this? Does this mean he dislikes us? What should we do? How can we help?" One thing the students had learned was that the word "no" had a negative effect on Allen and often led to tantrums, perhaps because he had heard the word so much during his life. So, the students, with their teachers' assistance, drew up a list of alternative ways to say "no" ("Please stop," "Do it this way," "un uh," "Come on, this is mine") and to redirect Allen when he was doing things he shouldn't do (Get him interested in something else; use gestures). The class discussion led to a list of ideas about why it is important to ignore Allen when he has tantrums and how to do so:

- Listen to the teacher instead of Allen.
- Tantrums may become less important to Allen if no one pays attention.
- Do our work and be positive role models for Allen.
- Pay attention to the good.
- Teach Allen to communicate with us in positive ways.

Over the next few weeks, students practiced using these ideas while Allen's team of teachers tackled his communication system. Soon, Allen's tantrums diminished to almost none.

Figure 3.10. Peer planning for Allen.

Steve, a high school sophomore who has a severe learning disability, yet excellent social skills and good peer relationships, does not need (or want) peer planning, even though he benefited from peer support activities in middle school. Some of his tenth-grade peers, however, could benefit from peer planning even though they are not labeled as having disabilities.

Peer planning sessions can be used to update peers on necessary information about their classmate with a disability or to tackle another problem that arises and affects one or more students. Peer planning can shift its focus to include other concerns that classmates have about their interactions, feelings, and classroom or school issues (Figure 3.11). One student, discouraged about his grandfather's illness and death, shared his feelings during peer planning; students later found ways to lend their support to him. In another case, fifth graders used some of their peer planning time to talk about the changes they feared would occur in middle school.

Peer Networks as Support Groups

In the peer network approach applied by Haring and Breen (1992), adult facilitators and teachers identified focus students with

Jim, who has extensive physical and cognitive disabilities, was mainstreamed for the first time in fifth grade. Jim's classmates had seen him only from afar during previous years because his special education class did not leave the classroom except to travel to the bus and the library. Jim's peers had an image of him as a "baby" because they had seen rattles and stuffed animals attached to his wheelchair in the past. It took several peer planning discussions to dispel the "mental age" versus "chronological age" stigma/myth. Jim's classmates, in turn, assisted in replacing these toys with age-appropriate versions that still provided Jim with the auditory feedback that he was seeking.

Figure 3.11. Providing information on a disability.

disabilities who needed support. Peer network members were recruited, starting with one or two socially appropriate peers without disabilities who knew the student needing support. These peers may have had prior or current contact with the focus student through a mainstreamed class, a school-based job, or a common interest or hobby (e.g., sports, playing music); in other cases, the student may have been acquainted with the focus student or requested by the focus student. Each of these students then recruited two to four close friends. Membership, however, was purely voluntary; peers and focus students were given opportunities to end their participation if they desired. The resulting group included four to five friends from an *existing social network*, a feature that appears to be advantageous for promoting interactions.

Peer networks (Haring & Breen, 1992) may work better in secondary schools than peer planning because the day is scheduled differently than in elementary schools. Peer planning, which involves an entire class, can be applied to classes in grades 2 through 6. Peer planning can address the needs of students with minor to more extensive disabilities, as well as those who simply need peer problem-solving. In middle school, peer support groups typically do not involve an entire class; support groups seem to work best when formed around small groups of peers who volunteer—a characteristic that matches peer networks.

Organization   The approach Haring and Breen (1992) used to organize and introduce the network is outlined in Figure 3.12. Through weekly meetings with students, adult facilitators worked to minimize their role in problem-solving and encouraged peers to take control of the group and its plans for the focus student. Haring and Breen's belief was that middle schoolers, with some adult mediation, are capable of providing an effective social network for a student who has little appropriate social interaction with his or her peers. Their findings support this belief: Two teenagers, one with autism and the other with mental retardation requiring intermittent support, each of whom was involved in peer networks, made noticeable increases in the frequency and quality of their social interactions with peers after the social network intervention was implemented.

The majority of the network members' contacts occurred during the 5-minute breaks between classes and during their half-hour lunch periods; available times were often limited because the focus students attended different classes than their peers (Haring & Breen, 1992). If focus students were included in general education classes, however, there would be even more opportunity for interaction. The specific schedule for interaction was arranged by asking members of each group to examine their daily class schedules to find a location during class transitions that was common to one or more of the peers and the focus student. Each class transition that had a common location was then identified as a time/place to interact with the focus student. Peer networks already were together during lunch, so this time was rich with social interaction opportunities. Peers met regularly to plan and evaluate their progress; the focus student they supported was included in these meetings, which members reported as being enjoyable—a time when a group of friends could gather at school.

When the average middle school or high school day is analyzed for unstructured socialization times, very few times typically are found. Lunch is often crowded and rushed, and friends may be scheduled for different lunch periods. School administrators are under pressure to stretch instructional time, and, together with many teachers, their belief often is that "free time" only yields problems. Therefore, in secondary schools, adult facilitators will need to scour the school day to find free times for support groups to connect; between classes and during lunch periods may be the best options.

Group Meetings   Network meetings generally include the focus student as long as discussion can be respectful and can result in positive outcomes. Meetings follow a set agenda.

With Pedro (a middle school student with disabilities) present, network members

---

Topics covered when introducing peer networks to middle school volunteers

1. **What are peer networks?**

   A group of students who are already friends include a new person into their social clique.

2. **Why?**
   - Quality of life
   - Teach skills through modeling
   - School inclusion
   - Disability awareness
   - Value of a new member in the clique

3. **Why us?**
   - Common interests
   - Common classes

4. **Who?**
   - Student (identify the focus student)
   - Four or five peers without disabilities
   - Adult facilitator
   - Classroom teacher

5. **How?**
   - Map student and peer schedules
   - Assign times to "hang out" together
   - Include student in normal routine
   - Group decides what and how to teach
   - Record data on interactions

6. **When?**
   - During assigned time per day
   - Whenever you feel like it
   - During group meeting one lunch period a week

7. **Commitment from peers:**
   - See this as a positive thing for each peer
   - See this as a positive thing for the group
   - Include the student as a friend
   - Attend weekly group meetings
   - Be open and honest
   - Record data

8. **Commitment from adults:**
   - Maintain peer routines
   - Develop interaction schedules
   - Provide all written information
   - Be sensitive to peer feedback
   - Teach skills as needed
   - Use peer suggestions
   - Be responsive to peer comments

Figure 3.12.   Peer network topics. (From Haring, T.G., & Breen, C.G. [1992]. A peer-mediated social network intervention to enhance the social integration of persons with moderate and severe disabilities. *Journal of Applied Behavior Analysis, 25,* 322.)

- *Talked about and assessed their interactions with Pedro during the week (appropriate and inappropriate interactions had been defined in the middle school earlier in the year)*
- *Looked at the data they collected during assigned transition times and other times (e.g., How many interactions occurred? Were they appropriate or inappropriate interactions?)*
- *Adjusted the interaction schedule depending on peer input*
- *Talked with Pedro about skills he needed and decided which ones they could teach and which ones teachers could teach*
- *Discussed strategies to improve Pedro's social skills*

- *Used role play and modeling to practice these strategies*
- *Brainstormed solutions to specific problems they had observed with Pedro's behavior or social interactions*
- *Informally determined group members' satisfaction about the meeting and assignments*
- *Gave each other reinforcement for their participation through praise, occasional letters home, and periodic group social activities*

Once schedules were arranged and the students met their peer network, weekly meetings got underway. The special education teacher taught the focus student to recognize photos of each peer in the network by name and to say members' names. By the time the support network met for the third time, group members and the facilitator discussed

- *Methods to establish eye contact with the focus student and ways of determining how close to stand by the focus student*
- *Appropriate topics to talk about (e.g., of interest, age-appropriate)*
- *Strategies for including the student in larger-group activities*

Pedro was involved in these meetings as much as possible. Following several weeks of consistent interactions with him, peers and teachers reduced their praise of Pedro to once a day. During the transitions between classes, adult facilitators and teachers did not prompt or provide cues or feedback to the peers or the focus student. Instead, group meetings were used to problem-solve any issues that arose and to discuss what had occurred, as well as what was successful and what was not. Twice weekly, the adult facilitator used modeling to teach the focus student a variety of appropriate social responses (generated by the peer group) to a range of social initiations (also generated by peers). Peer network members also generated ways to teach the focus student to respond and ways that the focus student might be more consistent in getting a response by modifying his or her initiation (e.g., "Ask who, what, or where questions but not why questions" [Haring & Breen, 1992, p. 324]). The network learned how to reestablish joint attention to a topic or item and how to improve the student's motivation to participate in a social exchange. The cardinal rule peers followed was that all interactions needed to be age appropriate and normalized. Figure 3.13 contains another example of a peer support network.

In addition to being an effective strategy for teaching social interaction and building peer relationships, Haring and Breen's (1992)

social network strategy has some other advantages for secondary students:

- The strategy is organized around existing peer social networks—students who know and enjoy being with each other and who offer positive peer models for social behavior.
- The focus student is matched to network members so their interests overlap and camaraderie develops.
- Peer-centered control and problem-solving within networks is shaped; at the same time, the adult's role gradually is minimized.

MAPS and Circle of Friends

Typically referred to simply as "MAPS," this peer support group process has been used in integrating and including students with a wide range of disabilities since it was introduced by Marsha Forest and Evelyn Lusthaus in 1989 (MAPS originally stood for the McGill Action Planning System). The goal of the MAPS process is to provide every student with the opportunity to be successfully integrated with their typical peers while enhancing the student's social relationships and friendships. The MAPS process involves a small group of peers who 1) get to know a classmate with disabilities, 2) learn more about that person and his or her relationships and routines compared to the peers' own relationships and routines, 3) brainstorm with the classmate and with adult facilitators (teachers and family members) an "ideal day" or schedule for the classmate, 4) design an action plan to achieve the changes, and 5) work to realize and improve that plan. There are some general guidelines for using the MAPS process, but the authors encourage users to adapt those guidelines to suit their particular students (Falvey, Forest, Pearpoint, & Rosenberg, 1992).

Team Decides if a MAPS Group Is Needed
As with any peer support approach, the student's educational team must first determine why and how they are going to use MAPS before adding it to the IEP. The team explains the process to and seeks permission from the

What the Research Says

Situation: Five junior high school students are participating in the peer support network.

Problem: The group facilitator has modeled "teacher typical" behaviors to get the student with disabilities to attend (e.g., "Look at me," "Good looking," "Put your hands down," "Stop!"). The peers begin to model this behavior when they are hanging out between classes with Josh. The peers report to the group that when they say things like that to the student their other friends look at them funny, and they won't talk to the student, it seems to make the student mad, and they feel like they are being too mean.

Solution: The group decides that the words and the actions they are using with the students are not natural—that is, they wouldn't normally talk that way. They decide that one reason they use those words is because that is what the adult uses, and the words seem to work when the adult uses them, and after all adults know more than kids do about teaching. But maybe a reason the student gets mad when they say those things is that they sound like a teacher and not a friend. Instead, they will try to use language that is the same as that they use with other friends. Things they do say when their other friends are not listening or when they are trying to get their other friends to do something with them is, "Hey John!," "That's cool!," "Knock it off!," "Let's go." In response to this issue, the adult facilitator becomes more aware of the language she uses in front of the peers and attempts to model the peers' actions and words in leading the group discussions and in role-playing.

Figure 3.13. A peer network's solution to "teacher language." (From Breen, C.G. [1991]. Setting up and managing peer support networks. In C.G. Breen, C.H. Kennedy, and T.G. Haring [Eds.], *Social context research project: Methods for facilitating the inclusion of students with disabilities in integrated school and community contexts* [pp. 54–105]. Santa Barbara: University of California; reprinted by permission.)

student's family; typically, one or several family members become involved, at least in the early meetings. In addition to a student's peers, MAPS group members often include one or several school staff members. Because special and general education teachers and paraprofessionals typically are familiar with the focus student and the peers, they are often included; one adult usually serves as the group facilitator.

Start with a Circle of Friends Exercise
The circle of friends exercise is a friendship awareness activity often used to introduce students and adults to the universal need for social relationships and peer support (Falvey, Forest, Pearpoint, & Rosenberg, 1992). First, peers are asked to put names of people and groups they know into four concentric circles that describe the relationship:

- The inner circle, the Circle of INTIMACY, reflects those who are closest to the student who the student really cares for and couldn't imagine living without.

- The second circle, the Circle of FRIEND-SHIP, lists the student's good friends—those who almost made the first circle.

- The third circle, the Circle of PARTICIPATION, lists the people, organizations, and networks the student is involved with (e.g., baseball team, choir, reading group, scouts, people at work, swimming team).

- The fourth circle, the Circle of EXCHANGE, contains people who provide services for the student for money (e.g., the dentist, hairstylist/barber, doctor, teacher, therapist) (Figure 3.14).

The general discussion that follows does not involve sharing specific numbers or names of those placed in the students' circles; students keep their circle information private because it is personal to them. Instead, the discussion is focused on why students put the people they did into the different circles. The teacher could ask the students: "Think about those in the inner circle and the second circle in particular. Why did you put them there?" The individuals in the center circle may be regarded as close friends. Those individuals in the second circle may be friends as well, but less intimate ones. The people in the two innermost circles, as well as many people in

Directions: Think about the people you spend time with in your life. Put their names or the group's names in circles that best describe their relationship with you.

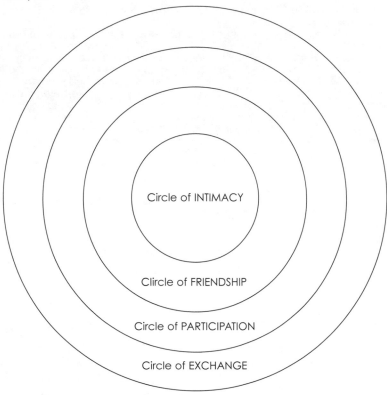

Figure 3.14.   Circle of support exercise. (From Falvey, M.A., Forest, M., Pearpoint, J., & Rosenberg, R.L. [1992]. *All my life's a circle: Using the tools: Circles, MAPS & PATHS.* Toronto: Inclusion Press; reprinted by permission.)

The Circle of PARTICIPATION (the third circle) who are the student's peers, can be viewed as the student's peer support group.

Often, a comparison of typical peers' circles to the circles of students with disabilities reveals several differences: People with disabilities often have 1) fewer individuals in the first two circles, 2) fewer groups in the third circle, and 3) either as many, though often more, paid people in the outer circle. The often stark contrast between typical peers' circles and the circles of a classmate who has disabilities can be used as a springboard to introduce the value of peer support and to initiate recruitment of members (Fisher & Snell, 1999). (Although the circle exercise can be a potent way to emphasize the value friends have in our lives, *this exercise alone, without any*

other planned activities, does not result in any changes in social interactions at recess and lunch between second graders and their classmates who have disabilities [Fritz, 1990].)

Conduct Group Meetings and Take Action Group membership is voluntary and meetings are loosely arranged on a weekly basis, at a common time, and in a fixed location. The focus student and participating adults also attend the meetings. The first few meetings are devoted to a discussion of the following topics and questions:

1. *What is the story/history?* Family members and friends relate the important milestones in the student's life.

2. *What is the dream?* Group members talk about their wishes for the focus student for

the present and the future. The "vision" should be based not only on current realities but also on their dreams for the person.

3. *What is the nightmare?* This question is difficult (some chose to omit it with younger groups), but it forces group members to think about what they must work hard to prevent from happening.

4. *Who is the person?* The group brainstorms for adjectives that describe the student; once a lengthy list has been generated, team members identify three words from the list that best describe the student.

5. *What is the person good at (strengths, gifts, and talents)?* The group facilitator asks members to review the list of descriptors as a means of identifying the student's unique strengths and talents. The facilitator encourages team members to think about what the focus student can do, what he or she likes to do, and what he or she does well.

6. *What are the person's needs? What do we need to do to meet those needs?* Team members focus on the activities, events, things, people, and so forth that they think are necessities or requirements for this person presently and in the future. The group then arranges the list by priority.

7. *What is the plan of action to avoid the nightmare and to make the dream come true?* Team members begin this task by outlining a routine school day for peers without disabilities who are the same age as the focus student. Then, the team begins to add things to make that day a good one for the focus student; they begin to explore options to meet the needs identified in question #6 in the context of a typical school day. Answering this question lays the groundwork for developing an action plan (Falvey, Forest, Pearpoint, & Rosenberg, 1992).

For all but the first question, team members will need to brainstorm first and then work to reach a consensus. Thus, the adult facilitator will want to review brainstorming rules (e.g., "We want quantity, not quality," "No judgments allowed," "Everyone participates") and consensus-reaching guidelines (e.g., "Let's find the best word," "What can we all agree on?" "Let's explain and compare our options, then locate our common ground"). As in other peer support group meetings, it is helpful to use large sheets of paper that can be displayed on the wall to keep track of the group members' answers to each of the seven areas of focus. These notes can be kept for future reference as the team moves on to its next task. Traditionally, the parent or relative of the focus student is part of this process along with the student's classmates. If parental participation is not possible, educators can solicit information about the student's history from the family ahead of time for use in the MAPS discussion.

Once the questions have been answered, the adult facilitator assists the student's peers in defining a *plan of action*, which consists of activities and actions individual members can undertake to make the student's ideal day become more of a reality. To devise the plan of action, the facilitator might ask group members to review a timetable of the student's actual day (contrasted with an *ideal day*) and ask questions such as, "Does it make sense for *Mike* to be doing this activity?" "Do any changes or modifications need to be made?"

Student Snapshot

 The MAPS group for Mike (a 10-year-old with disabilities) identified four main elements in his plan of action:

1. *Mike goes to fifth grade with us (he had attended a separate classroom).*

2. *His team (not our group) holds an IEP meeting to plan the "specifics"; we develop our plan of action.*

3. *We have a class meeting in September so Mike can meet all the new kids.*

4. *We start planning for middle school sometime next year. (Neary, Halvorsen, Kronberg, & Kelly, 1992, p. 113)*

The meetings that follow those that occur in the beginning of a school year are focused on making the plan of action work: planning needed steps, taking action, evaluating that action, and generating ways to improve the plan. The sense of responsibility to the focus person by the group and individual members, coupled with regular celebration and problem-solving, constitute the essential elements of a cohesive and effective MAPS process.

Personal Futures Planning

Personal Futures Planning (Mount & Zwernick, 1988), also called person-centered planning (Browder, Bambara, & Belifore, 1997; Kincaid, 1996), is another group support process quite similar to MAPS. Typically, *the focus person is of high school age or older, and group members extend beyond peers and family to include community members* (e.g., co-workers, people at local businesses frequented by the individual, support agency representatives). As with other peer problem-solving strategies, the group's focus is on identifying and achieving outcomes for the focus person.

During initial sessions of the support group, the emphasis is on the *personal profile of the focus person:* 1) people the focus person knows, 2) places he or she has lived, 3) a history of critical life experiences, 4) current health, 5) choices made by the focus person and by others, 6) behaviors that resulted in gain or loss of respect by others, 7) strategies that have worked and failed with the focus person, 8) group members' hopes and fears for the person, 9) barriers and opportunities the person faces, and 10) themes from the focus person's personal profile that group members discover. This personal profile, though more complex in its coverage, is comparable to the seven steps in the MAPS process. Large drawings accompanied by simple key words are constructed for each of the 10 areas of personal history so the group, including the focus member, can retain these discussions. This information allows the group to generate a Personal Futures Plan, which lays out a vision that encompasses home, work, community, relationships, and making choices and exercis-

ing competencies, thus achieving the following five outcomes:

1. Presence within the community
2. Ability to form and sustain satisfying relationships
3. Ability to make choices and express preferences
4. Opportunity to fill respected roles
5. Continual personal growth (Kincaid, 1996, pp. 440–441)

Similar to other structured peer support groups, the support group's task is to implement the plan through member action, group problem-solving, updating and improving the plan, and celebrating accomplishments.

Collaborative Problem Solving by Peers

The Collaborative Problem Solving (CPS) process (Salisbury, Evans, & Palombaro, 1997) was first initiated in an elementary school with teachers who had a child in their classroom with extensive disabilities; once these teachers mastered the process, they began using it in their classrooms with students. To initiate the CPS process, both general and special education teachers draw up criteria to guide their implementation of inclusion. For example, inclusion criteria might be stated as follows: All students will participate actively in each class activity, using adaptations when needed; the focus student's perspective is kept in mind when considering choices or decisions; and the results are judged by the amount and quality of the focus student's participation and inclusion. Any threat to these inclusion criteria would alert teachers that problem solving was needed.

Once the inclusion criteria were established, teachers learned the CPS process and role-played it until they used it consistently (Salisbury, Palombaro, & Evans, 1993). To make it easier for kids to use, the CPS process was streamlined from eight to five steps. Then, teachers began using it in the classroom whenever their inclusion criteria were not met (Salisbury & Palombaro, 1993). For example, teachers skilled at using CPS methods would initiate a CPS session whenever an issue of exclusion arose in their classrooms: "We need to do [activity]. If we do [activity], will everyone in our class be able to participate/be included?" (Salisbury et al., 1997). Depending on the class's answer to this question, the teacher might suggest that the class problem-solve a solution and then lead them through the five steps of the process (Figure 3.15). These CPS steps are "portable" and can be incorporated into any of the peer group methods. They also may be used by peers as a way of resolving problems that arise in any of the less structured strategies of peer support that are described later in this chapter.

Implementing Peer Support Groups

So how does an educational team determine what steps to take to include students who have little or no membership in a class? This section provides some general pointers for implementing peer support groups in a school. These guidelines are similar for each type of support group and for most age groups.

Preparation   Schools that practice inclusion are likely to have begun several practices that prepare the way for increased diversity. These practices might include staff in-services on disability, infusion of grade-level curriculum with content on disability (health, science, and literature), and disability awareness activities suited to students' ages. All of these activities will make peer support easier. The educational team, along with family members but *without* the involvement of typical peers, must sit down and discuss ways that they feel the student can be included and encouraged to interact with peers. The team should decide whether a peer support group is needed and should be formalized and, if so, what the peer support group would entail. Often, whole-class peer planning is the best; other times, a smaller, more carefully selected social network or MAPS group may be a better choice. For older students, networks or person-centered planning groups may be better options.

When typical students and the focus student are not familiar with one another, they will need time simply to be together and to get used to one another. This stage should take place during the first few weeks of school or upon the arrival of a student with a disability to a new school. During this initial phase, teacher modeling is one of the primary teaching strategies; although indirect in its approach, it is powerful—most students will be closely watching adults for direction on how to interact with the new student (Snell

---

The Five Steps of Collaborative Problem Solving

1. **What's happening here?**   This is where you decide what the problem is. Sometimes that's hard because you know something's not right, but you don't know exactly what it is. Talking about it with other people helped us figure things out.

2. **What can we do?**   This is the fun part. It's where you can brainstorm tons of ideas about possible solutions. They all get written down so that you can think about which one to try first.

3. **What would really work?**   In this step, you ask two questions for each possible solution. First, you ask, "Will the solution be good for all kids?" Second, you ask yourself if you or your group can really do this solution. "Do you have all the materials you need?" "Is there enough time to do it?"

4. **Take action!**   In this step, you first have to get everyone in your group to agree on which solution you want to go with. Remember, you pick the solution the group thinks is best and try it. You can always go back and try another way if you need to.

5. **How did we do? (Did we change things?)**   In this last step, you need to figure out if your solution worked the way you intended it to. Did everyone's needs get met or are there still things to be worked out? How did members of your group feel about the CPS process? Do you need to take further action?

Figure 3.15.   Collaborative problem solving for students. (From Salisbury, C.L., & Palombaro, M.M. [Eds.]. [1993]. *No problem: Working things out our way.* Pittsburgh, PA: Allegheny Singer Research Institute, Child and Family Studies Program; reprinted by permission.)

et al., 1995). (Some schools wisely adopt a plan for students to visit the school and classroom the year before, which may allow the child, staff, and student body to become more familiar with one another before the school year starts. [Refer to the last chapter of the booklet in this series on *Collaborative Teaming*; Snell & Janney, 2000.])

Seeking Permission from the Focus Student
Prior to providing information to classmates about the focus student, the peer planning process and the reasoning behind it need to be shared with the focus student (in a way that he or she can understand) and with his or her parents, thus allowing them time to consider whether they are comfortable with a peer support group approach. The focus student and his or her family members are given the option to refuse or to modify the way in which the student's disability, no matter how mild or severe, is discussed with classmates.

Recruitment of Volunteer Peers Sometimes, videotapes can help explain the purpose of peer support groups and enlist interest. For example, with middle school students, it is often useful to use the Circle of Friends exercise to sensitize peers to the similarities and differences they have with the focus student. Once the similarities and differences have been identified, a segment of videotape ("With a little help from my friends, Part I") (Forest, 1986) illustrating the MAPS peer support purpose and process can be played, followed by a group discussion. In peer support programs for high school students in Utah, a short, high-powered videotape entitled "Peer Power" has been central in informing students about and recruiting students into peer tutors/support program (Utah State Office of Education, 1994). Haring and Breen (1992) began their recruitment for networks by using teachers' recommendations of typically developing peers who had had prior contact with the focus student (peers who shared a class or a school job, had a common interest or hobby [sports, music], or who the focus student expressed an interest in getting to know). They met with the recommended students, explained the way the social support network would work, and, if interest was ex-

pressed, they asked these peers to enlist several close friends, thereby recruiting an established social network.

Once peers volunteer to participate in a support group, it may be appropriate to seek permission for the typical students' participation from their parents (Fisher & Snell, 1999). Membership and participation in these groups must remain completely voluntary for all students involved, and students should have periodic opportunities to withdraw from the group (Haring & Breen, 1992).

Sharing Information About Disability
One of the first activities in a support group, after the initial organization, should be to share basic information with the typical students regarding their classmate with disabilities, especially if the typical peers have a lot of questions or concerns about the focus student. The basic information should include facts about the student, such as the school or classroom he or she used to attend; the number of siblings he or she has; the student's likes and dislikes (e.g., favorite foods, games, hobbies, television shows); and other personal information. The focus student is often part of this initial disclosure of information and can contribute to the discussion, even if he or she uses an alternative method of communicating. If peer support has been built into a student's IEP (Chapter 1 describes this approach), the process should be ready for implementation when the school year begins.

The initial informational session should serve to dispel any myths or fears regarding the student's disability that are not factual.

When Daniel, a second grader with extensive physical disabilities and no formal communication system, was first included in his second-grade classroom, a few of the students were fearful of sitting next to him in case they might "catch" his illness. After a brief, child-oriented discussion about cerebral palsy, their fears were alleviated.

Scheduling Peer planning or peer support groups need to meet consistently, such as every Tuesday and Thursday for 20-minute sessions, in order to plan for and support one or several specific students. Because smaller support groups will meet separately from the whole class, they will need to arrange in advance when and where they will meet. Applications of MAPS and peer networks may use lunchtime to meet and plan or select a specifically arranged time—usually about 30 minutes weekly.

Peer Control It is crucial that the adults be facilitators, not controllers, and that they allow students to voice their opinions openly. Promoting peer control of the group, however, does not mean that adult facilitators cannot identify issues for the group to discuss or problem-solve.

Following initial organizational sessions, many teachers find it helpful to make notes of the discussions on the blackboard or on large pieces of paper (using an adult or peer recorder, depending on writing ability). Wall-displayed notes are particularly useful when the group is brainstorming or when they are formulating a set of guidelines (e.g., *Other ways to say "No" to Charles*) or a plan of action (e.g., *Involving Miranda at lunch, looking out for Carla in crowds* [Perske, 1988, p. 42]). These notes can serve as an ongoing set of reminders to the class or group and can be helpful when reviewing progress or making revisions.

Problem-Solving Strategies Problem-solving is central to all peer group processes. These processes, as they are used by teachers and peers, are discussed in more detail in another booklet in this series—*Collaborative Teaming* (Snell & Janney, 2000); however, they also will be reviewed briefly in this section. A problem-solving process consists of a series of general steps and some interpersonal considerations. Teachers will first need to model the steps, then teach their students to apply them and to engage in cooperative, interpersonal behaviors. Salisbury and her co-workers (Salisbury et al., 1997; Salisbury & Palombaro, 1993) found that elementary-age students from first to fourth grades could competently use a five-step collaborative problem-solving process to resolve problems relating to the physical, social, and instructional inclusion of classmates with extensive support needs. Giangreco, Cloninger, Dennis, and Edelman

and colleagues (1994) have successfully taught students to apply several creative problem-solving strategies of varying complexities (Figure 3.16). It is often useful to select a simple sequence of problem-solving steps, sometimes assigning numbers and phrases to identify each step, and then teach students to apply the steps consistently until they become independent in using the process.

FRIENDSHIP GROUPS AND PAIRS

The primary goals of friendship groups or pairs are to bring together students with disabilities and their peers for socialization and fun, to create informal support channels for a student with a disability, and to build social relationships and peer support. Although the idea of setting up "friendship" groups or pairs may seem somewhat artificial, these arrangements can provide a good opportunity to get students with and without disabilities to interact around a common theme. Friendship groups work particularly well when inclusion is minimal in school, as often happens during the high school years (Peck, Donaldson, & Pezzoli, 1990). Friendship groups are also especially crucial if a student with a disability is new to a school and the typical peers have been together for many years. It is difficult to move into a new school, but when a student has a disability to which his or her peers are not accustomed, it may be quite uncomfortable. Friendship or buddy groups reduce a student's isolation and help ease new students into an existing school culture.

A friendship group may be organized by the educational team, special education or general education teacher, or guidance counselor. Sometimes, these groups are coupled with a student club (Best Buddies or Key Club). Clubs can be formed to provide specific types of support to students; examples of potential clubs include a "signing club" for first graders who want to learn signs to communicate with a classmate or a "recess club" to help a fourth grader learn to use playground equipment and play games (Hunt, Alwell, Farron-Davis, & Goetz, 1996). The friendship group may meet

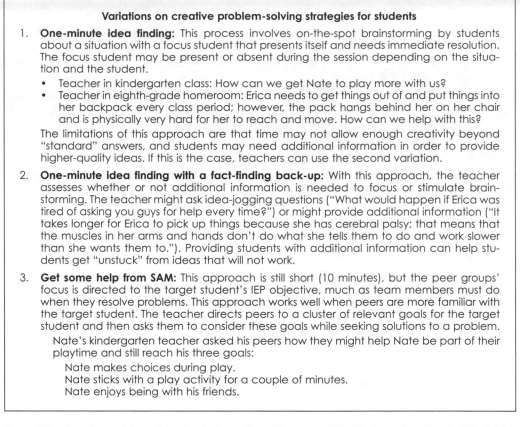

Variations on creative problem-solving strategies for students

1. **One-minute idea finding:** This process involves on-the-spot brainstorming by students about a situation with a focus student that presents itself and needs immediate resolution. The focus student may be present or absent during the session depending on the situation and the student.

   • Teacher in kindergarten class: How can we get Nate to play more with us?
   • Teacher in eighth-grade homeroom: Erica needs to get things out of and put things into her backpack every class period; however, the pack hangs behind her on her chair and is physically very hard for her to reach and move. How can we help with this?

   The limitations of this approach are that time may not allow enough creativity beyond "standard" answers, and students may need additional information in order to provide higher-quality ideas. If this is the case, teachers can use the second variation.

2. **One-minute idea finding with a fact-finding back-up:** With this approach, the teacher assesses whether or not additional information is needed to focus or stimulate brainstorming. The teacher might ask idea-jogging questions ("What would happen if Erica was tired of asking you guys for help every time?") or might provide additional information ("It takes longer for Erica to pick up things because she has cerebral palsy; that means that the muscles in her arms and hands don't do what she tells them to do and work slower than she wants them to."). Providing students with additional information can help students get "unstuck" from ideas that will not work.

3. **Get some help from SAM:** This approach is still short (10 minutes), but the peer groups' focus is directed to the target student's IEP objective, much as team members must do when they resolve problems. This approach works well when peers are more familiar with the target student. The teacher directs peers to a cluster of relevant goals for the target student and then asks them to consider these goals while seeking solutions to a problem.

   Nate's kindergarten teacher asked his peers how they might help Nate be part of their playtime and still reach his three goals:

   Nate makes choices during play.
   Nate sticks with a play activity for a couple of minutes.
   Nate enjoys being with his friends.

Figure 3.16.   Creative problem-solving for students. (From Giangreco, M.F., Cloninger, C.J., Dennis, R.E., & Edelman, S.W. [1994]. Problem-solving methods to facilitate inclusive education. In J.S. Thousand, R.A. Villa, & A.I. Nevin [Eds.], *Creativity and collaborative learning: A practical guide to empowering students and teachers.* (pp. 321–346). Baltimore: Paul H. Brookes Publishing Co.; adapted by permission.)

weekly around specific, longer-lasting themes, such as the homecoming dance or school grounds improvement. During these meetings, the students can brainstorm ways that their classmate with a disability can be integrated into cooperative group activities. Some schools have organized these groups to meet during lunchtime, recess, or after school. Other schools have scheduled meetings every Friday during the last 20 minutes of school that include refreshments.

Volunteering to Be
a Friend in High School

High school students also have been successfully paired with peers who have disabilities. Peck and his colleagues organized student volunteers into pairs and set schedules that enabled the pairs to meet several times a week during one or more school semesters (Peck et al., 1990). The pairs of students engaged in a variety of activities, including spending time together during breaks, lunch, or assemblies; participating in tutoring activities in the special education classroom, and getting together after school (e.g., going to school sporting events or out for ice cream). The participating students, who ranged widely in ability and social characteristics, reported many benefits from their partnerships, including gains in self-concept, social cognition, and tolerance of other people; reductions in their fear of human differences; and development of personal principles, interpersonal acceptance, and friendship (Peck et al., 1990).

Peer Connections:
A High School Peer Support Class[1]

At Eden Prairie High School in Minnesota, where students having mild to severe cognitive and physical disabilities have been included in general education for a number of years, staff initiated a program to further increase the opportunities for social inclusion (Keachie, 1997b). The family and consumer education department offered a course called Peer Connections, in which students both with and without disabilities were enrolled. The class, which met daily, focused on learning about disabilities, removing barriers to social inclusion, and improving social interaction. Students' main course assignments involved designing activities that would "build relationships and understanding between students" and "assist those with disabilities in developing their social skills in natural settings" (Keachie, 1997b, p. 18).

Peer Connections teaches students with milder disabilities or no disabilities to be "peer facilitators" to those students who have more extensive support needs. The combined group plans and implements social inclusion activities every week, such as attending a basketball game together, eating lunch together in the cafeteria, visiting after school in each others' homes, planning an after-school party at a student's home, and going to a movie or concert. Typically, friends of peer facilitators who are not part of the class join in on the activities, thereby expanding the social circles. Teachers, parents, and students have reported increases in the social networks of focus students. One student commented, "I've made a lot of friends through the Peer Connections program because people in the program introduce me to their friends, and then they become my friends" (Keachie, 1997a, p. 18). Peer facilitators have filled an advocate role for focus students in the group in situations of harassment, gossip, or teasing in school. School

administrators reported a large reduction in the number of incidents during which focus students were victimized by peers. Upon graduation, peers spoke of their continued contact with the focus students. (Also, see Figure 3.17.)

Student Aide Program:
Companions in a Middle School

The Student Aide program was started in a large junior high school with limited resources during a year when four students with fairly extensive disabilities were fully included in general education classes (Staub, Spaulding, Peck, Gallucci, & Schwartz, 1996). The students' disabilities encompassed mental retardation, seizure disorder, limited communication, blindness, aggressiveness, and cerebral palsy; however, all students could communicate, and three of the students had academic skills between second- and fourth-grade levels. The student aide program enabled peer volunteers to assist focus students with disabilities in numerous ways, including moving more quickly through crowded halls to get to classes, using adapted classroom materials, and getting involved in social interactions at lunch and during class transitions. Many strategies had already been implemented at this school to address the wide range of learning abilities in the student body (e.g., cooperative grouping, multi-age grouping, thematic instruction, and student-directed learning methods). Some student aides had special education needs; but, like the focus students, they received all their special education services in the general education classroom.

Responsibilities Student aide responsibilities included serving as a monitor, helper, friend, and teacher. Each student was asked to get parental permission before participating in the program. Focus students' class schedules depended on their needs and choices; for example, one student needed more opportunities to be active in class (opportunities that naturally occur in band, physical education, drama, and home economics). Getting the student aide program underway early in the first school year involved three steps:

---

[1]Peer Connections is a school board–approved adoption of the Yes I Can Program developed by the University of Minnesota's Institute on Community Integration, which currently is being implemented in 53 school districts in 9 states.

Voices from the Classroom

When Chris was a tenth grader at Eden Prairie High School, he became a member of the Peer Connections class. Before then, Chris, who has mild to moderate disabilities, often became uncomfortable in groups and would switch from age-appropriate social behavior to very immature behavior (e.g., hiding from others before and during class, being a "clown"). But during his 2 years in Peer Connections, he has grown up considerably. T.J., a senior in the same class, became good friends with Chris and served as a mentor for him. T.J. helped Chris learn that his immature behavior really did not get him what he wanted—friends and acceptance. Chris learned that when T.J. asked him "to get it together," he needed to act his age and things would improve. T.J. spent time with Chris after school as well. T.J. took some of his friends to watch Chris play soccer on the adapted recreation team; they went out for pizza and played video games at the mall; and, frequently they talked on the phone, ate dinner together at Chris's house, and went to an amusement park. By the end of the semester, Chris's social behavior had blossomed and he had become a leader in the class and in the Y's drama group that met after school.

During a person-centered planning meeting, Chris listed activities he especially enjoyed: going to the movies, bowling, and dancing. Chris had learned that a girl in his Peer Connections classes liked the same things; therefore, T.J. helped Chris and his mom plan dates with the girl, organize a boy-girl party at his house for friends with and without disabilities (which included dancing), and plan for the prom. At the prom, Chris spent time with T.J. and his girlfriend but also was comfortable with other peers who took part in the activities.

In his senior year, Chris became a facilitator in the Peer Connections class and assisted others who had support needs to "get connected" in the high school. Chris became an important member of the person-centered planning team for another student in the class. In the spring, Chris did not need help getting a prom date with a fellow student or preparing for the event. Chris gained a lot from his Peer Connections class: mature ways of acting around others, acceptance of responsibility among his peers, and the ability to share his social skills and knowledge with others.

Figure 3.17.   Pals, parties, and proms. (From Keachie, J. [1997a, Fall]. Pals, parties, and proms. *Impact, 10*[3], 19; adapted by permission.)

1. *Training the student aides:* During the first week, the focus students did not attend classes; but, under the direction of the special education teacher, they spent time getting to know several student aides through game playing. The teacher trained the student aides informally and apart from the focus students and talked openly about the aides' responsibilities, including specific methods of assisting, praising and encouraging, helping with academic work, monitoring behavior, communicating, relating socially, and providing companionship.

2. *Assisting focus students in adapting to their general education classes:* At the end of the first week of school, focus students attended classes accompanied by a student aide assigned for that class. The student aide's role was taken seriously; as the aide came to know the student and the course, he or she often modified or adapted the course curriculum and activities to enable the focus student to participate. Student aides earned course credit and were held accountable for their assistance though a point system; points were given by teachers, reviewed daily during their student aide period, and later converted to grades.

3. *Providing ability awareness preparation:* During the first month of school, the special education teacher provided ability awareness training to all students at the middle school, not to just student aides.

One student described her responsibilities as Kayse's PE aide:

"Well, first of all I have to make sure that she [Kayse] always brings her gym clothes and that she doesn't forget them. I also have to open her locker for her, because she doesn't

know the combination. We go out to the gym and I help her run and do her stretches." (Staub et al., 1996, p. 199)

Outcomes Following the implementation of a student aide program in a middle school, Staub and her colleagues observed many individually meaningful outcomes:

- One student aide took turns with her focus student reading the assigned science chapter aloud; then the student aide asked her questions, not "just the 'yes' or 'no' types of questions" (Staub et al., 1996, p. 199).

- Another aide assisted and monitored as his companion heated up a bagel in home economics class and spread it with cream cheese; they each ate half.

- One aide found a way to modify a computer project so his companion could operate the mouse.

- Another aide advocated for her companion by suggesting that she might want to take a test rather than be excused from it because she knew a lot of the information.

The low-cost student aide program meant that students filled many roles: aides acted as companions who provided opportunities for socialization, informal tutors who were creative in adapting tasks, and advocates. Although most comments about the program were positive, some students commented on the conflict that arose when their role required them to set limits like a teacher might do. Staub et al. (1996) reported perceived benefits for the focus students and the student aides:

- **The focus students:** Increases in independence, social growth, and larger social networks; academic skill gains; and behavioral improvements

- **The student aides:** Increases in social networks; improved feelings of self-worth; improvements in their awareness of, comfort with, and appreciation of people with disabilities; greater patience toward their

peers who learn differently; and increased responsibility

Partners at Lunch (PAL) Club

Having a small group of peers regularly eat lunch with a student who has disabilities is an excellent way to foster peer support and relationships. The PAL (Partners at Lunch) Club is one example of an extensively tested, somewhat structured approach that has been used in several of California's middle schools. Some of the features of the PAL Club are similar to those of peer networks (Haring & Breen, 1992); the PAL Club (Breen & Lovinger, 1991) began with pairs of students (one with disabilities and one without) and evolved into small peer networks in which a single student with disabilities was included. Students pairs were based on age, gender, and interests, along with the consideration of student preferences. After a PAL Club orientation meeting (*What do we do? Why? Who? How? When? What is my commitment?*), students who signed up recruited two to four of the friends they hung out with to join the PAL Club, as in social networks. At the next club meeting, in addition to voting on a name for the club, the group generated activities to do and organized themselves by

- Comparing their daily class schedules
- Deciding on how many and which lunch periods they would share with the focus student (one to four times a week)
- Determining how they would get together (which teacher and room they would go to and at what time), and where they would eat

Focus students were changed if there was a "mismatch in personalities between students" (Breen & Lovinger, 1991, p. 115).

During lunch, adult facilitators unobtrusively wandered by all the groups, intervening with their interactions as little as possible; *they found that when they prompted, corrected, or even modeled for group members, they stifled interactions and stigmatized the student and even the group itself.* Therefore, adults intervened only if

1. The focus student's inappropriate behaviors or interactions were not being handled by peers and threatened social acceptance.
2. Focus students needed subtle prompting to move closer and to turn and face the peer group to become part of it.

Facilitators made themselves available to PAL Club members for support during every lunch period. Adults taught the focus students any needed social interaction skills outside the lunch period but reinforced any appropriate interactions among the lunch group.

Once a week, all groups (including focus students) met together for a schoolwide PAL Club meeting, during which they ate pizza or ice cream, watched videotapes, listened to music, played games, or just interacted with one another. As described by Breen and Lovinger, weekly club meetings involved age-appropriate fun and interaction between peers and focus students. Adult facilitators circulated and sought unobtrusive comments from each group about their interactions during the previous week. Facilitators provided suggestions, on-the-spot problem-solving, and feedback on ways to improve group interactions:

Adult: *How's everything going at lunch with Susan?*

Peers: *Good.*

Adult: *That's great, I noticed she's keeping up with you guys better now when you're walking around.*

Peers: *Yeah, we only have to remind her sometimes.*

Adult: *Is that OK with you?*

Peers: *Well, I think she would fit in better if she talked to us more.*

Adult: *I think so too. What do you usually talk to each other about?*

Peers: *I don't know—classes, teachers, boys, music—stuff like that.*

Adult: *You know, Susan knows a lot about music—she's always listening to cool tapes—maybe you guys could ask her about it.*

Peers: *Really, she does? That's a good idea.*

Adult: *Great! I'll work with her some at this end also—give her some ideas about what she could talk about.* (Breen & Lovinger, 1991, p. 117)

The PAL Club concept provides a tested model for loosely organized friendship groups that have worked well with middle school students.

Best Buddies

The international organization Best Buddies was started by Anthony Shriver in 1987 when he was a senior at Georgetown University. The organization's mission is to match students with people who have mental retardation for the purpose of friendship. The single chapter at Georgetown expanded into Best Buddies Colleges, and today, there are more than 230 chapters across the country. Later, other Best Buddies groups formed (Best Buddies High Schools, Colleges, Citizens, and Jobs), each with the interrelated purpose of providing support and companionship. Best Buddies High Schools, which started in 1994, has chapters in 90 high schools and 4 middle schools, each with the purpose of involving teens with mental retardation in ongoing social activities with their peers (Grabowski, 1997).

The Best Buddies organization uses a process similar to other support programs with one exception: Best Buddies is an actual international nonprofit organization with its main office located in Washington, D.C. The organization's services include guidance in organizing Best Buddies groups; training officers; selecting faculty advisors (adult facilitators); recruiting volunteers (members and buddies); and recommending processes for member application and commitment, buddy matching, and chapter activities (regular buddy contacts and activities, chapter meetings, group outings, and fundraising) (Figure 3.18).

Evaluating
the Success of Friendship Groups

Most facilitators find that regularly seeking information on the "health" of the group or

---

At a Glance: "In today's high schools students with mental retardation often enter the same building and walk the same hallways as their peers, but they are left out of social activities. By introducing Best Buddies into public and private high schools, we are crossing the invisible line that too often separates those with disabilities from those without" (Grabowski, 1997). There are more than 140 chapters of Best Buddies high schools in the United States.

Mission: "To enhance the lives of people with mental retardation by providing opportunities for socialization and employment" (Grabowski, 1997).

How to Get a Newsletter: *Byline* is the official newsletter of Best Buddies International; call Mark Wylie, Editor, at (305-374-2233) or fax (305-374-5305) to inquire about getting a copy.

How to Start a Chapter: Call Ian Abrams, Director of Programs at the Best Buddies Headquarters, at (305-374-2233) or fax (305-374-5305). Ian can provide the information or refer you to the nearest regional office to assist.

     Address: Ian Abrams, Director of Programs
                  Best Buddies Headquarters
                  100 Southeast Second Street
                  Suite 1990
                  Miami, FL 33131

Best Buddies Web Site: *http://www.bestbuddies.org*

Figure 3.18. Best Buddies high schools.

club is a valuable way to improve the organization. Several types of information can be obtained for different purposes:

- *Peer opinion of the group's success with focus students:* Opinions can be collected through group discussion and short, anonymous questionnaires.

- *Peer satisfaction with their membership:* Satisfaction ratings can be collected through discussion or short, anonymous questionnaires. Facilitators regularly give participants the opportunity to reaffirm, change, or end their voluntary participation. Thus, these status changes also provide an indication of satisfaction.

- *Behavioral changes made by the focus student:* Data can be obtained by peers or facilitators and may be anecdotal, involve direct observation of behavior (Haring & Breen, 1992), or include self-report by focus students. For example, ongoing exchanges between two friendship group members (a typical peer and a focus student) can be assessed by adult facilitators with one of two or three behavior "grades":

  - *Did partners get together?:* Without prompts (+), with prompts (P), or did not do (−)

- *Were there interactions with the focus student?:* Independent interactions (+), prompted interactions (P), few or no interactions (−)

- *Were the interactions appropriate overall?:* Appropriate (+), inappropriate (−) (Breen & Lovinger, 1991, p. 118)

Adults who observed the group interactions did so in a manner as removed from the lunch group as possible. Breen and Lovinger found that facilitators did not have to hear actual verbal exchanges to obtain useful information and thus could avoid intruding. The form in Figure 3.19 was used to record interaction data and enabled facilitators to evaluate each group's success.

ENCOURAGING NATURAL RELATIONSHIPS AND SUPPORTS

The least structured ways of facilitating social relationships involve methods that simply encourage natural peer supports and relationships during school activities and routines. There are many options, including informal buddy systems, peer tutoring programs (described in Chapter 5), advocacy programs, and recreation as a means for integration. In-

Focus/Peer		Monday	Tuesday	Wednesday	Friday
		John	Martin	Carlos	Martin
Brian	Partner	+ Ⓟ −	⊕ P −	+ Ⓟ −	⊕ P −
	Interaction	+ P ⊖	⊕ P −	+ Ⓟ −	+ Ⓟ −
	Appropriate	+ P ⊖	⊕ P −	+ P ⊖	⊕ P −
Focus/Peer		David	David	David	Mike
Matt	Partner	+ Ⓟ −	⊕ P −	⊕ P −	+ Ⓟ −
	Interaction	⊕ P −	⊕ P −	⊕ P −	+ Ⓟ −
	Appropriate	⊕ P −	+ P ⊖	⊕ P −	+ P ⊖
Focus/Peer		Brian	Brian	Brian	Brian
Chris	Partner	+ P ⊖	+ Ⓟ −	⊕ P −	⊕ P −
	Interaction	+ P −	+ Ⓟ −	+ Ⓟ −	⊕ P −
	Appropriate	+ P −	⊕ P −	⊕ P −	⊕ P −
Focus/Peer		Sharon	Jeannette	Sharon	Kelly
Susie	Partner	+ Ⓟ −	+ P ⊖	+ Ⓟ −	+ Ⓟ −
	Interaction	+ P ⊖	+ P −	+ Ⓟ −	⊕ P −
	Appropriate	+ P ⊖	+ P −	⊕ P −	⊕ P −

Key: **Partner**s get together without prompts (+), with prompts (P), or did not do (−)
    Interactions were independent (+), prompted (P), or few or none (−)
    Appropriateness of interactions: appropriate (+) or inappropriate (−)

Figure 3.19.   Grid to collect data on PAL Club interactions. (From Breen, C.G., & Lovinger, L. [1991]. PAL [Partners at Lunch Club]: Evaluation of a program to support social relationships in a junior high school. In C.G. Breen, C.H. Kennedy, & T.G. Haring [Eds.], *Social context research project: Methods for facilitating the inclusion of students with disabilities in integrated school and community contexts* [pp. 54–105]. Santa Barbara: University of California; reprinted by permission.)

terestingly, although all of these approaches may improve interactions with peers without disabilities, Kennedy and Itkonen (1994) found that high school students with moderate and severe disabilities who had the benefits of peer tutors and "friendship" programs *did not make noticeable improvements in their social interactions with typical peers, nor did they meaningfully expand their social networks, until they actually participated in general education classes.* Therefore, in addition to structured and natural approaches for facilitating social interactions between students with disabilities and their peers, it continues to be important for educators to work toward inclusion in general education classes for students of all ages and disabilities.

Guidelines for Natural Support Approaches

Jorgensen defined *natural supports* for school-age students with disabilities as

Those components of an educational program—philosophy, policies, people, materials and technology, and curricula—that are used to enable all students to be fully participating members of regular classroom, school, and community life. Natural supports bring children closer together as friends and learning partners rather than isolating them. (1992, p. 183)

When harnessing natural or less structured supports to promote social relationships, educators will find it helpful to develop and follow some general program guidelines. The guidelines overlap with those that are used in more structured peer programs and emphasize the importance of sensitivity toward peer preferences, existing networks, and chronological age; showing respect for social exchanges between peers; and providing minimal but thoughtful assistance (Figure 3.20).

Buddy Systems

There are many different versions of buddy programs. Some buddy programs have goals of simply having fun or of providing assistance to a given individual. Most buddy systems are based within a classroom and involve incidental teaching during nonstructured, routine activities. Incidental teaching can address many skills, including social skills and any other skills that the specific activity requires (e.g., independent travel in the school, behavior in public, communication, simple self-care, learning to go down the slide). Buddies can

give social support, such as assisting students in getting on and off the bus, accompanying students to assemblies or after-school events, eating lunch, and "hanging out" in the halls before and after classes. Buddies may be assigned (they may always decline) or may volunteer and be given specific roles; however, buddy activities are never required or graded.

Cameron, who knows Jared from middle school and his ninth-grade physical education class, is asked to be Jared's PE buddy. He willingly agrees to the position for the month of October. Cameron helps Jared open his locker, reminds him to "stay cool," and helps him follow the teacher's directions when needed.

Being Helpful An important question teachers should address when implementing buddy systems is, *What is helpful help from peers?* It is worthwhile to give students clear direc-

1. Adult facilitators and/or experienced peers need to teach others to communicate with the focus student; they should be taught to both understand and use the student's communication system (e.g., facial expressions, vocalizations, movements, gestures, signs, picture pointing, augmentative or alternative communication device, words).
2. Group members should share and practice ways to amend conversations or interactions that are not working.
3. If the focus student is not able to get around without assistance, peers need to be taught respectful ways to assist and to encourage the student's participation while also promoting independence and choice. Peers also should be taught basic information about the equipment or procedures the person routinely uses.
4. Peers need to be taught the importance of balanced turn-taking, mutual enjoyment, and reciprocity in interactions.
5. Adult facilitators should determine and use or identify and try out preferred activities and materials that the focus students have in common with peers. Use the guideline: *If it is age appropriate, nonstigmatizing, safe, and fun, try it!*
6. Adult monitoring of interactive activities should be kept unobtrusive while enabling the adult to collect information about activity or program outcomes and participants' level of satisfaction.
7. Adults should schedule regular times to meet with the focus student's peers so that buddies, partners, or group members can problem-solve, plan, and discuss success stories, challenges, and things about which they are unsure (with the focus student present and participating if possible).
8. Adult facilitators should encourage and promote responsible peer control of the support activities.
9. Participation in the support activities should be fun, voluntary, and age appropriate.

Figure 3.20. General guidelines for using natural peer supports.

tion and modeling as to what kind of help is really helpful and what kind makes classmates dependent or even angry. The various kinds of help will be very individualized for the particular focus student to whom the buddy is assigned. Buddies may meet periodically with an adult facilitator for a discussion of concerns and successes and for progress updates. When students are also involved in peer planning groups with classmates, instruction may not be needed; however, some initial supervision is important in order to monitor the quality of interactions between partners as they get to know each other.

Getting Organized   A "buddy" system can work in several ways. An educator may work with a small group of students of mixed ages who are assigned to be buddies for a particular student who has developmental delays and cerebral palsy, such as second grader Daniel who needs an older bus buddy. The students who have buddies often need minor assistance in school routines, such as getting on and off the bus, getting to and from classes, completing some daily routines, going to the cafeteria and moving through the line, participating in physical education, getting to assemblies and having someone to sit next to and interact with, and getting to school club meetings.

Younger students are often eager to assist their peers; however, caution should be taken to teach them not to over help or baby the focus student. Assistance should be presented in the context of *We all need help sometimes.* Older students may be self-conscious about providing assistance to focus students unless they know how and unless "buddy behaviors" are viewed as being "okay" by their typical peers.

Advocates

An advocate is anyone who stands up for the rights of another. Advocacy roles are not assigned, but students may intervene as advocates whenever another student requires assistance to complete natural routines.

At recess, Marci observed a student with a cognitive disability being asked to do something inappropriate by a group of her

peers. Marci approached the student and told her that she did not need to do what they said; Marci then asked the student to play a ball game with her and her friends.

Adults, teachers, counselors, or coaches can offer advice on effective advocacy and can unobtrusively support or facilitate action by an advocate. Advocacy actions often evolve from participation in peer support and problem-solving groups. Care must be taken so advocates are not viewed by peers as "tattlers" or as violating the practice of "not telling on peers" (Schnorr, 1997, p. 8).

Informal Interactions in Secondary Schools

Despite the fact that students are older, adult facilitation of peer relationships and interactions is equally as important in middle and high school as it is in elementary school; however, the strategies and appearances will differ to suit the age and environment. Secondary school educators need to focus on *using natural opportunities* to promote interactions and on *creating other opportunities* by engineering times and places for various subgroups of students to interact with each other. Educators should focus on several different elements when brainstorming ways to increase interactions between secondary students with and without disabilities:

- The inclusive and social nature of each class

- The activities that occur after and outside of school

- The reputation of the educators who facilitate the experience with the secondary students (e.g., well-respected, aware, daily exposure to students)

- Other locations in a secondary school outside of classes (e.g., hallways, cafeteria, school store, locker rooms, snack areas)

- Preferred activities at the secondary level that draw kids together (e.g., music, trendy objects such as hacky sack or virtual pets)

• The effect that socialization outside of school has on secondary student relationships in the particular school and community

These six informational elements can be used to design in- and out-of-class activities that are appealing to secondary students and that will provide a context for social interactions between students with disabilities and their peers.

Schnorr's (1997) study of high school classrooms and student membership reveals some findings that are relevant to social relationships:

• Student membership in a class depended on one's affiliation with a subgroup of peers (a small group or a partner) in that class.

• Informal and class-related interactions, such as shared humor, occurred across the subgroups in a class and could influence one's status within the peer group.

• By itself, participation in informal and class-related interactions did not seem to influence membership in a class.

Of the six students with severe or multiple disabilities who were included in general education classes in the high school where Schnorr (1997) observed, only two students seemed to have affiliations with a peer subgroup; the other four students were "outsiders." Schnorr's findings regarding high school relationships are discussed in Figure 3.21.

Using Games and Recreation Activities to Promote Friendship Regardless of the age group, games can be an enjoyable way to create opportunities for students to interact with peers who have disabilities. The primary keys for using games and recreation activities as a successful medium include the game design (i.e., interesting to all, and all can participate) and when the game is scheduled to take place (e.g., as part of physical education, during other class periods, during outdoor periods, after school). Participation will vary depending on the student's disability, but planners need to aim for *active participation that every student can enjoy.* Typical peers themselves can be actively involved in problem-solving adaptations to assist focus students in improving their level of participation.

What the Research Says

Schnorr's findings regarding high school social relationships suggest that

• *Those who participated in the common types of class interactions* (e.g., greeting one another, loaning pencils/paper, and imitating others) were more likely to be connected to peer subgroups and viewed favorably.

• *Peer network strategies,* in which peers are connected to existing social networks or subgroups, seem to offer a more powerful means to expand a student's social membership in secondary schools than other strategies.

• *Getting connected* (i.e., developing relationships and achieving membership) was reported as the first priority by typical students new to a high school. This included *learning classmates' names, avoiding conflicts, "fitting in," "getting along,"* and *taking the initiative early in the school year,* or it didn't happen.

Support staff could help this process by

• Assisting teachers and peers in seeing the focus student as someone who is capable of understanding

• Sensitively providing any needed interpretations of the focus student's efforts to interact

• Tuning into the individual's efforts to interact with peers, providing support if and when necessary

Figure 3.21.   Findings regarding high school social relationships. (Source: Schnorr, 1997.)

Balloon Volley

Materials: Heavy balloon, chairs placed in a circle

Participants: At least four peers (eight works best)

Procedure:

Players are seated on the chairs. One student "serves" (tosses balloon up and hits it). The group volleys the balloon for as long as possible (when it hits the floor, is double-hit by one person, is caught, or if anyone stands up, the volley is over). After each volley, a different student serves. The group counts hits to identify which was their best volley.

Adaptations:

One person sits next to the target student and assists him or her by holding/tossing the balloon when it's the student's turn to serve or by guiding the student's arm to help him or her hit the balloon.

If the target student is unable to volley, he or she could serve on every other volley (or more frequently as the group will tolerate it).

Positive Outcomes:

Each person has equal control/turns; everyone participates.

Pace is suitable for a group of students with mixed disabilities.

Students receive counting practice.

Contributor: Deb   **Tested:**   Yes

Adapted Uno

Materials: Uno cards with "reverse" and "skip" cards removed. Cheaptalk communication device (XX company) on which messages "Reverse" and "Skip" are recorded.

Participants: Target student and at least two peers

Procedures:

Players sit at table. Target student has access to two switches connected to Cheaptalk; each switch activates one of the messages. After cards are dealt, dealer says "Go!" Game proceeds according to Uno rules (but players hurry!). Target student is instructed to use switch every 15 seconds (or an appropriate interval for that student). Cheaptalk (Enabling Devices, Inc.) message applies to whomever is taking a turn when the message is heard.

Adaptations:

One student assists target student with prompts to hit a switch at regular intervals (or variable intervals for more excitement).

Positive Outcomes:

Target student controls important component of game.

Switch activation results in immediate reinforcement (excitement from other players).

Target student receives one-step switch activation practice.

Contributors: Dee, Cassandra, Deb   **Tested:**   Yes

Figure 3.22.   Simple adapted games for middle school students with and without disabilities. (From Morris, D. [1997, Fall]. *Invented and adapted games that allow active participation by students with severe disabilities and their peers.* Unpublished manuscript, University of Virginia, Charlottesville; reprinted by permission.)

Communication   Successful *communication* is central to any social interaction. Teachers can teach social interactions naturalistically— as a game gets underway and during the game—but they can also work on improving the focus student's communication apart from typical peers. The same is true of the *game skills;* they can be taught as students are playing the game, or they can be taught beforehand. Some facilitators have found it helpful to figure out any necessary game adaptations ahead of time and to teach the required game skills to the focus students before combining them with their peers. For example, five high school students with a range of disabilities (e.g., cerebral palsy, communication difficulties, and cognitive limitations) were first taught to play adapted pinball and bowling by their special education teachers at a YMCA near the high school; they quickly learned to generalize those skills to after-school games with peers without disabilities who were recruited through a friendship program from the same school (Vandercook, 1991).

Figure 3.22 shows two simple games that a teacher adapted so that middle school students could play and have fun with three of their peers who had fairly extensive support needs. Teachers will find the manual by Heyne, Schleien, and McAvoy (n.d.) very helpful in planning recreation activities to promote friendships between students with and without disabilities.

DISCUSSION

Some readers may feel that the approaches presented in this chapter ask children to take on too much responsibility for their classmates with disabilities; however, we have found that these experiences enable typical peers to learn valuable life lessons about respecting and being attentive to others' differences. Both children and teenagers learn skills and form attitudes and values from peer support activities that they will use throughout their lives. By contrast, many of us who did not grow up playing and studying alongside peers with disabilities may still experience some uneasiness and fear around people who are different from us.

Relationships among children and adults change from year to year. When students with disabilities move with the same peer group from grade level to grade level, the ensuing comfort level makes it easier for relationships to be maintained and to evolve. So, what happens to these relationships between students with and without disabilities when they move into middle school and high school? Some of them continue as they had been, and some gradually or even abruptly come to an end. Friendships do not necessarily have to be sustained in order to be meaningful; what one learns from friends is built upon in other relationships. However, when students lose friends, it is also important that others take their place.

Peer support should continue to be an IEP accommodation throughout school for students with significant disabilities, poor social skills, or no supportive relationships. Because social relationships change and become more complex as students mature, creating opportunities for interaction between peers with and without disabilities should become more intentional over time and should not simply be left to chance.

The phrase "nothing about us without us" is used by several self-advocacy groups of adults with developmental disabilities to signify that 1) decisions about their daily lives are truly *their* decisions, and 2) they should be included to the greatest possible extent in making those decisions. The same phrase can be applied to school-age students with disabilities, especially those at the secondary level: Student voices must be listened to when creating and sustaining social relationships. In creating experiences to promote social relationships, educators need to find proactive strategies to discover each focus student's needs and preferences.

Chapter 4

Teaching Social Skills

Social skills are important for all students to learn. When children and adolescents have inadequate social skills for their age, they are less able than their socially competent peers to develop positive relationships with fellow students, and their learning at school is often threatened. Researchers who study social skills in children agree on the following:

1. Children and adolescents who are at risk for not learning positive social behavior or who have identified disabilities often need some instruction and guidance in social interaction.
2. Social skills instruction can have positive outcomes on children's acceptance by peers.
3. To improve inadequate social skills, it is important to assess, target, and directly teach the necessary skills.

This chapter describes methods to assess and build social skills. First, however, the concept of *social competence* is explained and then used as a basis for detailing the social difficulties that many children must learn to overcome. The three students described below—Daniel, Melanie, and Rick—are used in this chapter to illustrate these skill difficulties and ways that teachers can address them.

Student Snapshot

Daniel is an 8-year-old who has multiple disabilities, including cerebral palsy, visual impairment, and a seizure disorder. Because he does not use speech, he uses some augmentative devices to communicate. Daniel uses a wheelchair; however, he relies on others to operate it. Daniel's parents communicate with their fellow core team members daily via a written log book in addition to attending regular meetings. The physical therapist, occupational therapist, speech-language therapist, and vision consultant are active members of Daniel's team, though they are generally less available

than the other team members; they provide updates at weekly meetings through written notes to the team. Daniel is learning to react to an object schedule, to initiate interactions with and respond to his peers and teachers, to make choices, and to reject things he does not want. Daniel's team has devised ways to actively involve him in classroom activities.

Student Snapshot

Melanie, a full-time member of the fourth grade, has autism. To communicate, Melanie shakes her head yes and no and uses a picture communication book, some signing, and infrequent words. Melanie's parents have been active participants on her team and attend core team meetings every month in addition to frequent verbal exchanges between meetings. Melanie's general education and special education teachers meet weekly to plan and problem-solve, and her classroom teachers interact daily as they work together to implement her program within the fourth-grade class. Melanie is working on following school routines and actively participating in them (e.g., arrival, lunch, recess, class job). Melanie has some reading and writing skills and enjoys using the computer. Socially, Melanie is a loner, and her interactions with peers are often unsuccessful unless she has adult support. Melanie is learning self-calming methods to use when she becomes angry or fearful.

Student Snapshot

Rick, a highly articulate 15-year-old, has pervasive developmental disorder, obsessive-compulsive disorder, and Tourette syndrome. He is enrolled in six general education classes and a one-to-one resource period; Rick receives 100% support and monitoring throughout the day and during class transitions—a time that is difficult for him. Rick's team is highly cohesive and pro-

vides strong support, and his parents contribute and are very pleased with his progress. Rick often interacts like a small child or an adult, rarely like a teen. He needs situations that allow guided practice to develop his proper role. Rick is learning to reduce his references to his and others' biological functions and to refer to them in appropriate ways if and when necessary. Teachers use redirection and other specific approaches to prevent Rick from getting into an agitated state; his disability is characterized by periodic and intense mood swings, which usually require him to remove himself from the situation and go calm down. During these periods, Rick can become highly inappropriate and may be aggressive. Rick is learning to recognize and control his inappropriate behavior during classes; he keeps track of his behavior by giving himself points for appropriate behaviors, which earn him special outings with his teacher and friends.

THE CONCEPT OF SOCIAL COMPETENCE

Social competence is not a simple concept; however, a basic understanding of the concept is important in order to assess a student's current abilities and to identify specific needs for instruction. *Social competence* encompasses both an individual's effectiveness in influencing the behavior of a peer and the appropriateness of the behavior (given the environment, culture, and context) (Odom, McConnell, & McEvoy, 1992, p. 7). Figure 4.1 illustrates one way to envision social competence that has clear implications for assessing and teaching (Gustafson & Haring, 1992). The model is a combination of several social competence ideologies, but relies primarily on work by Dodge (1986) with input from Greenspan (1981). This model regards social competence as having multiple components: cognitive, affective, *and* behavioral.

Notice that a person's goals going into a social situation are influenced by the three "input" boxes in Figure 4.1. The goals that the student sets also correspond with the student's

understanding of the social cues and interaction and ultimately influence his or her choice of responses. Goals may not be directly "visible" but might be expected, given the student's past behavior or reputation. A lack of social skills may mean that a child seeks a self-centered goal at the cost of another more relationship-enhancing goal (e.g., "I am going to win" versus "I want to have fun with everyone in this game"). Some children may fail to notice significant social cues from their peers or from adults because of a sensory or cognitive disability and, consequently, might fail to adjust their goals for the interaction. For example, if an adolescent girl with a visual loss does not notice that the peer to whom she is talking is bored or is attending closely to a videotape or another peer, the girl may persist inappropriately in her goal of carrying on a conversation.

The first two components of the social competence model are intertwined: *Encoding* encompasses the information an individual takes in from a social situation; *interpreting* entails understanding that information in a way that reflects one's personal perspective. Synonyms for these terms and overlapping concepts include *social sensitivity, social insight, social cue discrimination,* and *social perception.* These processes are covert; that is, they involve thinking and are not obvious or outwardly expressed by the student's behavior. As students encode and interpret a social situation, they *set or revise* their goals for that situation. Goals vary widely and may include, *"I'm gonna have fun," "I need some help to do this," "I want that toy and I'm gonna get it,"* or, *"I wish they would just smile at me."*

The second pair of components also have a reciprocal influence on each other. Related terms include *social communication, social problem-solving, generating alternatives,* and *evaluating alternatives.* Searching and deciding on a social response involves a consideration of the possible ways one might react to a social situation and the choice to react in one of several ways. A child's experience and goals have a big impact on both of these processes, as is the case for tenth-grader Rick.

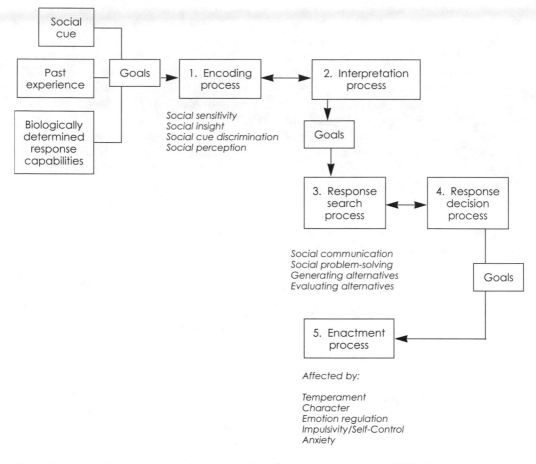

Figure 4.1.   A model of social competence. (From Gustafson, R.N., & Haring, N.G. [1992]. Social competence issues in the integration of students with handicaps. In K.A. Haring, D.L. Lovett, & N.G. Haring [Eds.], *Integrated lifestyle services for persons with disabilities* [pp. 20–58]. New York: Springer-Verlag; reprinted by permission.)

At class break in earth science, Rick approached two guys he knew as he went to sharpen his pencil. His goals favored positive social exchange because he knew the boys and had had positive experiences with them before in earth science class. The cues from this situation favored interest and low "risk." Thus, the array of responses Rick mentally searched probably included "friendly" and "nonaggressive." For Rick, transitions between classes are stressful and confusing. During these times, his goal is to reduce stress by getting to his next class; Rick's goals shift from being prosocial to being antisocial toward those who get in his way.

Notice that the response search and decision steps *are not directly observable*, making them challenging to teach and to monitor.

In this model, the *Encode—Interpret* process is followed by a *Response Search—Response Decision* process, with the possibility that the person's goals for the social situation might be adjusted along the way. The student's interacting behavior ("the enactment process" in the model), which is influenced by many factors, follows the first two processes. For example, the individual's temperament—a combination of his or her ability to focus attention and act with forethought coupled with his or her generalized mood or affective tendency—may sway the way that he or she actually behaves. A student's *character*—the quality of his or her moral responses—also may affect how he or she behaves. Other influencing factors include *anxiety, impulsivity, self-control,* and *emotion regulation.*

> *Rick's anxiety in making the transition between classes means that he probably will not notice people he knows and will be less likely to smile or greet others. When other students approach him, Rick has difficulty controlling his anger and has even struck out and cursed at them.*

How well-executed the response is can be another concern during this behavioral process. If a student selects a prosocial response (to join a peer group) but does not know how to engage in this response or tries incompetently to do so, the outcome is often not successful. Alternately, if the student's attempts to enter the peer group are inefficient (too slow, incomplete), the student also might be unsuccessful. Consider fourth-grader Melanie, who is learning ways to approach her peers and initiate interactions.

> *Melanie has learned to use a successful strategy to join an ongoing play group at recess; she watches and then suggests a novel way her peers might change the activity. Often, however, she is not persistent enough or her peers do not understand her ideas for play, and she is not included successfully.*

As mentioned in Chapter 2, an individual's past reputation in the eyes of his or her classmates is not easily reversed; therefore, if Melanie has a history of either not trying or trying and giving up in joining an ongoing peer group, she is likely to fail again. Her peers will have come to view her as a withdrawn classmate, *not* an enjoyable play partner. Her teachers would be wise to consider a combination of approaches:

- Teach Melanie to be more proficient in her communication with peers.

- Teach Melanie's peers to better interpret her communication.

- Use adult facilitation to promote positive peer support for Melanie through classroom-based peer planning groups.

Because "enactment" is the observable behavior, it is what adults and peers focus on most despite the complex process that precedes the behavior. For example, prior to reacting to a social situation (*enactment*), a child may observe that situation (*encode*), have expectations about it (*set goals*), think about it (*interpret*), modify his or her expectations (*possibly modify goals*), formulate how to behave or what to do (*make a response search*), decide what to do (*make a response decision*), again adjust his or her goals, and then finally behave (*enact*). This last step, the actual behavior, is usually the primary step in the social competence model toward which teachers and parents direct their instruction and their reactions; however, the other steps in this model are also worthy of attention for many students. To focus on these other steps, however, requires that the steps or processes be made overt by teaching students to discriminate aspects of their own thinking. For students who are less sophisticated conversationalists (e.g., Daniel, Melanie), much of social skills training may address enactment.

The next section describes two ways to classify or view social interaction difficulties that will be helpful to teachers as they assess and plan teaching methods to address social difficulties.

SOCIAL INTERACTION DIFFICULTIES

Ways to Classify Social Skill Problems

There are many ways to classify social skill problems. One way, which is described in Chapter 1, is a straightforward classification of social skill problems borrowed from Brady and McEvoy (1989) (Figure 4.2). Children might exhibit one of the first three patterns (although usually not more than one) but also may dem-

---

Social difficulties some children have when interacting with peers

Aggressiveness: The display of one's negative emotions or anger through a variety of behaviors (e.g., tantrums, hitting, verbal attacks, threats, fighting), which are excessive in their rate and/or intensity.

Social Withdrawal: The tendency to be quiet and shy and not to participate with others in most situations (e.g., avoiding play at recess, keeping to oneself at lunch and during transitions, not volunteering in class) though typically having the skills to observe social situations and respond to others' social bids.

Nonresponsiveness: A more extreme form of social withdrawal involving a lack of response to peers, withdrawal from peers' invitations to interact, or making inappropriate responses; nonresponsiveness often requires instruction on *how* to respond.

Poor Quality of Interactions: Interactions with peers occur but often are unsuccessful in one or more ways. The duration may be too short (unable to complete an interaction) or too long (clinging); the interaction style reflects a lower level of maturity than the student's peers and the interaction becomes stigmatizing (e.g., overly affectionate, unable to understand or tell jokes that peers share; prefers toys and activities that are suited for younger children).

Generalization and Maintenance Problems: Social skills are used in some situations but do not transfer to other situations (classroom play and play during recess or in the after school program) or are learned but not maintained (seeking assistance, keeping track of anger as a means of controlling it).

Figure 4.2.   Interaction difficulties. (From Brady, M.P., & McEvoy, M.A. [1989]. Social skills training as an integration strategy. In R. Gaylord-Ross [Ed.], *Integration strategies for students with handicaps* [pp. 213–231]. Baltimore: Paul H. Brookes Publishing Co.; adapted by permission.)

onstrate poor quality of interaction and generalization and maintenance problems.

A second approach sorts children and adolescents by the amount or type of learning that they will require to perform the social skills in question. Each group defines the learning difficulty responsible for the inadequate social skills: 1) the skills are not known; 2) the skills are known but are not performed, not performed well, or are not fluent; and 3) the skills may or may not be known but are overpowered by successful, competing behavior problems (Gresham, 1997). These two frameworks will be used to classify student's social skill deficiencies because they help teachers to design teaching programs.

Inadequate Social Skills   What are inadequate social skills? They are the shortcomings a person exhibits in his or her interaction with and enjoyment of others. Social skills follow a developmental progression and, therefore, will change as children grow into adolescence and adulthood. As children get older, social skills take on more mature forms (that also vary somewhat by culture and gender). The skills, however, continue to serve the same function: being polite, humane, and gregari-

ous; greeting; listening; following rules; offering assistance; complimenting others; expressing anger appropriately; joining in; and having conversations. The following sections relate examples from the three students (Daniel, Melanie, and Rick) to this framework for classifying social skill inadequacies (Gresham, 1997).

Skill Acquisition Problem   In the first group are individuals who do not have necessary social skills because the skills have not been taught to them or the students have not learned them. Students with skill acquisition problems may not know how to make friends, know how to start or carry on a conversation with peers, or have any clue as to how to join into a group of socializing classmates.

Daniel has extensive limitations in his voluntary movements and is learning to use a communication system and make choices; he is perhaps the most in need of learning to socialize.

Performance Deficit or Fluency Problem The second group includes students who have the skills but don't use them or perform them poorly and need periodic coaching and feedback. Motivation and a lack of opportunity to use the skills often seem to be reasons why some students fall into the performance deficit or fluency problem category.

Melanie's difficulty in joining in with her peers illustrates that she partially knows what to do but is not fluent in using social skills or in generalizing them across situations and peers.

Interfering or Competing Behavior The third group includes students whose inappropriate behavior outweighs or overpowers their use of appropriate behavior and social skills. Problem behaviors (e.g., grabbing, pushing) may be easier to use and more effective for getting what a student wants (e.g., toys, a place in line) than the appropriate behavior (e.g., asking, waiting).

Rick sometimes receives assistance with getting out of a busy hallway or gets out of completing a class task if he explodes into an episode of hitting and refusing to work. Rick is less able than other students to say he needs help on an assignment or to indicate that it is hard for him to be around crowds.

Although not perfect, categorizing social skill difficulties into problem types (e.g., aggressiveness, social withdrawal) or into learning problem types can help teachers as they design teaching programs. Both methods are used along with the model of social competence to structure the discussion of assessment and teaching strategies.

DESIGNING SOCIAL SKILLS INSTRUCTION

Figure 4.3 sets forth the steps of a six-step process for designing programs to teach social skills. The process involves assessing social skills, targeting needed skills, designing a teaching program directed toward those skills,

implementing the program, and evaluating its effectiveness. First, it is necessary to address some preliminary issues: strategies to build positive social relationships and teamwork.

Broad Strategies to Build Positive Social Relationships

Experience has taught many of us about the effectiveness of several broad strategies for building positive social relationships between students with adequate social skills and students who are "at risk" for or who demonstrate social skill difficulties. The first three strategies, discussed in Chapter 3, may prevent or even improve social skill problems and, therefore, are ongoing tactics that schools will want to implement *before* targeting and directly teaching social skills:

1. Create opportunities for peers to interact, and support these interactions.

2. Improve the school atmosphere so that it is cooperative and accepting of diversity.

3. Build peer social support for students who need it.

The fourth strategy is to provide social skills instruction based on assessment and a collaboratively developed plan; this strategy can either be applied in combination with the first three strategies or alone if the improvements made in the social environment are not enough to build needed social skills.

Social skill instruction can be focused on an individual student, a small group, or an entire class. When an entire class is targeted for social skill instruction, a "universal" or global approach is used. Ideally, teachers select a proven curriculum that is suited to the age group and involves adequate amounts of teaching time (Walker, Colvin, & Ramsey, 1995). Often, a large group of age-appropriate skills (e.g., listening, greeting others, having conversations, joining in, complimenting, expressing anger, keeping friends, doing quality work, following rules, using self-control, offering assistance, disagreeing with others, being organized) are systematically addressed.

Step 1. Team identifies the student's social skill difficulties and the type of learning problem:

A. Assess student on social skills expected for his or her gender, age, and cultural group.

B. Identifies the type of learning problem:

Acquisition problem: Student doesn't have the skill or is missing a step in performing a social skill sequence.

Performance or fluency problem: Student has the skill, but may not know when to use it, may be too slow in using it, may be unable to adjust the skill to suit the situation, or may simply lack proficiency in using it.

Interfering or competing behaviors: Student has lots of competing, inappropriate behaviors; social skills may be known but are not efficient or effective enough to compete with the problem behaviors.

> If a social skill problem is not identified, then explore other strategies that might be effective:
>
> Improve peer/staff acceptance; modify schoolwork and add supports; or arrange for opportunities to interact

Step 2. Team gathers and discusses information, then sets goals for the student:

A. Pools existing information
B. Observes to collect additional information
C. Discusses information and sets goals

Step 3. Team generates teaching ideas that match the student's specific social skill difficulty:

A. Reviews successful social skill teaching methods
B. Selects methods that match learning problem, social competency, and context
C. Considers the implications of peer network
D. Considers the use of commercial programs

Step 4. Team evaluates the feasibility of its ideas and selects teaching options for improving social skills.

Step 5. Team develops a teaching plan and considers the following:

A. Is staff training or additional staff/volunteer support needed?
B. Is parental involvement adequate; is a home component needed in plan?
C. How will we schedule instruction and integrate it into student routines?
D. Will we group students, teach individual students, or both?
E. What materials and adult resources will we need?
F. How will we promote generalization?
G. What easy-to-use and meaningful ways will we use to monitor student progress before, during, and after training?

Step 6. Team implements the plan, monitors student progress, improves the plan as needed, and evaluates outcomes.

Figure 4.3. A team process for designing social skills instructional programs. (Sources: Gresham, 1997; Walker, Colvin, & Ramsey, 1995; Walker, Schwarz, Nippold, Irvin, & Noell, 1994.)

Research suggests that classmates without disabilities can be a major motivating force for students with disabilities and can often help teach their classmates whose skills are insufficient; peers contribute to creative problem-solving, cue and model during naturalistic opportunities for the social skills, and reinforce the social skills when they do occur.

Roles of Team Members in Social Skills Instruction

Social skills instruction often is more challenging than academic skills instruction. Good teaming is essential to success. Goals should reflect the broader view of the team and should include family, student, and peer input. Teaching needs to be frequent enough to produce learning and widespread enough—across times, people, and places—to yield generalization (Forness & Kavale, 1996). The collaborative process allows educators to work together and with parents and students to productively focus on particular students who exhibit social skills difficulties. Peers, teachers, and administrators all have roles in promoting social competence within schools (Brady &

McEvoy, 1989; Snell et al., 1995). Their combined involvement should promote the needed consistency and intensity in training across staff and school activities.

Role of Special Educators　Special education teachers play a large role in this process by 1) facilitating the team's selection of social skill goals and the design and implementation of teaching plans, 2) pulling in related services staff whose expertise may be critical for students with physical and communication disabilities, 3) designing their schedules to provide routine opportunities for focus students to be with peers and have support for their interactions, 4) modeling interactions with focus students, 5) sensitively answering peers' questions about classmates with disabilities, 6) providing and teaching others to give positive behavioral support to students with problem behavior and instruction to students learning social skills, and 7) teaching peers strategies to support their class members.

Daniel's special education teacher works closely with Daniel's therapists to determine ways that Daniel can communicate yes *and* no *and make clear choices. The special education teacher coordinates times to explore these social interaction ideas with classroom staff, to try them out with Daniel and his peers, and to work with the second-grade teacher to integrate them into Daniel's schedule.*

Roles of General Educators　Classroom teachers and paraprofessional classroom staff are present in the classroom more than the other team members; therefore, they are fundamental to the process of fostering social skills. They 1) model acceptance of all students, 2) answer peers' questions, 3) plan activities to meaningfully include students, 4) provide direct support to students as they learn social skills, 5) monitor day-to-day progress of social skills, 6) identify times and places in the schedule when social skills instruction is best or create new opportunities, and 7) encourage classmates to lend support to peers who need it.

All of Rick's teachers are involved in planning prevention strategies that can work in their classrooms to prevent behavior crises. Melanie's and Daniel's teachers are central to the design of their social skill instructional programs, always suggesting ways to integrate teaching into daily routines.

Roles of Peers　Peers participate in social skills teaching activities as models and "prompters" for students who are learning social skills, as "encouragers" to classmates for their mastery of skills, and as collaborators with each other and with adults to seek solutions to focus students' social difficulties. Peer involvement in planning social activities helps guarantee that the content of the activity and the language used are age-appropriate, that the exercises are enjoyable for peers, and that participation in the activity is not stigmatizing.

Early in the school year, Melanie's and Daniel's classmates learned how each of the students communicated. Classmates practiced ways to offer Daniel choices and "read" his choice. Melanie's classmates learned a turn-taking approach for communicating with her as she used her communication book to tell them about her activities out of school. (Figure 4.4 describes the method Melanie's teachers taught her peers to use.)

Roles of Administrators　Building principals lend administrative and school system support. In their leadership capacity, they can 1) arrange schedules so opportunities exist for social integration among students, 2) work with teachers to integrate special services in terms of classroom assignments and adequate availability of special education support, 3) distribute teacher duties so special and general education teachers regularly interact with general education students and students with disabilities, 4) promote the teaching of social skills by providing in-service training, and 5) facilitate collaborative teaming in the school. Finally, when classwide social skills instruction is desired, principals can appoint a group of

What the Research Says

Hunt and her co-workers perfected an approach for making it easier for students to interact with their peers whose communication is difficult to understand. First, *conversation books* were created for the students with disabilities whose speech was unclear. These books contained photos of activities, people, pets, sports, and other events that the students enjoyed during and after school and a *menu of conversation topics*; photos were regularly added and removed to keep the books current and interesting. Conversation topics were selected by pointing to photos. Next, the student was individually taught to use a *turn-taking structure* to interact with a teacher, using the conversation book to augment his or her communication system (e.g., words and phrases, signs, conventional gestures). The conversation structure involved back-and-forth interactions between two people; topics were changed or clarified by pointing to photos.

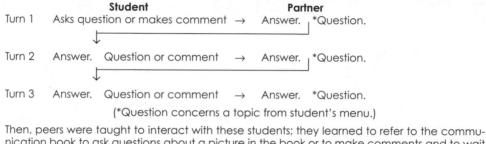

	Student		**Partner**	
Turn 1	Asks question or makes comment	→	Answer.	*Question.
Turn 2	Answer. Question or comment	→	Answer.	*Question.
Turn 3	Answer. Question or comment	→	Answer.	*Question.

(*Question concerns a topic from student's menu.)

Then, peers were taught to interact with these students; they learned to refer to the communication book to ask questions about a picture in the book or to make comments and to wait each time the student answered to give him or her time to ask another question or to make a comment. This training was given during 5-minute sessions during the school day and repeated with all of the involved peers across many settings where informal interactions could take place.

The training resulted in meaningful increases in conversational exchanges between students with fairly significant cognitive disabilities and their peers without disabilities, some of whom also had limited motor skills or behavior problems; students ranged in age from elementary school (ages 6–10) to high school (ages 15–18).

Figure 4.4. Taking turns and communicating closely with peers. (From "Establishing conversational exchanges with family and friends: Moving from training to meaningful communication" by P. Hunt, M. Alwell, & L. Goetz, 1991, *The Journal of Special Education, 25,* 305–319. Copyright 1991 by PRO-ED, Inc. Adapted with permission.)

teachers, parents, and students to work with guidance counselors in reviewing and selecting an effective published program or curriculum.

The assistant principal at Rick's high school contributed to the planning of Rick's crisis management plan because, when necessary, it required the immediate availability of a staff member to assist in removing Rick to a location where he could calm down. The principal also arranged for a special in-service session for staff.

The next section defines the steps involved in designing programs to teach social skills.

A TEAM PROCESS FOR DESIGNING SOCIAL SKILLS INSTRUCTION

This section reviews each step of the team process found in Figure 4.3, starting with assessment and ending with implementation. Steps 1 and 2 of this planning process involve assessment of social behavior. Teams will make use of a variety of specific assessment strategies to define the difficulty and to understand the circumstances under which the student's behavior is and is not a problem. Most of these strategies will be informal, relying on focused interview and observation that requires defining the problem behavior(s) first. Assessment information helps the team determine objectively if there really is a problem that warrants attention and teaching and, if there is, which social skills need to be taught.

Step 1
Team Identifies the Student's Social Skill Difficulties and the Type of Learning Problem

This step is initiated when experienced classroom or special education teachers notice social inadequacies or unusual peer-to-peer behavior in students. During this stage, the general and special education teachers share their concerns and may decide to further observe the student, to use one or more of the teacher assessment procedures addressed in the next section, or to involve the school psychologist or guidance counselor in the assessment. Informal interactions about the focus student by team members or between teachers and parents can be very helpful at this early stage.

Strategies Used by School Psychologists and Counselors

In assessing students whose social skills and behavior problems are more extreme, it is sometimes useful for teachers to seek the assistance of the guidance counselor or school psychologist. The first two sections of Table 4.1 list screening and identification measures and social skill rating scales. These measures have norms that can be interpreted by those who are trained in using them. The measures involve interviews, rating scales, and questionnaires; however, they require prior observation and knowledge of the student. These assessments may or may not be helpful in clarifying a student's social difficulties. Assessment activities could include the following:

- Counselors, psychologists, or teachers complete norm-referenced or less formal *screening or behavior rating scales* that measure relevant

aspects of social and emotional competence and screen for social skill or behavioral problems and indicators of risk.

- Parents, peers, and/or teachers (and possibly the focus student) are interviewed.

Observing Behavior[1]

Planned observations of the student's social interactions or the lack thereof can verify whether further teacher intervention is necessary. Initially, informal observation involves *discussing* the social interaction concern and *defining* it in observable terms and *planning when and how to informally observe* the student during the school routine.

Define and Measure Behavior   Direct observation is one of the educator's most useful tools for identifying and pinpointing social skill difficulties (and later for assessing the impact of a teaching program). There are many approaches to observation, some of which are not practical for use in school environments due to the attention, equipment, training, or time involved. Simpler observation procedures will still require some care and precision to yield accurate results. The third section of Table 4.1 describes several informal social skills assessment procedures.

The first method in the informal assessment section requires the direct observation of student behavior during recess or other unstructured times. Equipped with a clear definition of the behavior of interest (hitting, being alone, cooperative play with peers), a teacher uses a hidden stopwatch to time the duration of a student's difficult social behavior for 10 minutes during recess (Walker et al., 1995, p. 226). This approach can be used to determine *if* there really is a social skills problem. As noted by Walker, Colvin, and Ramsey,

> As a general rule, it is a red flag if a target student spends more than 12 or 15% of a recess

---

[1] *Behavioral Support*, a companion booklet in this series (Janney & Snell, 2000), provides a useful framework for assessment and intervention with disruptive and serious problem behavior such as verbal abuse of others, aggression toward others, tantrums, and self-injury.

Table 4.1.   Assessment methods relevant to the identification of anti-social behavior and to social skill training

Early Screening and Identification of Risk Behaviors and Social Problems

1. **Achenbach Behavior Checklist** (Achenbach, 1991): Teacher and parent forms to nominate and then rate students suspected of having an antisocial profile; excellent psychometric characteristics. Ages 2–18.

2. **Student Risk Screening Scale (SRSS)** (Drummond, 1993): Teachers rate a whole class of young elementary students on early antisocial behavior; easily used and reliable; identifies behavioral indicators that lead to conduct disorders.

3. **Early Screening Project (ESP)** (Walker, Severson, & Feil, 1994): Screening of preschool and elementary school–age children on their behavior and social competence via a sequence of three "gates" or stages: 1) teacher nomination and rank ordering based on behavior problems; 2) highest ranked then rated to check against norms; and 3) those who exceed normative criteria are both rated by parents and observed by teachers in structured and unstructured situations on their responsiveness to teacher demands and peer relationships. Reliable.

4. **Systematic Screening for Behavior Disorders (SSBD)** (Walker & Steverson, 1990): Similar to the ESP but is for use with children in grades 1-6; reliable.

5. **School Self-Rating** (Meyer, Harootunian, & Williams, 1991; Meyer & Henry, 1993): Middle school students rate themselves on 13 items that are moderately predictive of passing to the next grade; items address academic self-appraisal, attitude toward school, and cooperation. Can be administered after at least the third week of school.

Social Skills Rating Scales for Use by Teachers

1. **Social Skills Rating System** (Gresham & Elliott, 1990): Preschool, elementary, and secondary school versions with self-report version for fifth graders and older; parent rating scale included; national norms and excellent psychometric properties.

2. **Walker-McConnell Scale of Social Competence and School Adjustment (SSCSA)** (Walker & McConnell, 1988): Two versions (K–6 and 7–12); national norms and excellent psychometric properties.

Informal Social Skill Assessment Procedures Involving Interview/Observation

1. **Direct behavioral observations during recess or other nonstructured times:** When directly observing students, there are numerous ways to measure and record defined behaviors or social skill deficiencies. The important elements are 1) a clear definition of relevant behavior(s) in observable terms, 2) observation in an unobtrusive, nonstigmatizing manner over a long enough period to obtain a representative picture, 3) a procedure that is simple for teachers to use while still allowing an accurate observation, 4) a simple description of each observation context (e.g., time, date, location, people present, activities, unusual events), 5) involvement of the classroom teacher, and 6) cost-effectiveness.

    One such method of direct observation entails using a stopwatch and recording the cumulative duration of the problem behavior over a recess or social interaction period of a set length of time (e.g., the second 10 minutes of recess) (Walker, Colvin, & Ramsey, 1995). Often, two rather broad behaviors indicate that children are in need of social skill instruction ("negative social behavior" and "alone" behavior); both behaviors can be observed simultaneously using two stopwatches (one assigned to one behavior and the other assigned to the second behavior). In this approach, two totals result from every observation—one for each behavior. Observational data are graphed for easier understanding.

2. **Matrix to target social skills deficits by rating individual students across the class** (Walker, Colvin, & Ramsey, 1995): This flexible observation procedure entails listing core social skills appropriate to an age group or taught by a curriculum (e.g., listening, greeting others, joining in, complementing, expressing anger, keeping friends, doing quality work) on the left side of a matrix. Students' names are written across the top of the matrix (see Figure 4.5). The teacher who observes uses a formal structured process for judging each student on each skill; therefore, judgments are not subjective. A numerical rating of 1 to 5 could be used, with "1" equaling "unskilled," "3" equaling "moderately skilled," and "5" equaling "very skilled." Teachers will look for low student scores (across skills for a single student);

(continued)

students who receive a rating of 3 or less on 75% of the skills will benefit from training on all skills in the curriculum and may initially be taught using one-to-one or small-group formats. Low average scores across the class (skills on which 70% of the class earns a rating of "3" or less) indicate skills in which the whole class, using a classwide approach, will benefit from additional training.

Matrix information can help teachers form socially balanced student groups.

3. **Transition Checklist** (Chandler, 1992): This checklist, in combination with listings of social skills that are expected in kindergarten, can be used to assess preschoolers' skills, characteristics of the sending preschool program and the receiving kindergarten program, and differences between the two programs.

4. **Social Contact Assessment Form** (Kennedy, Shukla, & Fryxell, 1997): A rating and recording scale for social interactions or "contacts" lasting 15 minutes or longer during which information about the interaction was noted (i.e., location, activity, people involved, school period, and perceived quality rating).

5. **Social Interaction Checklist** (Kennedy, Shukla, & Fryxell, 1997): A paper and pencil event-recording system to assess two dimensions of social interactions: (1) interaction duration and 2) occurrence of social support behaviors (i.e., greeting, information, access to others, material aid, emotional support, companionship).

6. **Interactive Partnership Scale (IPS)** (Hunt, Alwell, Farron-Davis, & Goetz, 1996): An observation procedure during which each focus student is observed for 10 minutes (observe for 20 intervals of 15 seconds each with 15 seconds to record data after each interval). For each communicative initiation (from a focus student to another student or from another student to the focus student) that occurs during an interval, several things are recorded: who the interaction partner is (e.g., paraprofessional, general or special education teacher, therapist, other adult, student without disabilities, student with disabilities) and the structure (e.g., initiation, acknowledgment, reciprocal interaction), function (e.g., request, protest, comment, assistance, greeting), focus (social or task-related), and quality (mismatch, neutral, affirming/affectionate, praising/complimentary, sharing pleasure, humorous, displeased, angry) of the interaction. The resultant data can be analyzed and used in various ways.

Measures of Relationships and Friendships

1. **School-Based Social Network Form** (Kennedy, Shukla, & Fryxell, 1997): This instrument measures students' friendship networks at school. Information is collected on individual students via interviews with peers and school staff who are familiar with the student, the student's schedule, and his or her social interactions. Information gathered includes numbers of social contacts in a 2-week period, with whom, length of time for which the individuals have known the focus student, the way in which they regard the focus student (e.g., a friend, liked), and whether or not the individual has provided social supports to the focus person or vice versa. Instrument has good reliability and validity.

2. **Acceptance Scale for Kindergartners (ASK)** (Favazza & Odom, 1996): A scale used to assess the attitudes of kindergartners toward peers with disabilities. The instrument appears to be reliable for use with children in this age group.

3. **Sociometric Assessment of Social Status:** A commonly used general approach for measuring social status among children and adolescents. Sociometric measures use peer nominations on positive dimensions (e.g., liked, a friend) and possibly on negative dimensions (e.g., not liked, not a friend). Peers also can be asked to rate the extent to which they like to play with a familiar child who is named or viewed in a picture. Sociometric measures are not good ways to assess social competence, as they give summary scores; peer nominations are better than peer ratings, but both are questioned as to their validity with preschoolers with disabilities. (For more information, refer to Gresham [1986] and Odom, McConnell, & McEvoy [1992].)

4. **Student Friendship Perception Survey** (Hendrickson, Shokoohi-Yekta, Hamre-Nietupski, & Gable, 1996): A series of open-ended questions and forced-choice questions suitable for middle and high school students that address ways to be a friend to a peer with severe disabilities, reasons why student could be a friend, and reasons why it might be difficult to be a friend.

5. **Assessment of Loneliness** (Williams & Asher, 1992): Students are interviewed to assess their understanding of loneliness; instrument has satisfactory internal reliability for both typical students, ages 8–13, and their peers with mental retardation. Questions address feelings of loneliness (questions 2, 5, and 9) and perceptions of inclusion or exclusion (questions 1,

(continued)

Table 4.1.   *(continued)*

3, 4, 6, 7, 8, 10). Italicized questions use a reverse response format in which response order is reversed when scoring.

1. Are the kids at school friendly to you?
2. Is this school a lonely place for you?
3. Are there kids at school who care about you?
4. Are there kids at school who understand how you feel?
5. Do you feel alone at school?
6. Are the kids at school mean to you?
7. Do you get along with the other kids at school?
8. Do you feel left out of things at school?
9. Are you lonely at school?
10. Do the other kids at school want to be with you?

In a private interview format (taking 15–20 minutes), each student is told that their answers to the questions will help adults understand their experiences in school. First, some practice questions are posed to teach students how to use the response format. Students are told to listen as questions are read one at a time and then to record one of three possible answers: "yes," "sometimes," or "no." Interviews conclude on a positive note; children are asked to talk about their favorite school activities. Following the interview, students' responses are scored; "yes" is scored as a 1, "sometimes" is scored as a 2, and "no" is scored as a 3.

Functional Assessment Devices

1. **Functional Assessment and Program Development for Problem Behavior: A Practical Handbook** (O'Neill, Horner, Albin, Sprague, Storey, & Newton, 1997): This three-part assessment and program development manual provides guidelines for 1) interviewing family members and school staff who are well acquainted with the focus student 2) observing the student's problem behaviors (noting time, location, and antecedents and consequences of the behavior) and making an educated guess as to the behavior's function, and 3) for designing behavior support plans. Suitable for all ages.
2. **Motivational Assessment Scale (MAS)** (Durand, 1988; Durand & Crimmins, 1988): This scale assists in the indirect assessment of one or more motivating function(s) that potentially maintain a student's problem behavior. The rating scale is completed by individuals who know the student well. Research in which the intervention has been based upon the MAS-identified function has established the validity of this instrument. Suitable for individuals of all ages.
3. **Communication-Based Intervention: Describe, Categorize, Verify** (Carr et al., 1994): A three-stage functional assessment procedure for use with individuals of any age; provides guidelines for use with individuals who have minimal communication and social skills. In the first stage, the antisocial problem behavior is identified through interviews with staff, peers, and family members who are well acquainted with the person. Next, incidences of these behaviors are observed and documented using a card system; one card is used per incident and documents the location, time, and people involved; the antecedents; the behavior; and the consequences. Interviews are continued whenever new behaviors or questions arise. A team of individuals then examines each card and categorizes each behavioral incident by its apparent function (e.g., attention; tangible; escape; or unknown, nonsocial motivation). Cards on which the team agrees are sorted into categories by function; each function category is further analyzed for distinct patterns. Programs for each category are written by the team and implemented to verify the team's categorization.

(Sources: Odom, McConnell, & McEvoy, 1992; Walker, Colvin, & Ramsey, 1995; and Wittmer, Doll, & Strain, 1996.)

period in solitary activity. Similarly, if the student is negative more than 10% of the time, it is also a red flag. Non-antisocial students in general rarely spend time alone at recess, and they are positive with each other approximately 90 to 95% of the time. (1995, p. 226)

This focused observation method can be used in later steps of the team planning process to gather additional information during other school routines (Step 2) and to monitor outcomes (Step 6). When direct observations indicate a student's antisocial behavior occurs often enough to warrant concern, the next step is to determine which social skills need to be learned, improved, or taught to correct the problem behavior.

Assess Social Skills Assessments of the particular social skills a student is missing or in which he or she is deficient can be made (Measures of Relationships and Friendships in Table 4.1). Assessment methods involve observing the student's behavior for the presence of specific social skills and then measuring the amount and types of social contact and interaction between students. Most commercial programs to teach social skills will provide a means for assessing the targeted skills. For example, the matrix method shown in Figure 4.5 can be used to rate an entire class on specific age-appropriate social skills and to identify potential teaching targets (Walker, Colvin, & Ramsey, 1995).

Identifying the
Type of Learning Problem

During Step 1 of the team process, teachers will identify which learning problem is involved (i.e., acquisition, performance, interfering). This initial identification might change after gathering and sharing additional information and holding a team discussion. Step 3 explains how the type of learning problem a student experiences influences which teaching method the team chooses to implement.

Step 2
Team Gathers and Discusses Information, Then Sets Goals for the Student

During Step 2, team members share their knowledge about the focus student and any relevant data. The team discussion may indicate that more information is required to design a teaching program (e.g., the amount of time a student spends alone at recess; a survey of the social opportunities available in middle school; an ABC analysis of a student's problem behavior). Once the information pool is complete and understood, the team can set social skill goals.

Pooling and Discussing Information

The student's core team (general education teacher, special education teacher, and par-

ent) are often the most knowledgeable and concerned about a student's social skill problems; however, sometimes other extended team members will have information that is relevant and that should be included in team discussions.

Daniel's speech-language, occupational, and physical therapists provide needed information and ideas about how to promote back-and-forth exchanges between Daniel and his peers.

The school psychologist who tested Rick's social skills and the assistant principal who will help plan for support staff often join Rick's team.

These team discussions will be ongoing throughout the process, sometimes as sit-down meetings and other times "on the fly." Collaborative teams often work best; collaboration involves building trust and respect among team members, communicating effectively, making the most of meeting time, problem-solving, sharing responsibility, and following through. (The companion book in this series, *Collaborative Teaming,* may be helpful.)

Gathering Additional Information

Sometimes additional assessment beyond what has been described is necessary. The fourth section of Table 4.1, Measures of Relationships and Friendships, describes measures that can be used to assess student' existing social networks, social acceptance by students' peers, and students' understanding of friendship and loneliness. For example, it can be valuable to observe closely students' social interactions with their peers.

Daniel's teachers were worried that there were too few interactions between Daniel and his classmates and that his classmates helped him too much; therefore, they gathered information on the amount of social interaction that occurred between Daniel and his peers and on the kinds of social support behaviors that peers showed to

Student Names

Social Skills	Jenny	Jeff†	Julie	Mary	Sarah†	Frank	Dave	Suzy	Jerry†	Eric	Myles	Ed†	Ann	Maria	Bonnie	Carl	Kelly	Phillip	Vicki	Tom†	Kate†	Will	Average social skill score
1. Listening	4	2	3	3	3	4	2	5	1	3	3	2	4	5	3	2	4	3	5	3	2	4	3.2
2. Greeting others	3	1	3	4	2	3	5	3	1	4	3	3	5	3	2	4	3	4	4	3	2	3	3.1
*3. Joining in	3	2	3	3	1	3	4	3	2	3	2	1	4	3	2	1	3	4	3	2	1	3	2.4
*4. Complimenting	3	3	2	3	2	4	3	4	1	3	3	2	3	4	3	3	2	3	4	3	1	2	2.8
*5. Expressing anger	3	1	3	4	2	3	4	4	1	3	3	1	3	4	3	3	3	4	4	3	2	3	2.9
6. Keeping friends	3	2	4	4	1	4	4	3	2	4	3	2	4	4	3	3	4	4	4	3	2	3	3.3
7. Doing quality work	3	3	3	4	2	4	3	4	1	4	4	3	3	4	3	4	3	4	3	3	3	4	3.3
8. Following rules	4	2	3	3	1	3	3	3	2	3	3	3	4	4	3	3	3	3	2	2	1	3	2.8
9. Using self-control	3	3	3	4	1	4	4	4	2	4	3	2	5	5	3	4	3	3	3	2	1	4	3.1
10. Offering assistance	4	3	4	4	2	4	5	3	2	5	4	3	4	3	4	4	3	3	5	2	2	4	3.5
*11. Disagreeing with others	3	2	3	3	1	3	4	3	2	3	4	2	3	3	3	3	3	4	3	3	2	3	2.9
12. Being organized	4	3	4	4	2	4	4	3	3	5	4	2	4	4	2	3	4	3	4	3	3	4	3.5
13. Having conversations	4	2	3	3	3	3	4	4	2	4	4	3	4	3	3	4	3	4	4	3	1	3	3.2
Average Student Score	3.4	2.2	3.1	3.5	1.8	3.5	3.8	3.5	1.7	3.7	3.3	2.2	3.8	3.8	2.9	3.2	3.2	3.5	3.7	2.3	1.8	3.4	

*Low average social-skill score.
†Low average student score.

Figure 4.5. Matrix assessment observation of social skills completed on a whole class to target skill needs. (From *Antisocial Behavior in School: Strategies and Best Practices*, 1st edition, by H.M. Walker, G. Colvin, and E. Ramsey. © 1995. Reprinted with permission of Wadsworth Publishing, a division of Thomson Learning. Fax 800 730-2215.)

Daniel (e.g., greeting, material aid, emotional support). They decided to use the Social Interaction Checklist (Kennedy, Shukla, & Fryxell, 1997) rather than invent their own measure.

Whether students are making the transition from preschool to kindergarten, from elementary to secondary school, or from school to community environments, teams may want to know more about the social environment the students will be entering.

Because Melanie would be making the transition to middle school soon, her team decided an environmental inventory of the middle school would be useful. The special education teacher would visit the school, observe social routines, and interview potential classroom teachers and classmates regarding social interaction opportunities.

Other disciplines can aid with assessment when there is a need to improve student difficulties in communication, movement ability, sensory ability, or physiological/medical or psychological health. Functional assessments, another valuable assessment procedure that will be described in the next session, can help teams understand the conditions that predict when behavior problems will occur and the consequences that seem to motivate or maintain the behavior problems.

Making Functional Assessments of Behavior Problems

A functional assessment is essential when social skill problems involve excessive inappropriate behavior, such as highly disruptive classroom behavior and aggression toward others. The last section of Table 4.1 lists several tools for functional assessment.

The basic strategy in functional assessment is to study the antecedents, behaviors, and consequences (ABCs) of the situations where the behavior problems *do and do not occur*. During functional assessment of a problem behavior, the team seeks to observe three types of information (Horner & Carr, 1997). A sim-

ple ABC form (as shown in Figure 4.6) may be used to record this information; a blank form is located at the end of the book.

Information About Consequences   What happens following each instance of the problem behavior? What do teachers and staff do? What do peers do? What do parents and siblings do? In the "ABC" patterns that students learn, adults (teachers and parents), and oftentimes peers, actually become part of the consequences that maintain the problem behavior. Adults' roles in maintaining problem behavior may not be realized until the team studies the results of a functional assessment. One (or several) common functions usually act to maintain most problem behaviors. The student learns that engaging in problem behavior results in one of several consequences:

- *Escape from or avoidance of a situation* that may be boring, too difficult or demanding, disliked, painful, or scary; this may include avoidance of social interaction

- *Obtaining attention, comfort, or nurturance from others*

- *Obtaining some desired tangible item* such as food, toys, or a preferred activity

- *Sensory reinforcement* by repetitive movements such as rocking and even self-injury

When observing a focus student, teachers should note on the recording form the consequences for each instance of problem behavior. This entails writing down what actually happened following the behavior (i.e., what adults or peers said and did to the focus student, even if this involved ignoring). Teachers also might guess as to which of the four common functions seem to be operating.

After several disruptive weeks in school, Rick's team decided to do a functional assessment over a 3-day period, recording any instance of Rick's disruptive behavior (aggression, cursing, yelling). They noted six instances in 3 days, and each instance involved a fair amount of disruption to the staff and/or students. The observed conse-

Student: _____Rick_____   **Observer:** _____Ms. Otis (SE)_____   **Date:** __9/13/99__
From: __9/13__ **To:** __9/15__ **Class/Routine:** __All-day schedule__ **Location:** ____school____
Behavior(s): __Aggression, yelling, cursing__ **Possible Setting Event:** ____Forgets meds?____

Antecedents	Behavior	Consequences
What happened before?	**What is problem behavior?**	**What happened afterward?**
Monday 9/13/99		
9:30 transition between classes; R. was accidentally pushed, moving slowly	Cursed at teacher, peers Hit student	Teacher took him to resource room [escape]
11:45 Lunch room; no empty tables in corner	Yelled at students sitting in corner table	Students laughed, R. laughed; teacher talked to R., who moved to area without students [attention, escape]
2:00 P.E. class in gym; volleyball game; teacher asked R. to go to his court	Yelled and tried to hit teacher	SE aide took him to corner of gym; he did not play game [escape]
Tuesday 9/14/99		
9:30 transition between classes	Refused to move in crowded halls; yelled	Teacher helped him to next class [escape]
1:45 Earth Science; during lab group with guys he likes	R. made comments about female classmate's body; peers laughed	Teacher gave him dirty look [attention]
2:30 Regular bus aide left early; sub aide met R. at his locker	R. yelled at sub, refused to go to bus with her	Ms. Otis talked to him [attention]; he got on bus
Wednesday 9/15/99		
10:50 Field trip in English class	R. struck out at teacher and peers as they helped him on bus	R. was removed from bus and stayed at school in resource room; shot baskets in gym for part of day [escape]

Figure 4.6.   ABC assessment of Rick's problem behavior. (Contributed by Johnna Elliott.)

quences seemed to reduce or stop Rick's disruptive behavior. Later, when the team looked at the assessment it agreed that Rick's problem behavior seemed to either get him out of a situation he disliked (i.e., escape) or get him attention.

Information About Antecedents   Antecedents are the conditions or stimuli that precede a behavior. When seeking this information, the team focuses on the antecedents that seem to predict or trigger the problem behavior. These "trigger" stimuli include specific people, locations, types of comments (e.g., requests to work, reprimands such as "no"), types of tasks, and types of assistance used to teach the task (e.g., physical prompts). After each instance of the problem behavior, the person making the observations should note the antecedents that preceded the behavior: The observer should identify the people who are present and interacting in addition to the time, context, and location of the problem behavior.

The team looked at the functional assessment (which they continued even as they planned a teaching program). They found several situations that preceded Rick's problem behavior that led to escape: crowded, often noisy situations (e.g., in between classes, in the cafeteria, during PE) and new or unique situations (e.g., field trips, staff changes).

Information About Setting Events Setting events are factors or conditions that may or may not be present, that may be less obvious and more distant from the problem behavior, and that seem to alter the likelihood that certain categories of antecedents will result in problem behavior. Influential setting events can be biological (e.g., constipation, sleep deprivation, allergies, hunger, hormonal imbalances), social (e.g., crowding, sequence of activities, people present or absent, classroom social structure), and physical (e.g., room temperature, humidity, noise level, comfort of clothing).

Rick knows that when his special education teacher, Ms. Otis, is absent, he will probably eat lunch right after earth science instead of attending a tutoring session with her; this means he must eat during the time that the cafeteria is noisiest and most crowded. Therefore, when Rick learns that Ms. Otis is absent (social setting event), his behavior is more difficult all morning. Also, if Rick misses his morning medication (physical setting event), he is more likely to become anxious; this often leads to disruptive behavior.

Information obtained from a functional assessment allows the team to predict when the problem behavior will and will not occur and what function it serves for the person or why the behavior is perpetuated (Horner & Carr, 1997). This information influences the design of the behavior support program in several ways. It suggests

- The social, communication, or other skills that are missing and need to be taught
- Ways in which staff might change the school environment or schedule to prevent the problem behavior
- When skill teaching should take place (when the circumstances predict the problem behavior might occur)
- When instruction and social interaction will be less difficult

(A companion booklet in this series, *Behavioral Support* [Janney & Snell, 2000], offers a detailed and systematic approach for assessing and addressing problem behavior.)

Setting Social Skill Goals

Based on the information gathered during the functional assessment, the team sets goals for teaching the necessary social skills. Assessment data can help teams precisely identify the social skills with which a student is having difficulty or lacks fluency in performing. If a student's excessive problem behavior competes with appropriate social behavior, functional assessments will help determine which skills should be targeted to replace the problem behavior and to provide acceptable alternatives for achieving the same outcomes. Many of these "replacement" skills will be communicative or social in nature (e.g., requesting a break, asking for help or attention, telling a teacher about menstrual pain, earning an opportunity to choose a leisure activity).

Rick's functional assessment suggests that he could benefit from learning to ask for a break from stressful situations (e.g., high noise levels, crowds) and from keeping a daily schedule so he can be ready for changes.

Some skills will be targeted as deficient, weak, or in need of review across a large group; other skills will be individually prescribed for a single student. The following are examples of social skill goals that all students will profit from learning:

- Knowing how to enter a group of peers

- Being capable of taking turns with others

- Being able to exhibit social reciprocity in conversation (balanced mutual exchange of information and ideas)

- Having and using the ability to manage conflicts

- Knowing how to cooperate and support others

Sometimes *peer input* will contribute to the team's discussion of skill goals and criterion conditions (when, where, with whom, and how well the student will need to perform these skills). Observation of the student's peers, as well as solicitation of their ideas during peer planning sessions, can assist the team in selecting age-appropriate social skills and in setting realistic criteria to judge whether teaching has been successful. Questions for peers might include the following:

- What do you think ____ could learn to do instead of the problem behavior?

- What is important for ____ to learn in order to fit better into our class/school?

- What is difficult about talking to, playing with, or being around ____?

- How well does ____ need to know this skill?

- How often does ____ need to use this skill and with whom?

- Where and when should ____ use this skill?

The next section presents several guidelines for designing programs to teach these and other social skills appropriate to various age groups.

Step 3
Team Generates Teaching Ideas that Match the Student's Specific Social Skill Difficulty

 During Step 3, team members take several steps to match teaching ideas with the focus student's social skill shortcomings and type of learning problem (i.e., acquisition, performance, interfering behavior). First, they review potential methods effective with social skills. Then, they select methods that fit the student's current abilities and social competence and that match the learning problem and context. The team will then consider both the influences of peer networks on the focus student and the use of commercial social skills programs.

Reviewing Successful Social Skill Teaching Methods

Teams have many teaching strategies from which to choose that have been proven successful in teaching social skills and in modifying socially inappropriate behavior. Figure 4.7 provides brief definitions of some of these methods.

Broad Methods   The first two methods are quite broad and actually include many other approaches:

- *Manipulation of events that happen before (antecedent to) the target behavior:* These events include cuing, prompting, directing, pretask encouraging, reviewing rules, rearranging classroom furniture, and task step rehearsing.

- *Manipulation of events that happen after (in consequence of) the target behavior:* These events include praising, smiling, patting on the back, confirming, and correcting.

Some of the approaches that are included within these two general approaches are reviewed next; others are listed in Figure 4.7.

Interactive Methods   The next five teaching methods in Figure 4.7 (*modeling, creating so-*

Broad Methods

Manipulation of Antecedents: This broad category of interventions may prevent problem behavior by reorganizing the student's environment in ways that influence the conditions under which problem behavior or antisocial behavior occur. These strategies are often combined with others and need to be matched to the student and the circumstances to be effective. Strategies include things such as using a curriculum of sequenced lessons on social skills taught as an academic subject, providing prompts or reminders, rearranging the desks or the entire classroom (e.g., into cooperative teams of four to six balanced groups), stating and reviewing class rules, providing a choice of activities, allowing more mobile activities, teaching self-management, developing behavior contracts, and using relaxation activities.

Manipulation of Consequences: This broad category of interventions involves the presentation and removal of positive and negative events based on the student's behavior. Both adults and peers are involved in manipulating consequences, but self-management strategies teach the focus student to manipulate his or her own consequences contingent on certain performances. Consequence strategies may involve reinforcing students who follow class or individual behavior rules (e.g., by praising, giving a "high-five" sign, smiling, or checking a recess card). Consequence strategies also include enforcing rules by using correction methods (e.g., student rehearses the broken rule and tells why it should have been followed), warnings, or unpleasant consequences such as the loss of time during recess. In the long run, positive consequences are most effective because they build the needed skills, whereas punishing consequences do not teach appropriate behavior and may weaken a student's rapport with the punishing adult. Consequence strategies are usually combined with other strategies and need to be matched to the student and circumstances to be effective.

Interactive Methods

Modeling: Training focuses on filmed, tape-recorded, or live demonstrations of targeted social skills. Modeling is an antecedent approach and often is used with coaching or while giving the student opportunities to perform the target skill and providing feedback.

Scripts for Prompting Interaction: Students with few interaction skills are taught specific scripts to use during social or academic interactions with their peers. These scripts may be written sentences, word cards, or pictures that are used to teach and prompt students; scripts also may simply be a series of verbal phrases and/or actions used with a game or some material (hand held video game, pack of gum) that a student is taught to use during interaction with a peer. Scripts can be social (conversation topics, recess game suggestions) or task oriented, which are used within reciprocal tutoring pairs or study groups (e.g., "Check my work," "Help me," question cards about a reading assignment).

Coaching: This strategy involves direct verbal discussion of the target behavior or skill, which typically is accompanied by discussion and feedback. This method primarily consists of manipulating consequences (e.g., giving praise, feedback, correction) but also uses antecedent approaches (e.g., instructing, prompting, discussing the target skill). Modeling and coaching often are used together and can be directed toward an individual or a group.

Role-play: An individual (adult or student) acts out a targeted social skill, an inappropriate social behavior, an emotional response, or a feeling. The actor may be given conditions for the performance, such as to respond to a specific social situation, and may be asked to take his or her own or another student's perspective, to play the role of a specific person or portray a particular emotion, or to dramatize alone or in cooperation with a group. Role-playing is an antecedent teaching approach that usually involves feedback (consequences) to the student or actor regarding his or her performance.

Opportunistic Teaching: This is an incidental teaching approach to develop socially competent performance of skills during daily "teachable moments," such as when interactions take place in natural circumstances (e.g., recess, classroom, hallways, cafeteria, standing in line). The adult (or peer mediator) uses a combination of methods, depending on the situation (e.g., prompting, cuing, coaching, shaping, praising) to improve the student's performance of the skills/social strategies being taught or approximations of those skills and strategies. Opportunistic teaching is used to prompt students when they miss an opportunity to perform a targeted social skill (e.g., could have joined in a group but looked and walked away), when they misuse a skill and need correction, and to "debrief" students who use inappropriate behaviors when an alternative target social skill would have worked.

(continued)

Figure 4.7.   Teaching methods to build or refine students' social skills. (*Sources:* Gresham, 1981; Kamps, Potucek, Lopez, Kravits, & Kemmerer, 1997; Koegel, Koegel, & Parks, 1995; McConnell, Sisson, Cort, & Strain, 1991; Schneider, 1992; Schrumpf, Crawford, & Usadel, 1991; Walker, Colvin, & Ramsey, 1995.)

Figure 4.7.   *(continued)*

Self-Management Methods

Self-management strategies: These strategies set approaches for teaching students to become independent or less dependent on adults' constant vigilance of their behavior. The steps for designing and teaching these strategies include defining the target behavior, identifying practical reinforcers that the child can earn, designing a self-monitoring device (e.g., photo or picture series, checklist, self-beeping timer, wrist-worn counter), teaching the student to use the device, fading the student's use of the device while maintaining self-management, and encouraging use of the device across other natural environments.

Self-monitoring strategies: Another variation of these strategies, whereby a student learns to check his or her own behavior whenever a predetermined signal occurs—for example, the student checks to see if he or she is on task, is making verbal responses to adults' or peers' questions, and is not engaged in self-stimulatory behavior (e.g., rocking, humming).

Cognitive Strategies

Social-Cognitive Processes: Training is focused on any of the cognitive processes involved in social competence that lead to improved awareness of social situations (e.g., taking the perspective of another, social problem solving, anger control, peer mediation).

> **Anger control strategies:**   These strategies are emotional control techniques that help individuals identify when they are angry; recognize the conditions that trigger their anger and the negative outcomes related to intense expressions of anger; and identify ways to cope with negative feelings, express anger, and reduce aggression. Included are strategies such as self-talk, cognitive meditation, relaxation training, behavior rehearsal and opportunities to control oneself across a range of social situations.
>
> **Behavioral rehearsals:**   This technique involves role-play and problem-solving. The student practices the target skill under controlled conditions (e.g., just before attending a class during which the problem often arises) and verbalizes what he or she will do in the upcoming social situation or actually performs the target skill as a means of reminding him- or herself what to do, thereby preventing problem behavior.
>
> **Social problem-solving strategies:**   These strategies teach students to resolve problems by generating alternatives to the conflict; skills taught include the process skills needed for negotiation, listening skills, turn-taking skills, the ability to assume the perspective of another, and the ability to maintain a positive attitude.
>
> **Peer-mediation strategies:**   These strategies are voluntary methods to resolve conflicts and disputes between peers by means of a trained mediator who is an "unbiased, empathic listener, and respectful of all parties to the process" (Walker et al., 1995, p. 205). The mediator takes a neutral and objective position and keeps all information confidential. The process does not allow interruption when someone is talking and requires an agreement by each of the involved parties to cooperate (Schrumpf, Crawford, & Usadel, 1991).

---

cial scripts, coaching, role-playing, and opportunistic teaching) are particularly effective when students first are acquiring social skills (Schneider, 1992). These strategies overlap somewhat, but they all involve back-and-forth interactions between an adult (e.g., teacher, parent, counselor) and the student or a group of students. Interactive methods place an emphasis on *seeing, then doing, then getting feedback.*

Sometimes, peers are taught or guided to assist in instruction; they might be taught to demonstrate (model), remind (cue), or praise (reinforce) specific social skills. This approach is called *peer-mediated instruction* (see Figure 4.8). Other times, peers might simply provide spontaneous models to which the adult calls attention.

In Melanie's fourth-grade class, four girls are learning ways in which they can help Melanie interact with them. They all have learned a turn-taking, "conversational" approach that involves using Melanie's picture conversation book (with pictures from home and school activities) while "reading" signs and limited words and speaking slowly. Several of the girls have brought pictures from home to make the conversations more interesting, and the class has started its own conversation book.

What the Research Says

Peer-mediated instruction *means that peers are taught and supervised by their teachers to assist one or several classmates in learning social skills. Teachers do not directly intervene with the target student but teach through peers.*

Preschoolers and young elementary-age children have learned to use peer social interaction skills to approach a focus student, to wait for a request (e.g., child reaches for a toy), or give a social bid or initiation (e.g., "Let's play blocks"), to persist in order to get the student to respond, to prompt the student (e.g., "Say 'ball,' . . . Good, you can have the ball!"), and to praise the student whenever he or she makes a social initiation (Strain & Odom, 1986). Some peer trainers have been taught to be a "buddy" to a particular classmate with disabilities and to use the strategy of "stay, play, and talk" during snacktime, play, art, small-group activities, sociodrama, and cleanup (English, Shafer, Goldstein, & Kaczmarek, 1997). Peer training is often one-to-one with some role play; during actual playtime, the teacher coaches (e.g., prompting, shaping, praising) the peer trainer. After playtime, the teacher gives the peer feedback and reinforcement on his or her efforts and provides more training as needed.

Elementary, middle, and high school peers also have been taught to be successful teachers of social interaction, conversation, eye gaze, initiation, response and other interaction social skills with their classmates in between classes, at lunch time, and in class (Haring & Breen, 1992; Hughes, Harmer, Killian, & Niarhos, 1995; Kamps, Potucek, Lopez, Kravits, Kemmerer, 1997).

Most peer-mediated social skill strategies follow several steps:

1. Focus students and their interaction skill needs are identified.
2. Peer trainers or buddies are selected.
3. Peers are trained by teacher.
4. Peers direct social initiations/bids (enactment process) to focus classmate(s) during class activities.
5. Teachers reinforce peer trainers for successful initiations and provide additional training as needed.
6. Peers learn to be persistent in obtaining a response from the focus student and to give prompts for the social response.
7. Teachers reinforce peer trainers for being persistent and provide additional training as needed.
8. Peers learn to praise their classmates' successful social behavior.
9. Teachers reinforce peer trainers for successful mediation.

Figure 4.8. Peer-mediated instruction. (Sources: Goldstein, English, Shafer, & Kaczmarek, 1997; Haring & Breen, 1992; Hughes, Harmer, Killian, & Niarhos, 1995; Kamps, Potucek, Lopez, Kravits, & Kemmerer, 1997; McGee, Almeida, Sulzer-Alzaroff, & Feldman, 1992; Odom, McConnell, & Chandler, 1993.)

Opportunistic teaching involves teaching social skills when students are in the presence of other students and are engaging in daily routines. This approach employs actual interactions between the focus students and their peers rather than contrived interchanges between adults and focus students. During natural opportunities, teachers also can use other interactive strategies (e.g., *modeling, coaching, role play, social scripts, opportunistic teaching*) to promote skill generalization. Teaching during natural opportunities is very useful when a social skill is partially acquired but needs to be made more fluent.

Once Melanie and her four friends are skilled at interacting with one another using the conversation books, the girls demonstrate their method of interacting with Melanie to the rest of the class; Melanie then picks other students with whom she would like to interact before school, at break times after seatwork, during recess, and at lunch.

Self-Management Methods *Self-management methods* involve teaching directed toward improving the student's independent use of a social skill. Sometimes, students learn to use devices such as class schedules or watches that beep to help remind them or prompt them to perform a target skill or check on their behavior. *Self-monitoring* is one type of self-management that entails checking on one's own behavior whenever a predetermined signal occurs (e.g., "Am I paying attention?" "Am I talking out loud?"). Self-management usually means that students learn to *self-reinforce* or apply rules to give themselves positive consequences for performing the target behavior (e.g., talking to peers who approach them, keeping hands to themselves). These skill-based methods (the first three groups in the table) all require direct instruction and may be used by adults (e.g., teachers or guidance counselors), by peers who have been taught to apply the methods with their classmates or by adults in combination with peers.

Cognitive Strategies   Cognitive strategies are referred to by multiple names: *interpersonal cognitive problem-solving, social cognitive processes, and cognitive-behavioral processes.* These are strategies that focus students learn to use so adults do not have to control or alter the situation (e.g., praising the student, giving him or her reminders). Cognitive strategies "focus on developing improved cognitive awareness of social situations and understanding adaptive strategies for responding to them" (Walker, Colvin, & Ramsey, 1995, p. 240). First, the strategy is taught, and then focus students learn to use the strategy in a situation during which they interact with others. Students may learn to generate a range of alternatives/behaviors and then decide which is the best response. Other students who are taught to self-manage will learn somewhat artificial ways to cue themselves; if these artificial signals are faded and students are taught to discriminate the natural stimuli that cue their behavior, the method used becomes a cognitive strategy.

Rick is learning to predict the situations that make him anxious and, consequently, angry. He also is learning to choose one of several options when an anxiety-provoking situation arises: He chooses between 1) asking to go to one of several places to calm down (e.g., study hall, resource room, shop teacher's office), 2) staying where he is and using a relaxation breathing routine, or 3) going and sitting by one of several peers with whom he is comfortable. Soon, Ms. Otis will work with Rick to try out these methods during natural opportunities in his schedule.

Selecting Teaching Methods that Fit a Student's Social Competence and Abilities

The specific teaching strategies selected need to complement the student's social competence abilities (to observe, interpret, search options, plan a response, and carry it out), his or her means of communication, and his or her specific social skills needs.

Many of the strategies for teaching social skills that rely on direct instruction are focused on *enacting/behaving* socially, or *interacting.* For example, modeling, coaching, and most of the approaches that involve peers as social skill "teachers" focus on the behaving process. Involving peers in the enactment/behavior process is especially appropriate, not only because social skills are overt and less difficult to teach but also because peer approval and peer cuing or reminding may be more effective than approval and cuing given by adults.

Communication Problems   When students are lacking in communication ability and/or do not have a reliable means of communicating, team members should focus and problem-solve here first. *Although speech is not essential to social participation with typical peers, students without speech must have reliable ways to communicate.* When many of these students first learn to communicate, they will begin by using "body language" and later by combining several symbolic communication systems such as speaking a few words or short phrases; using some manual signs; pointing to a set of picture symbols; using a simple switch-operated system such as the Cheaptalk (Enabling Devices, Inc.); or working a complex, computer-based, portable communication system with speech such as a Dynovox (Sentient Systems, Inc.). Time needs to be set aside to teach peers to interact using this often highly personalized system of communication.

Some teachers teach the focus students about their new communication system while providing separate training to peers through role playing; then, the teachers bring peers and focus students together and, if needed, offer more instruction while the students interact (Garrison-Harrell, Kamps, & Kravits, 1997). During these social interaction sessions, teachers helped students develop conversational topics related to the focus students' interests and also taught students to make eye contact with focus students, use their names, and be persistent in maintaining a conversation (Garrison-Harrell et. al., 1997).

Melanie points to photos in a notebook for some conversations but uses signs, gestures, and some words to express herself as well. She can read a printed daily schedule of activities, recognizes many printed words, and understands a lot of spoken language. Melanie's teachers will use modeling coupled with simple words and gestures to teach Melanie's peers to interact with her by using conversational turn-taking and a communication photo album; Melanie will use her photo album to add meaning to her signing and limited speech.

Other students will not be as sophisticated as Melanie in their communication. They might simply use a personal set of "body language" behaviors to express themselves; however, these behaviors may be primarily nonsymbolic and may include sounds, facial expressions, gestures, and movements. Meaningful interactions can take place once peers learn the student's "personal communication dictionary," particularly within the context of familiar routines and preferred activities. Instruction is geared toward the interaction itself (each partner learning how to initiate and respond so he or she is understood) and toward refining the communication responses so they are more conventional and consistent while also expanding them.

Daniel's peers have learned to give him choices for leisure activities by showing, telling, and letting him feel (one at a time) each of two choice items that represent activities he likes (e.g., audiotape for a talking book, switch to operate musical video games). "Should we listen to the book" (Daniel feels the tape) "or do the video game" (Daniel feels switch)? They know to repeat the choices and pause after each, waiting for him to lift his head, which is Daniel's signal for making a choice.

Cognitive Strategies Teaching strategies that address one or more of the cognitive processes preceding social interaction (thinking and planning) fall into the category of cognitive/behavioral processes; students must make their thinking and planning processes conscious through verbal rehearsal or role play. These strategies are complex and often involve a combination of teaching methods. For example, a teacher might show a videotaped social scene and ask students to report what they see in the scene (encode), what the scene means to them (interpret), what they could do (search responses), and what they will do (decide on response). Instruction could be directed at any of these four thinking/deciding processes. Role play can be used to practice the last process of engaging in social interactive behavior.

Despite their complexity, cognitive strategies have been successfully applied to younger children with disabilities and students with autism and mental retardation by reducing the difficulty of the language involved in the cognitive strategy and by adding objects or pictures. If a student is less able than his or her typical peers to examine his or her own thoughts or to communicate, using concrete (tangible or visual) reminders can reduce the abstractions involved. For example, photos or drawings can be shown to represent "angry" feelings or to symbolize the skill of "sharing" and can serve as a reminder for a target social skill. Picture charts and cognitive picture rehearsal scripts have been successfully used with children who have autism to practice a successful adaptive behavior routine; the pictures (Hodgdon, 1994) or the pictures and script, are used to teach and to remind students of an adaptive routine (Groden & Le Vassuer, 1994) (Figure 4.9). Students with less language ability may also benefit more from teaching methods that first directly shape students' desired behavior in the social situation to which the behavior applies and then teach the students' classmates to model and to prompt students' behavior in social situations.

Selecting Methods that Match Learning Problem and Context

Many variations of role-playing, rehearsal, and self-management strategies have been successful for teaching students with social skills difficulties. As with other skills taught in school, it is important to create the best conditions possible for students to learn social skills. This means that the methods and the context (location, time of day, activity, people present) chosen for teaching a student should correspond to the type of social skills learning problem the student has (Gresham, 1997). This section explains some of the available methods and describes contexts that are suitable for each type of learning problem: acquisition, performance or fluency, and interfering or competing behaviors.

The three types of learning problems can be broken down into different stages of learning that apply to many skills, not just to social skills. First, students acquire a skill (making change, telling time, reading printed directions), then they focus on perfecting it and using it in many changing school and community contexts. Social skills are no different; once a social skill has been acquired, its performance often needs improvement. Therefore, it is not unusual for students to have some skills in the acquisition stage of learning and others in the performance stage. Students with interfering behavior will first need to learn that there are alternate social skills that also achieve the desired outcome (peer attention, escape from unpleasant situation) and that the problem behavior no longer works), but these students may be unprac-

ticed in the acquired social skills and may need to improve their performance of the skill after it has been acquired. Table 4.2 summarizes the intervention methods and teaching contexts that match each type of social skills learning problem.

Acquisition Learning Problems   *Social skills that are unknown or that are very poorly performed pose acquisition learning problems.* These skills will require more intensive, individualized training involving any or all of the following approaches:

- Labeling and talking about the social skill
- Watching teacher, peer, or videotaped models of the skill
- Learning to discriminate positive examples from negative examples of the skill in specific, familiar school and home routines (e.g., "watch these kids play: this is one way to share your toys; this is another way to share; but, this is NOT sharing")
- Practicing using and labeling the skill in role-plays and then in a variety of natural situations

Proficiency or Fluency Learning Problems Once students who require acquisition learning strategies have mastered some targeted skills, they may benefit from teaching strategies from the second group: strategies that make them into proficient skill performers across many school routines. Those with *proficiency or fluency learning problems know the skill but either don't use it or use it inadequately (e.g., too slow, complete in some situations but not in others);* these learners will benefit from somewhat different teaching strategies:

- Learning to discriminate between more refined examples of the social skill
- Expanding their understanding of what is socially okay and what is not okay
- Practicing the skill enough so it can be performed smoothly and quickly
- Teaching the student ways to remember to use the skill in actual social situations

You're at your desk working on addition.

The teacher looks at your paper and says, "Tom, check the last problem. That's not the right answer."

You take a deep breath, relax your arms. You breathe out slowly and say, "No big deal, I can fix it."

You use your calculator and do the problem again.

Now you have the right answer; you feel good about that. You tell the teacher.

She smiles and puts a sticker on your paper. You're happy. You can't wait to show Mom when you get home today.

Figure 4.9.   Cognitive picture and script rehearsal strategies. (From *Teaching Children with Autism*, 1st edition, by K.A. Quill. © 1996. Reprinted with permission of Delmar Publishers, a division of Thomson Learning. Fax 800 730-2215.)

Table 4.2.   Matching social skill problems to effective interventions and training contexts

Social skill problem	Description	Intervention match	Proper context
Acquisition or skill problem	Student doesn't have the skill or is missing a necessary step in performing a social skill sequence.	Use interactive methods (e.g., modeling, coaching, behavioral rehearsal), manipulate antecedents and consequences.	Structured small group initially, then informal and naturalistic
Performance or fluency problem	Student has the skill but may not know when to use it, may be too slow in using it, may be unable to adjust the skills to suit the situation, or may simply lack proficiency in using the skill.	Use antecedent control strategies (e.g., peer social initiations, proactive classroom management, self-management, incidental teaching) and reinforcement-based procedures.	Informal, naturalistically occurring approach using incidental teaching with performance feedback
Interfering or competing behaviors	Student has lots of competing, inappropriate behaviors; social skills may be known but are not efficient or effective enough to be used instead of the problem behaviors.	Use a combination of procedures while also teaching and strengthening alternative behaviors (e.g., improve school/home environment to prevent problem behavior, use curriculum adaptations or academic tutoring, behavior contracts and self-management approaches, response cost, relaxation and calming methods).	May use both formal and informal approaches; however, an informal approach to training in naturally occurring contexts is essential to replace existing behavior problems with needed social skills

• Teaching students to *self-manage*—requires students to 1) identify and label the ways they currently behave in a particular context (e.g., "I'm too slow," "I get nervous and forget what to say"); 2) recognize the desired social skill and context in which it is needed (e.g., "If I say it the simple way, they will listen"; "I will take a deep breath and then say what I have learned"); 3) cue themselves to perform the appropriate skills (e.g., "Now it is Sara's turn to talk"), and 4) evaluate their actions (e.g., "I said it simply and they listened to me").

Students are taught to self-manage their behavior by rehearsing directions that they first say aloud and later say to themselves: "She spoke to me, now it's my turn to speak" or, "I want to say something, I need to raise my hand." This "say, then do" approach is a simple method of learning to direct oneself. Sometimes, students learn to self-record and keep track of the times they were successful in managing their social behavior. Students also might learn to self-reward (e.g., "I filled up my hand-raising card, so I can trade it in for computer time") or seek a positive consequence after reporting their success to the teacher.

Those students who need to improve the fluency and performance of social skills will also require an emphasis on *skill generalization:* performing the skill fluently in many situations with different groups of peers and adults at home and in the community. To emphasize skill generalization, teachers will use *opportunistic teaching:* cuing, prompting, coaching, shaping, and praising students as they use the skill or as they approximate the skill in everyday routines.

Interfering or Competing Behaviors Students who do not use appropriate social skills due to interfering or competing behavior will need other approaches. Their teachers will first study the ABCs of the behavior problem very closely. A functional assessment allows team members to discover the maintaining patterns of behavior that the focus student has learned and that others, including the student's peers, staff, and family members, "feed into." This information, in turn, is used to design an individual positive behavioral support program in which the ABCs are intentionally changed from maintaining the problem behavior to teaching alternate social behaviors. Social skills instruction alone will not suffice.

Rick's team has devised a comprehensive set of prevention, teaching, and management plans to address both Rick's disruptive behaviors (aggression, yelling, and confrontational behavior) that appear to be maintained mainly by escape and his socially immature behavior (talking about biological functions) that appears to be maintained by peer attention (Figure 4.10). Then, Rick's team identified 11 social skills that they believed he needed and brainstormed methods to teach these skills to Rick. All three types of learning are addressed in these 11 target skills: acquisition learning (knowing peers' names), improving performance (opening doors, helping classmates), and learning appropriate alternatives (asking for a break, managing rejection or stressful class work).

For students in this latter group, such as Rick, whose inappropriate behaviors "drown out" the social skills they do possess, the good and bad influences of peer networks may need to be examined.

Considering the Influences of Peer Networks

Social competence leads to membership in stable social networks, which often has a positive influence on school-age students and prevents them from being isolated from peers. Sometimes, however, existing student networks can work against social skills training; prosocial skills are not always maintained by the peer network while problematic behavior may be. In such cases, intervention is more complicated. The educational team may have to address specific questions regarding a student's social networks and adjust the social skills teaching plans accordingly:

- *Does the student's social network limit his or her social opportunities?* What factors influence the networks that exist in the classroom (gender, race, athletic ability, socioeconomic status, aggressiveness)? Can these factors be manipulated to expand the social and behavioral roles the student can occupy?

- *What social roles or events might assist the student in developing new skills or social characteristics?* What events or roles are connected with desirable behaviors or skills? Is it possible to place the student in these events or roles to enable the student to be favorably viewed by his or her peers in a way that is not possible during routine class activities?

- *Does the student associate with classmates who encourage or maintain problematic behavior?* If so, social skills training, even if successful, may never generalize to everyday peer exchanges because the student's network does not support the new skills. Could intervention be directed toward the whole group or social network? As an alternate solution, could the student be supported in associating with another group (one that supports his or her positive characteristics)?

- *Are there peers in the classroom who can "positively elicit and support the student's new skills or characteristics without a social cost to themselves"* (Farmer et al., p. 251)? The focus student could be placed in the proximity of supportive and helpful students who can promote appropriate social behaviors. Classwide cooperative group activities, along with social skills instruction, can further these behaviors. Teachers must be careful

Rick's Behavioral Support Plan

Prevention Strategies

1. *Prompt behaviors before R. has a chance to make a mistake:* Most problems occur when R. is unclear about directions. State directions precisely in second person telling R. what he needs to do; wait for his initiation. If he gets stuck, jump in with a cue.

2. *Assist with organizational and personal management:* Changes in routine, staff, or schedules will likely cause difficulty for R. Warn him in advance. Tell R. what the new routine will be so he knows what to expect. He should check his daily agenda, add any changes, check assignments in his blue folder, review his day during seventh period, and complete any unfinished work. Monitor R.'s transitions between classes.

3. *Provide instruction as to appropriate social behavior:* For new or unstructured situations, explain what will happen and how R. should behave or role play; give him a choice if he seems unable to cope with the situation and follow through with the choice. If R. is involved in inappropriate conversation with peers, or peers seem to be aggravated with his conversation, interject and monitor his tone. If R. is out of line, quietly pull him aside, get his attention, and explain what he is doing to cause problems and how he can change his behavior.

4. *Promote peer support:* R. has many peers who understand him and like him; others do not know him and have stumbled into altercations with him. If students in class do not seem to understand R., ask Johnna (special education) to talk to the class about the nature of R.'s disability in his absence (with approval of R. and his parents). Try to intervene in difficult interactions before situation escalates; let peers know you will take care of the situation (they don't need to), and try to communicate that R. has some special issues and they need to "cut him a break." Johnna will help as needed.

Teaching Strategies

1. Provide clear, active, specific *instructions*.

2. R. responds well to *clear sequences*. For multistep problems, make a numbered list of steps for him to follow. Refer to the list so R. can gauge his progress.

3. Use *interrupt, ignore, redirect, & reward*. Interrupt or ignore R.'s inappropriate behaviors, redirect him to the specific behavior you would like him to do (make something up if there is no task at hand), and quietly reward him for engaging in the correct behavior.

4. *Social stories:* Write a list of behaviors that you expect R. to follow during class. Build R.'s understanding of these behaviors by creating, with R.'s assistance, stories about his engaging in appropriate behaviors in familiar current situations during which the behaviors are needed. Rehearse and revise these stories periodically to reinforce his understanding. Have R. read the list as he enters the instructional situation.

Responding to Difficult Situations

1. *Is R. tired?* Sometimes, when R. is being hysterical or unreasonable, he is tired. A caffeinated beverage or a brief nap is often a good remedy.

2. *Problem solving:* When faced with a problem he cannot easily solve, R. is likely to go from a state of calm to a state of panic and despair almost instantly. Keep in mind that R. has relatively poor problem-solving skills. When faced with a threatening situation (which might be anything he does not understand), he will likely respond without employing the cognitive skills that are necessary to solve the problem.

3. *Use behavior interruption* if the problem is unclear or it is not possible to redirect R.'s attention toward a solution and R. is hysterical. Interrupt a behavior with the introduction of novel, unexpected, low-demand stimuli (e.g., activity, suggestion, materials). One way to do this is to tell R. to do something completely unrelated to the setting or situation. The solution should probably involve some travel. For example, if R. becomes angry and upset after being prompted to work on a class assignment, instruct him to go to the hallway and get a drink or to deliver an envelope to Ms. Elliott (he often calls her Johnna and that's okay). Once R.'s in the hallway, walk with him until he calms down. Then, ask what the problem was and what kind of help he needs to fix it.

(continued)

Figure 4.10. Rick's behavioral support plan. (Contributed by Johnna Elliott).

Figure 4.10. *(continued)*

4. *Change the adult:* Often when R. is very upset, it is helpful to have a different person jump in and take over. This is another type of behavioral interruption; instead of changing the setting, change the person. For example, if R. is upset over a particular set of directions delivered by one teacher, another teacher might jump in and quickly reassess the situation: "R., you seem to be upset. What's the problem? Do you need a little help here? Pick up that pencil and let me help you get started." This approach requires that the second teacher take over the duties of the first for a short period of time.

Crisis Plan

If R. is in a state of hysterics that is beyond redirection, send a student to get Johnna (special education teacher). She will come immediately. Since R. sees Johnna sporadically throughout the day in short periods of time, she can usually be the novel person who interrupts the behavior and gets him back on track. If this happens, R.'s team will need to assess their plan and see what changes they need to make to eliminate the cause of the problem. When R. calms down, let him explain the reasons for his disruption. Discuss ways to prevent the problem from happening or alternative ways he could respond to the situation in the future.

If R. uses inappropriate language, immediately escort him to a time-out area (i.e., in-school suspension) for 5–10 minutes.

Policy on Suspension: If R violates school rules or policies, he will be dealt with on school premises according to the recommendations of a team including the school principal or designee, special education teacher, classroom teacher involved, and instructional aide.

neither to set the focus student up for engaging in the problem behaviors nor to let the helping students become socially vulnerable themselves (Farmer, Pearl, & Van Acker, 1996).

Considering the Use of Commercial Social Skills Programs

Most commercially available social skills programs address a specific age group and range of social skills and use a combination of teaching strategies. Unfortunately, not all programs avoid mistakes. In their review of 53 social skills training studies administered to students who have learning disabilities, Forness and Kavale (1996) offered several explanations for the poor outcomes:

1. Use of training packages with no track record of success

2. Faulty measures that didn't relate to the training focus

3. Failure to match training to the student's social skill difficulties

4. A lack of training intensity (less than 3 hours per week for 10 weeks)

Several of the various social skill programs are listed and partially described in Figure 4.11. Though this list should not be regarded as complete, the programs that are listed have been identified as having one or more characteristics that distinguish them as potentially effective training packages (Forness & Kavale, 1996; Gresham, 1997; McIntosh, Baughn, & Zaragoza, 1991; Walker, Colvin, & Ramsey, 1995; Zaragoza, Vaughn, & McIntosh, 1991). These characteristics include

1. *Support for the program's effectiveness:* The program has some published support confirming that it improves the social skills it addresses.

2. *Socially valid methods used to select target social skills:* The program addresses skills rated as important by reliable sources. For example, the authors of ASSET (Hazel, Schumaker, Sherman, & Sheldon-Wildgen, 1981) identified their core skills by reviewing published social skills literature; obtaining ratings of importance on these core

Let's Be Social (Social Integration Project, 1989)
Relevant Ages: Preschool and early grades
Skills Addressed and Methods Used: Interacting, sharing, cooperative play, making friends, and so forth.
Program Effectiveness: Cited by Brown and Odom (1994) as incorporating many of the strategies known to promote generalization and maintenance of social behavior
Publisher: Communication Skill Builders, Tucson, AZ

Playtime/Social Time (Vanderbilt/Minnesota Social Interaction Project, 1993)
Relevant Ages: Preschool and early grades
Skills Addressed and Methods Used: Interacting, sharing, cooperative play, making friends, and so forth.
Program Effectiveness: Cited by Brown and Odom (1994) as incorporating many of the strategies known to promote generalization and maintenance of social behavior
Publisher: Communication Skill Builders, Tucson, AZ

Social Skills Intervention Guide (Elliott & Gresham, 1991)
Relevant Ages: Preschool through high school
Skills Addressed and Methods Used: A social skills curriculum designed to be used in combination with the Social Skills Rating System (SSRS) (Gresham & Elliott, 1990)
Program Effectiveness: Tested; SSRS has excellent psychometric properties; cited by Forness and Kovale (1996) as having "potential effectiveness"
Publisher: American Guidance Service, Circle Pines, MN

Skillstreaming in Early Childhood: Teaching Prosocial Skills To the Preschool and Kindergarten Child (McGinnis & Goldstein, 1990)
Relevant Ages: Preschool through second grade
Skills Addressed and Methods Used: Persisting despite difficulty, joining in, coping with teasing, knowing when to tell, waiting your turn, and so forth. Methods include modeling, role-playing, feedback, and transferring skills (homework)
Program Effectiveness: Skillstreaming series cited by Forness and Kovale (1996) as having "potential effectiveness"
Publisher: Research Press, Champaign, IL

The First Steps Program (Hops & Walker, 1988)
Relevant Ages: Kindergartners at risk for antisocial behavior
Skills Addressed and Methods Used: Consists of three components including school intervention, family support and parent training, and support and assistance from community social service agencies
    1) **CLASS** (Contingencies for Learning Academic and Social Skills): school component
    2) **Homebase**: parent training model
    3) Matching family needs with available community support services if the family is eligible (e.g., services for poverty, abuse, alcohol and drug problems, single parent home)
Program Effectiveness: The first component is based on 5 years of research and the second on 25 years of research; the third is the least well developed
Publisher: Educational Achievement Systems, Seattle, WA

RECESS: A Program For Reducing Negative-Aggressive Behavior (Reprogramming the Environmental Contingencies for Effective Social Skills) (Walker, Hops, & Greenwood, 1993)
Relevant Ages: Kindergarten through third grade
Skills Addressed and Methods Used: This program teaches prosocial forms of peer-related behavior and uses sanctions (point loss and time-out) for negative and aggressive behavior, breaking rules, teasing, and bullying. Cooperative social behavior is taught to children who are aggressive and their classmates using scripts, discussion, and role-playing. A response cost point system is used whenever rules are broken or inappropriate social behavior occurs. Children are praised by adults for appropriate social, interactive, and cooperative behavior. Group contingencies (rewards and privileges) are used at school while individual contingencies are applied at home. This program is gradually extended from recess to the classroom and includes a phase during which supports are faded and maintenance is established.

(continued)

Figure 4.11. Commercially available social skills teaching programs. (Sources: Brown & Odom, 1994; Forness & Kavale, 1996; Gresham, 1997; Walker, Colvin, & Ramsey, 1995; Zaragoza, Vaughn, & McIntosh, 1991.)

Figure 4.11. *(continued)*

Program Effectiveness: Support for powerful effects on the social behavior of aggressive children in grades K–3 (Walker, Colvin, & Ramsey, 1995)
Publisher: Educational Achievement Systems, Seattle, WA

The ACCEPTS Program (A Curriculum for Children's Effective Peer and Teacher Skills) (Walker, McConnell, Holmes, et al., 1983)
Relevant Ages: Kindergarten through sixth grade
Skills Addressed and Methods Used: This program teaches three areas: classroom skills (e.g., complying with teacher requests, working on assignments), relating to others (e.g., friendship-making, getting along with others), and coping skills (e.g., coping with teasing and not getting one's way). The program teaches a total of 28 social skills in a sequence that enables the building of more complex skills. One-to-one and small-group formats are used, but the program may be adapted to the whole class.
Program Effectiveness: Supportive research with elementary children (Walker, McConnell, Walker, et al., 1983) and with preschoolers (McConnell, Sisson, Cort, & Strain, 1991); also cited by Forness and Kovale (1996) as having "potential effectiveness"
Publisher: PRO-ED, Austin, TX

Skillstreaming the Elementary School Child: New Strategies and Perspectives for Teaching Prosocial Skills (McGinnis & Goldstein, 1997b)
Relevant Ages: Elementary-age children, third grade through fifth grade
Skills Addressed: Asking for help, saying thank you, using self-control, accepting consequences, making a complaint, and coping with group pressure
Teaching Methods: Modeling, role-playing, feedback, and transferring skills (homework)
Program Effectiveness: Skillstreaming series cited by Forness and Kovale (1996) as having "potential effectiveness"
Publisher: Research Press, Champaign, IL

ASSET: A Social Skills Program for Adolescents (Hazel, Schumaker, Sherman, & Sheldon-Wildgen, 1981)
Relevant Ages: Adolescents
Skills Addressed and Methods Used: Basic social skills (e.g., giving positive and negative feedback), accepting negative feedback, resisting peer pressure, problem solving, negotiating, following instructions, making conversation) and serious behavior problems; methods include videotaped modeling (scenes in which adolescents model appropriate and inappropriate behavior with peers, parents, teachers, and others), group discussions, role plays, and homework assignments
Program Effectiveness: Excellent content validity on core social skills and situations in which skills could be applied; cited by Forness and Kovale (1996) as having "potential effectiveness"
Publisher: Research Press, Champaign, IL

Skillstreaming the Adolescent: New Strategies and Perspectives for Teaching Prosocial Skills (McGinnis & Goldstein, 1997a)
Relevant Ages: Middle school and high school, sixth grade through twelfth grade
Skills Addressed and Methods Used: Starting a conversation, apologizing, expressing feelings, standing up for a friend, responding to failure, and setting goals; teaching methods include modeling, role-playing, feedback, and transferring skills (homework)
Program Effectiveness: Skillstreaming series cited by Forness and Kovale (1996) as having "potential effectiveness"
Publisher: Research Press, Champaign, IL

The Prepare Curriculum: Teaching Prosocial Competencies (Goldstein, 1988)
Relevant Ages: Middle and high school students who are aggressive, withdrawn, or weak in their prosocial competencies
Skills Addressed and Methods Used: Problem-solving, interpersonal skills, situational perception, anger control, moral reasoning, stress management, empathy, recruiting supportive models, cooperation, and understanding and using groups; teaching methods include games, simulations, role plays, and group discussions
Program Effectiveness: Skillstreaming series cited by Forness and Kovale (1996) as having "potential effectiveness"
Publisher: Research Press, Champaign, IL

(continued)

Figure 4.11.   *(continued)*

PALS: Problem-Solving and Affective Learning Strategies (Vaughn, Levine, & Ridley, 1986)
  Relevant Ages: School ages
  Skills Addressed and Methods Used: Problem-solving skills and positive and cooperative social interaction with peers
  Program Effectiveness: Cited by Forness and Kovale (1996) as having "potential effectiveness"
  Publisher: Science Research Associates, Chicago, IL

The ACCESS Program (Adolescent Curriculum for Communication and Effective Social Skills) (Walker, Todis, Holmes, & Horton, 1988)
  Relevant ages: Seventh grade through twelfth grade
  Skills Addressed and Methods Used: Friendships, getting along, compliance with teacher requests, appropriate ways of making assistance needs known, and self-control
  Effectiveness: Socially validated core skills (Walker, Colvin, & Ramsey, 1995, p. 229)
  Publisher: PRO-ED, Austin, TX

---

skills from parents, teachers, and students; and seeking the critical judgments from experts in the field.

3. *Prescriptive nature:* The program enables teachers to decide "that a deficit in a particular skill or domain actually exists and that it creates problems, and also to determine whether it is a skill-based or a performance-based deficit" (Walker, Colvin, & Ramsey, 1995, p. 228). Teaching students to use skills they already perform acceptably reduces their motivation to improve.

4. *Assessment of outcomes:* The program provides a means for measuring students' achievement of long-term, valued outcomes, such as being socially accepted by peers, developing positive relationships, and attaining improved social adjustment and mental health.

Most of the programs listed are meant to be used prescriptively with either a whole class (universal approach) or with small groups of students. One-to-one instruction, particularly when it involves pulling the student out of class on a regular basis, has some serious side effects. Many researchers suggest that this approach be avoided unless school staff build in certain features to reduce stigma and to improve skill generalization (e.g., use in combination with classwide program, build in peer support, vary training schedule, involve general education teacher).

Melanie's fourth-grade teacher has designated a half hour each day to social skills training. In combination with the guidance counselor and the special education teacher, Melanie's teacher offers 30-minute activities using the ACCEPTS program. Often, teachers are able to integrate academic skills such as reading, speaking, and writing into the social skills teaching. The ACCEPTS program teaches skills in three core areas: classroom social skills, relating to others, and coping.

Step 4
Team Evaluates the Feasibility of Its Ideas and Selects Teaching Options for Improving Social Skills

During Step 4, the team reviews each of the teaching options it has generated to address the focus student's social skills limitations and/or problem behaviors. In inclusive schools, the implementation of social skills teaching programs always relies on multiple staff members. A social skills program is much easier to implement and, therefore, more likely to realize improvements when all team members participate in planning the program and reach consensus on the final plan. When teams apply their own set of "feasibility criteria" to the options they are considering, it is often easier to reach consensus objectively and to avoid staking out personal territory among the teaching options generated.

Step 5
Team Develops a Teaching Plan

Teaching plans vary depending on each particular student's social skill needs and capabilities. Often, it is helpful for team members to use an Issue/Action planning form (see Figure 6.2); this allows them to focus their discussion and notetaking on a student's specific social skill issues, the actions they will take to address each issue, the person(s) responsible, and a target date. For students who have IEP objectives that pertain to social skills, these teaching plans will simply delineate how those objectives should be taught and evaluated. This teaming strategy is discussed in detail in Chapter 6.

Rick's comprehensive behavioral support plan (Figure 4.10) reflects the complex nature of his social skill limitations and his disruptive behavior at school.

As the team draws up teaching plans for a student, it should address several questions:

- Is staff training or additional staff/volunteer support needed?

- Is parent involvement adequate? Is a home component needed in the plan?

- How should instruction be scheduled and integrated into the student's routines?

- Should students be taught as a group, as individual students, or both?

- What materials and adult resources will be needed?

- How should generalization be promoted?

- What easy-to-use and meaningful ways will we use to monitor student progress before, during, and after training?

Step 6
Team Implements the Plan, Monitors Student Progress, Improves the Plan as Needed, and Evaluates Outcomes

In Step 6, team members implement and monitor the teaching plans they have designed. For example, they will consider the difficulties the focus student may have with generalizing new social skills and plan ways to promote skill transfer. Teams will identify meaningful outcomes measures to assess the success of the program. Finally, teams will generate ways to strengthen programs that are not producing the skill improvements for which they have aimed.

Generalization Problems with Social Skills

The biggest challenge in social skills training arises when students have demonstrated target skills during instruction, yet fail to use them on the playground, at the bus stop, in the hallways, at lunch, or at the basketball game or school dance. Gresham describes these two phases of learning as "polar opposites" (1997, p. 245). Initially, students are taught to discriminate a skill (examples of it and nonexamples of it), and learn the context for its use (use it here but not there); but, later, students need to learn to generalize that skill to a variety of contexts, which requires that they be more liberal about when to use the skill and which particular form of the skill to use. This learning process is no longer a "black and white" or sharp discrimination but might instead be called a "poor" or "fuzzy" discrimination.

For most students, teachers will follow or accompany classroom instruction (discrimination training) with conscientious teaching across many contexts (generalization training). The method of "opportunistic teaching" is a primary tool to get students to generalize social skills across the day; it involves *seeing, then doing, then getting feedback, and is repeated over and over in different locations at varying times whenever the skill is needed.* For students who have learned cognitive strategies, generalization training may involve reminders to recognize when to use a particular strategy. Another approach that seems to promote generalization of social skills is to involve peers in the modeling and prompting process (peer-mediated training). Kamps, Potucek, Lopez, Kravits, and Kemmerer (1997) discovered that they could greatly increase incidental opportunities for peers to interact with classmates who had autism by forming special peer networks associated with many routine activities (e.g., lunch bunch, recess buddies, classwide peer tutoring). During these peer network activities, peers used simple modeling and script prompting methods to initiate interactions while teachers monitored the sessions and gave out praise and points.

Teaching Context and Generalization
Teaching context influences the degree to which students learn to generalize a social skill. Context can be either structured, formal, and thus more artificial; or, it can be less structured, informal, and naturalistic or contextualized:

- Structured, formal, and artificial: *Melanie and two girls are sitting with the teacher at a small table in back of the classroom with Melanie's conversation book; they are practicing a turn-taking approach to conversing using words, gestures, and photos.*

- Less structured, informal, and naturalistic: *When Melanie's peers yell to her to join them at recess, the classroom assistant reminds Melanie to respond and act ("If you want to play, wave to them, and go after them").*

Formal interventions are recommended for students who have social skill acquisition problems; learning is focused and direct, even though somewhat *decontextualized* or removed from the natural context where the skill is needed. Later, to promote generalization, teachers can switch to informal or incidental contexts, a practice also referred to as *contextualizing* instruction.

The practice of contextualizing instruction first means that teachers will embed instruc-

tion within the range of natural peer contexts in which a student routinely functions or within new contexts that are expected. (Using reality-based teaching does not mean that teaching cannot also be focused or that formal skill instruction cannot also happen.) Also, in addition to teaching during ongoing interactions, *past* social incidents can be used as teaching material. For example, teachers can use recent school situations and peer-to-peer exchanges as the medium for modeling and structuring role plays. Sometimes, video or audio recordings, simulated or not, can be made to help students recall what transpired in a dialogue between classmates that was successful or that ended in dispute. Other times, students can recall the sequence of events, script them, and then reenact the scene with a different ending. Photos or slides taken of typical interaction scenes can be used as a way to recreate the situation for students. Classroom furniture can be arranged and role plays can be used to simulate the context for a social skills lesson based on a recent social conflict (e.g., an argument that happened during lunch). Teaching in real or realistic contexts promotes skill generalization; students learn the broader range of situations in which social skills are appropriate and can practice adapting the skills to fit the situations.

When planning ways to expand naturalistic teaching into social contexts beyond the classroom, teachers can identify or sketch the overlapping social environments to help determine a student's need for additional instruction.

Melanie's team sketched the classroom and recess locations where Melanie was involved in direct social skills instruction and then drew the many other locations where Melanie needed to use her new skills and could benefit from social peer support. The team wrote in pluses (+) and minuses (−) to indicate the contexts where they had seen evidence of good and poor generalization. Because the social demands and the type of supports available changed across these environments, this view gave Melanie's team a better feel for how they could contextualize her instruction and plan additional train-

ing to obtain the desired generalization to environments in which Melanie needed the skills.

Alternately, teachers could construct a matrix listing the environments where a particular student needs to use new social skills (e.g., classrooms, cafeteria, hallways, school bus and bus stop, bathroom, band room, gym, outdoor track) and rate each environment on its characteristics when the student is in the environment. From these ratings, a team can identify the contexts and characteristics that are more difficult for the student and can, consequently, extend generalization more precisely.

By contrast, students who have social skill performance problems will benefit more from opportunistic or naturalistic teaching; this method teaches students to perform the skill in *contextualized* situations (real circumstances that are part of the daily routine and involve peers and/or adults). Informal contexts make use of naturally occurring behavioral events to teach social skills, thereby promoting skill generalization. It is recommended that teachers use natural contexts with students who have performance problems so that instruction is contextual and the student's learning shifts to the more complex and less predictable set of stimuli that exist in ongoing school routines and social exchanges. At this point in social skills training, peer support and peer-mediated training can be a less obtrusive, more appropriate means for promoting generalization than having adults provide focus students with prompts, cues, coaching, rehearsal, and feedback.

Competing Behavior as a Generalization Threat Teachers may need to pay attention to the focus students' past behavior in the generalization environment as they shift their attention to getting students to use their new skills.

Many generalization errors seem to result when the acquired social skills are not as strong or efficient as the former behaviors used by the student in a particular social situation. Researchers have described these former responses as "competing behaviors." Competing behaviors are often more efficient

than the new social skills a student has learned; the new skills may be harder to perform, slower to use, and less habitual. When the student is in an environment where he or she has a long history of problem behavior that often "works" in obtaining what he or she wants, it is unlikely that the student will "call up" the new skills. This is because the strong competing stimuli elicit the old undesirable behaviors, particularly in situations in which no instruction has occurred. The teacher's goal, therefore, should be to teach students social skills that are "functionally equivalent" to or just as effective as the problem or competing behavior in obtaining a desired outcome (Horner, O'Neil, & Flannery, 1993).

Since elementary school, Rick has demonstrated his dislike for active, noisy games in physical education by covering his ears, growing anxious, making noises, and refusing to participate. Beginning in middle school, Rick perfected a set of highly effective ways to get out of PE; these methods include yelling, refusing to participate, asking to go to the rest room, and behaving aggressively toward others. By mid-October, Rick's team (including his physical education teacher) designed a program based on his functional assessment. The team taught Rick several alternative ways for him to "escape" loud group games: Instead of participating in the group activities, he could ask for a short break, run on the track, perform exercises using headphones, or use a self-monitoring plan to keep track of actual participation in order to earn preferred activities. Because the competing behaviors were so ingrained in Rick and still occasionally worked with some teachers, the replacement behaviors were not automatic for him.

In cases of poor skill generalization, team members might ask several questions and then strengthen the student's program based on the answers:

1. Does the student engage in undesirable behavior that achieves the same results as the socially skilled target behavior (e.g., ends disliked activity, gets attention)? Are the unde-

sirable behaviors equally (or more) effective in obtaining reinforcement? (If the answers are positive, ask the second set of questions.)

2. If the undesirable behaviors are equally or more effective in obtaining reinforcement, are they easier for the student? Are they more likely to achieve the same function faster and more consistently than the socially skilled alternative behavior? (Gresham, 1997, pp. 246–247)

If the answers to these second questions are also affirmative, the solution lies in the following rule: *Decrease the efficiency and reliability of competing, inappropriate behaviors.*

• Don't allow problem behaviors to "work" for the student.

• Ensure that the social skills and appropriate behavior (even if imperfect) result in the function that the student seeks (e.g., attention, escape, tangibles).

Finally, the team should learn about trigger stimuli that might play a role in preventing the generalization of learning. To do this, they should ask the following questions:

3. Are competing problem behaviors related to the presence of a specific stimulus (e.g., person, place, or thing) or are they associated with many stimuli and situations? (Gresham, 1997, pp. 246–247)

When the team members determine that singular people, places, or things act as triggers for problem behavior, they might try to change these stimuli to prevent the problem; however, if many circumstances provoke the problem behavior, then the best plan is to *increase the efficiency and reliability of socially skilled alternative behaviors (#2).*

Because they could not discontinue loud group activities during physical education, Rick's team decided to increase the efficiency and reliability of Rick's alternative behaviors. They determined ways to address his problem behavior when it did occur. Then, the physical education teacher and class assistant taught Rick several appropriate ways he could request "escape"

from loud group games. Next, they planned and gave Rick's peers some instruction on ways in which they might support Rick by ignoring his problem behaviors; several peers agreed to run or exercise with him if he requested these alternatives. Additionally, Rick was not allowed to leave PE and sit in the principal's office when he engaged in his old problem behavior. Instead, he was taken by a teaching assistant to the far end of the gym (or to another gym) and was expected to complete an exercise activity.

Use of Meaningful Outcome Measures

When social skill teaching plans work, the improvements in student behavior will be noticed and appreciated by others. This meaningful outcome is sometimes called *social validation;* society (e.g., teachers, parents, peers, principals) deems that the change is important. Another outcome we want to achieve is a positive change in the person's social relationships, which has been called *habilitative validity* (Hawkins, 1991). Answering the following types of questions will help educators evaluate their social skill teaching efforts by examining social relationship outcomes:

• Did the social skills or behavior change make a difference in the individual's social functioning, particularly in their participation and interaction in peer networks?

• Did social skill training produce changes in the person's status within his or her peer group? Are there any positive changes in his or her social relationships?

Often, a very large difference in a person's social skills performance is necessary for the change to be noticed by significant others (e.g., parents, teachers, peers). Teams should keep track of the targeted social skills but also monitor the students' improvements in social relationship outcomes.

Daniel's team keeps track of how often he responds to peers' comments and initiates social interaction; they also get a monthly count from Daniel's home of invitations to play that Daniel receives from classmates and those that classmates accept from him.

Melanie's team counts her isolated behavior at recess and her success in conversational turn-taking. At the monthly team meeting, Melanie's mom describes the social contacts Melanie initiates and those she receives from classmates and neighborhood children.

Rick's aggressive acts and confrontations with staff members are being monitored, *along with his use of appropriate alternative ways to escape disliked situations. Ever since Rick has joined the high school Key Club, Rick reports his weekend volunteer and social activities to his teacher.*

To be meaningful, a behavior change or social skill must be noticed by others and reach what is called the "just noticeable difference" level of performance; however, a "just noticeable difference" is often rather large and is regarded as significant only when it occurs across most or all environments that the student routinely uses.

Chapter 5

Models of Peer Support in Instruction

with Monica Delano

The term *peer-mediated instruction* applies when teachers involve students in lending instructional support to other students. Two broad models of peer-mediated instruction are described in this chapter: cooperative learning and peer tutoring. Both approaches accommodate learner diversity and foster opportunities for social relationships among peers.

Our daily newspapers routinely editorialize about the state of public schools; they suggest that students are not achieving acceptable academic outcomes and will be unprepared for life after school. They also propose that schools attempt to accomplish too much and, in doing so, miss their central function—academic achievement.

A lot is known about the ideal conditions for learning. Imagine a classroom in which the following occur:

1. Students spend most of their time *actively engaged in learning academic material* (e.g., reading, writing, participating in academic discussions, asking and answering questions).

2. Time is used efficiently with a *minimum amount of time spent in transition* between activities.

3. Students' *errors are kept to a minimum.*

4. Students spend most of their time *successfully engaged in tasks* that are relevant to what will be tested.

5. Students are frequently *monitored to determine if they are engaged* and performing correctly.

6. Lessons are structured so that *students know what they are to do and the purpose behind the lesson.*

7. Students are *frequently asked questions* to test their knowledge and comprehension.

Many researchers agree that students in classrooms such as these will make meaningful gains in measurable levels of academic achievement (Berliner, 1988; Greenwood, Carta, & Kamps, 1990), but are classrooms such as these *exactly* what teachers are aiming for? Many teachers feel pressure to look for outcomes that extend beyond academic achievement and to define "effective" instruc-

tion as being more than academic learning time, engaged time, time management, success rate, monitoring, structuring, and questioning.

A great deal has been learned about how to facilitate academic outcomes among a wide range of abilities. However, if we envision a society in which "no one gets lost, structured so that each citizen has an active role, and all people would be guaranteed access to the resources of society" (Sapon-Shevin & Schniedewind, 1992, p. 21) regardless of gender, ethnicity, and abilities, then perhaps our schools must look beyond the academic outcomes and seek to foster a sense of community and social responsibility as well. Restructuring schools so that the well-being of students is taken into consideration requires school administrators to redesign the culture of their schools and classrooms into places that create empowerment, cooperation, compassion, and respect (Berman, 1990). A first step in this direction may be to implement instructional models that have been demonstrated to be highly effective in producing gains in academic achievement and to have the potential to facilitate the development of caring communities in which all students are accepted, active members of the school.

Cooperative learning and *peer tutoring* are based on solid research foundations, and both offer innovative strategies for meeting the diverse needs of today's classrooms. Some practical guidelines for implementation and several case examples are provided following a brief summary of the empirical support for both approaches.

COOPERATIVE LEARNING

Though several structured models of cooperative learning exist, the purpose of this section is not to describe specific approaches to cooperative learning but, rather, to present an overview of the technique, guidelines for use, and some practical applications.

Components of Cooperative Learning

Cooperative learning is an instructional method in which students work in small, mixed ability groups and are responsible for their groupmates' learning as well as their own learning (Campbell & Campbell, 1995). Cooperative learning classrooms are places where heterogeneous groups of students learn to work together, accept one another, and achieve positive academic and social outcomes. Competition is replaced by cooperation, mutual support, and shared accomplishments. Though this may sound idealistic, there are several structured models of cooperative learning that support these outcomes (see Sharan, 1994, for detailed descriptions). All models for cooperative learning share what Johnson and Johnson (1989) identified as the five essential components of cooperative learning, which distinguish cooperative learning from generic group work:

1. *Positive interdependence:* All group members work together toward a shared goal. Each student plays a key role in the group's success and takes responsibility for supporting the other group members. The group is successful only when each member achieves the goal.

2. *Individual accountability:* Each group member is required to learn the material or meet his or her individual goal. Group members may quiz one another to check for understanding. As the classroom environment becomes a cooperative community, students begin to develop a sense of caring for others and encourage each other to do their best.

3. *Cooperative skills:* Cooperative skills are the subset of social skills that involve synergistic interactions between group members participating together in group activities (e.g., taking turns, active listening, resolving conflicts). Teachers may instruct students in the use of cooperative skills through modeling, guided practice, and feedback.

4. *Face-to-face interaction:* Cooperative learning tasks require students to physically group together and interact with one another during the activity. Depending on the specific activities, desks or chairs can be rearranged in small circles with a shared working surface; younger students often cluster together on the floor.

5. *Group processing:* During a cooperative learning activity, students are asked to reflect on how well they are functioning as a team. Group strengths and weaknesses are identified. Based on the identified group needs, students set improvement goals for the group.

Outcomes for Cooperative Learning Classrooms

Cooperative learning is perhaps one of the most extensively studied instructional methods. Hundreds of research studies on cooperative learning, in addition to numerous books and various reviews of the literature, have been published in the 1980s and 1990s. Though continued systematic research is still needed, especially in the area of including students with disabilities, results are quite encouraging. An extensive review of the literature is beyond the scope of this chapter (refer to Slavin, 1991, 1995); however, some of the promising benefits are highlighted in Table 5.1. Continued research in this area will increase our understanding of the impact that cooperative learning has on specific student outcomes (Figure 5.1).

GETTING STARTED WITH COOPERATIVE LEARNING

To initiate cooperative learning groups in a classroom, teachers will need to take several steps. First, the lesson will need to be planned—setting group and individual objectives, assigning students to groups and roles, readying materials, targeting cooperative skills, and planning how to monitor groups. Then, teachers will want to ensure that group instruction addresses the diversity students bring to the classroom, both in learning needs and culture.

Organizing a Cooperative Learning Lesson

Organizing class activities so students learn cooperatively is not a trivial process. Teachers cannot simply place students into groups and

Table 5.1.   Outcomes often associated with cooperative learning

Increased academic achievement
Improved intergroup relations
Improved self-esteem
High-level reasoning strategies and increased critical reasoning competencies
Greater ability to view situations from others' perspectives
Greater intrinsic motivation
More positive attitudes toward subject areas, learning, and school
More positive attitudes toward teachers, principals, and school personnel
Less disruptive and more on-task behavior
Greater collaborative skills and better attitudes, necessary for working with others
Greater feeling of individual control over one's success in school
Increased altruism and supportive behaviors toward others
Increased prosocial behavior
Improved skills at resolving conflicts
Increased attendance

Source: Johnson, Johnson, Holubec, & Roy (1984).

have them all work together on a task. Often, it takes several years for a teacher to become competent in using cooperative learning strategies. Once these strategies for implementing cooperative learning are understood, teachers are encouraged to explore more specific cooperative learning models (see Sharan, 1994). Some specific models of cooperative learning may correspond to a class's specific learning tasks, topics, and age groups more closely and, thus, be more useful than other models.

The organization of cooperative learning groups usually includes eight steps.

Step 1
State Group
Lesson Objectives

 The first step in planning a cooperative activity is to set the goals for the lesson. Each member of the group is responsible for meeting the goal, though each student does not need to take the same approach. Goals should be stated in measurable and observable terms and should include a criterion for success (e.g., 30% increase over pretest score) so that students know what they need to accomplish. Depending on the nature of the lesson, shared group goals may include achieving a

specified score on a test, creating a product (e.g., constructing a model, performing a one-act play), or solving a problem.

Step 2
Assign Students to Groups

Cooperative groups are usually heterogeneous with respect to ethnicity, gender, ability, and socioeconomic status. At the beginning of the school year, when the teacher is unfamiliar with the individual students in the class, students may be randomly assigned to groups; however, once the teacher is familiar with students' academic levels and social skills, heterogeneous groups can be systematically created to form base groups. Occasionally, teachers may appoint temporary or "ad hoc" groups for short-term projects while still relying on the base groups. Teachers also might allow students to create their own groups (self-selected groups) for some projects; however, this often leads to homogeneous groups (e.g., a peer network of high achievers in one group). Typical groups range in size from two to six students. Base groups should be rotated routinely to ensure that every student has an opportunity to work cooperatively with each one of his or her classmates.

Cooperative learning and academic achievement

When cooperative learning is appropriately implemented, students achieve better outcomes than in individual or competitive situations.

- Slavin (1990) analyzed 68 studies of cooperative learning and found that in 72% of the studies, cooperative learning groups outperformed control groups.
- Johnson and Johnson's (1989) meta-analysis of research found that achievement was higher when students worked cooperatively than when they worked individually.
- The key components of cooperative learning that are credited for these learning outcomes are positive interdependence, individual accountability, equal opportunity for success, cooperative skill instruction, and learning strategy instruction (Johnson & Johnson, 1989; Slavin, 1990).

There is strong support for cooperative learning as an approach to achieve academic gains in diverse classrooms, but how diverse should the classroom be?

- More study will help address the following questions:
  1) Can cooperative learning facilitate the development of higher-order thinking skills (Davidson, 1985)?
  2) To what extent is academic achievement in students with disabilities meaningfully supported by cooperative learning (Cosden & Haring, 1992; Lloyd, Crowley, Kohler, & Strain, 1988)?
- Much of the learning and instruction in cooperative groups occurs "within a social dialogue of group interaction, rather than the more passive responding of traditional didactic instruction" (Cosden & Haring, 1992, p. 55). Students with difficulty in attending to others, socially interacting, or communicating in general will be especially challenged by cooperative learning and will require some accommodations.

Cooperative learning and acceptance of diversity

Cooperative learning provides a way to structure classrooms so that students can develop and understand each other's differences and learn to support each other's learning.

- These features enable students to look beyond race, gender, and ability stereotypes and develop positive relationships by working toward common goals.

Research suggests that cooperative learning is associated with gaining interpersonal skills and acceptance of differences.

- Acceptance of students with disabilities
- Positive relationships among members of different ethnic groups
- Improvements in interactions between students with disabilities and those without
- Increased academic engagement during group sessions
- Increased learning by all group members, including elementary students with autism and multiple disabilities (Dugan et al., 1995; Hunt, Staub, Alwell, & Goetz, 1994; Slavin, 1995)

Figure 5.1.   Cooperative learning: Research findings and issues.

Step 3
Role Assignment

Assigning group roles allows students to take responsibility for specific tasks during the group activity and fosters positive interdependence. Roles can be task related or process related. Teachers may assign roles that are well suited to the students' skills, or students may be asked to select roles that match their particular interests and skills. Table 5.2 lists several cooperative group roles typical to cooperative groups (Putnam, 1997).

Step 4
Individual Goals

To ensure individual accountability and to monitor progress, teachers should set individualized, measurable goals for students. Usually, group members with IEPs will have individual achievement goals related to the group task and may have accommodations or modifications in place. Research has shown that inequities in effort and participation by team members may have a negative impact on group motivation and achieve-

ment (Cosden & Haring, 1992). However, this does not mean that everyone has to have the same goals. When classmates are used to classrooms where "we don't all learn the same things or in the same ways," individualization is accepted as a means of enabling all group members to contribute.

Step 5
Materials

Getting, distributing, and returning materials is often a group role assigned to students; however, teachers will want to list and make accessible the materials students will need to meet both their group and individual goals.

Step 6
Target Cooperative Skills

Cooperative skills are those social, teamwork skills that are necessary for effective group participation. Younger students, typically, will need to learn skills such as staying with the group, sharing materials, taking turns, contributing ideas, and encouraging others. Sec-

Table 5.2. Cooperative group roles

Recorder	Documents the work of the group, takes notes, writes answers
Reader	Reads the written material, reads the answer for the group
Summarizer	Recapitulates what has been decided in the group, summarizes the ideas shared
Encourager	Reinforces group members for performing well or staying on task, instills a strength of purpose, invites members to participate
Courier	Brings materials to the group, carries messages or assignments to their destination
Checker	Makes certain that everyone is on task, agrees with the answer, understands the assignment, discussion, or answer
Interrogator	Challenges group members to defend their answers and to avoid superficial responses or to explore matters more deeply
Manager	Assures directions are followed, organizes group process
Time keeper	Watches the time and keeps the group on task and moving forward
Voice control technician	Monitors the noise level in the group and indicates when students need to quiet down.
Equalizer	Makes sure group members are treated fairly and courteously, that they have opportunities to participate, and derive benefit from the groupwork

(From COOPERATIVE LEARNING IN DIVERSE CLASSROOMS by JoAnne Putnam, © 1997. Reprinted by permission of Prentice-Hall, Inc., Upper Saddle River, N.J.)

For *students with more severe disabilities*, these skills include the following:
- Recognizing group members
- Greeting group members
- Developing skills to partially participate in group activities

For *students with mild disabilities*, these skills include the following:
- Asking appropriate questions
- Asserting ideas
- Attending to others in the group

For *students without disabilities*, these skills include a small repertoire of individualized skills:
- Communication skills that let group members interact effectively (e.g., being familiar with another student's yes/no or picture system or with their augmentative device; knowing how to prompt another student to participate without being obstrusive)
- Collateral peer support behaviors that let group members motivate each other to persist in cooperative group tasks.

Figure 5.2. Skills needed to benefit from interactions in cooperative learning groups with members who have disabilities. (From Cosden, M.A., & Haring, T.G. [1992]. Cooperative learning in the classroom: Contingencies, group interactions, and students with special needs. *Journal of Behavioral Education*, 2, 53–71; adapted by permission.)

ondary students may need skill development in active listening, giving and receiving constructive criticism, paraphrasing, time management, and conflict resolution. Some students with disabilities may need help with cooperative skills related to their specific disabilities or skill repertoires; others will simply need to improve the cooperative skills in which they are weak (Cosden & Haring, 1992) (Figure 5.2).

Student Snapshot

Susan is a 10-year-old who has cerebral palsy and an emotional disturbance. She walks independently but needs some assistance with fine motor tasks. Handwriting is especially challenging; therefore, Susan is learning keyboarding. Susan's social skills are delayed in comparison with those of her peers, and she sometimes has difficulty reading social cues and working cooperatively with others. Susan's accommodations include the use of oral and typed responses in place of written responses, a calculator, alternate level reading materials, a peer buddy, shortened assignments, and self-monitoring behavior checklists. A teaching assistant works unobtrusively with Susan in the fifth-grade classroom as needed and lends sup-port to the group as a whole. Susan also attends a daily language arts tutorial with a special education teacher and participates in small-group counseling sessions twice per week. Because Susan is accustomed to using checklists (for behavioral performance and to complete school tasks), she may benefit from having a checklist of her role responsibilities (e.g., being voice control technician *means that you will . . .) and the cooperative skills on which she is working (e.g., ask others questions and listen to their answers; give compliments to others who make contributions to the group project, and smile when you do so; take your turn and let others have their turn). (Figure 5.3 shows Susan's Program-at-a-Glance.)*

Step 7
Plan How to Maintain Groups

Cooperative learning goals often are monitored best through observations; teachers rotate among groups and jot down notes on the cooperative skills they observe students exhibiting as they work in their groups. A grid with the alphabetized class list on one side and the target cooperative skills written across the top of the grid can provide a simple way to code what

---

Program-at-a-Glance

Student: _Susan_   **Date:** _1998–1999_ **Grade:** _5_

IEP Objectives (briefly)

Reading and Writing:
- *Decode words with long vowel patterns*
- *Use correct consonant blends in writing*
- *After reading a short story, identify setting, problem, and order of action*
- *Write or type five simple sentences on one subject*

Math:
- *Master basic math facts for numbers up to 20*
- *Use a calculator to add and subtract numbers greater than 20*
- *Identify coins and match values*
- *Tell time in 5-minute increments*

Accommodations

- *Oral and typed responses in place of written responses*
- *Calculator*
- *Alternate-level reading materials*
- *Spell-check on first draft*
- *Peer buddy (e.g., reader, peer to assist with manipulating notebooks and jacket as she requests)*
- *Shortened assignments*
- *Self-monitoring behavior checklists*
- *Reading tutorial*
- *Counseling and peer mediation sessions as needed*
- *Teaching assistant in classroom*

Academic & Management Needs

- *Susan needs high rate of success in academic tasks and structured choices (often has difficulty complying with directions and sometimes displays aggressive behavior).*
- *Give her permission to take brief breaks in a designated classroom area; prompt her to ask for a break when she needs it.*

Comments

- *Occasionally displays aggressive behavior, which interferes with instruction of others and may be harmful (throwing things, hitting). Susan may ask to or be prompted to go to a place to calm down; if she asks preventatively, let her go.*
- *Peer mediation has helped reduce conflicts with peers in past year.*
- *Weekly telephone conferences with Susan's mother are helpful to share information about assignments and behavior.*

Figure 5.3.   Program-at-a-Glance for Susan.

---

teachers observe. Correctly used skills can be marked with a "+," those prompted by peers or adults marked with a "P," and those missing or deficient marked with a "−." Analyses of these grids will help teachers determine when group or individual instruction may be needed.

Step 8
Comments and Feedback

Group members can be asked to provide their teacher with comments regarding their group's functioning; the teacher can then share feedback with the groups. This task is often more difficult for younger students. Some teachers have found that discussions along with T-charts can help students define the social skills in terms that they understand (see first section of Figure 5.4 for example of a T-chart). Simple group processing charts can help groups self-evaluate their progress in using particular social skills. (The second section of Figure 5.4 provides some examples applied to younger elementary students that are applicable, with modification, to older students.)

For students in several fourth-grade classrooms in which one classmate had autism,

1. **Use a T-Chart to define social objectives with children:**

Teachers ask students to focus on one specific behavior on which they are working and brainstorm how it looks and sounds. The teacher uses a T-Chart (as shown below) to record the student's definitions.

Using Quiet Voices

Looks Like	Sounds Like
Faces together—one foot apart	Whispering
Sitting close together	"One foot voice"
Knees touching	Soft voices
Looking at each other	Very quiet

2. **Process cooperative group lessons:**

Have groups process at the end of the group session for a few minutes.
- Initially, ask groups to use a smiley-face chart to evaluate themselves (chart below on left).
- Later, ask groups to answer two open-ended questions (chart below on right).

Have the entire class process afterward by discussing what happened.
- Students remain in their groups, and teacher facilitates discussion of instructional and social objectives of lesson.
- Students refer to their group data to talk about how well their group did and what they will work on for the next lesson.
- Use teacher data to provide feedback to groups and point out positive examples of how students worked together.

Initial Group Processing Chart	Later Group Processing Chart
How did we do? We used quiet voices: ☺ 😐 ☹ We did our roles: ☺ 😐 ☹ Sign here: _____	**Our social skills:** How did we do? What will we work on next? Sign here: _____

3. **Monitor the use of social skills:**
- Discuss the skills before groups start.
- Inform students that the class will talk together about how well they did after the groups meet.
- Tell students that teachers will observe how they work throughout the group lesson.
- Have teachers move about from group to group and provide reminders and assistance on instructional and social objectives if needed.
- Have teachers collect data during the lesson on students' social objectives by jotting codes by students'/groups' names (see chart that follows).

Key: 1 = Quiet voices + = Good
2 = Stays with role − = Needs improvement

Chai Lee Doug Luis	Eva Brad Terri		Rachel Katie Arum	Jamel Kiara Russell
Kathleen Daniel Darnell	Tony Christopher Tamara	William Cerise Dayquan	Erin Juan Beth	Kirk Delesta Shannon

Figure 5.4. Methods teachers used with first graders to define, monitor, and process cooperative group skills. (From Ayres, B., O'Brien, L., & Rogers, T. [1992]. *Working together, sharing and helping each other: Cooperative learning in a first grade classroom that includes students with disabilities.* Syracuse, NY: Syracuse University, The Inclusive Education Project; reprinted by permission.)

Dugan and her colleagues (1995) first used classroom games to teach the social skills and then refined the skills in the context of cooperative learning social studies groups. The acronym SCORE was used to remember the five social skills:

- **S**hare your ideas with others.
- **C**orrect each other's work.
- **O**ffer praise to each other.
- **R**eact to others, but do so calmly.
- **E**ncourage and help other groups members.

Listed in Figure 5.5 are the teaching and reinforcement strategies teachers used to shape the students' performance of these five skills along with a description of how they organized the cooperative learning groups.

Addressing Diversity in the Classroom

If schools are to have classrooms in which all students can learn, be accepted, and accept others, teachers must fulfill several requirements through their cooperative group instruction: 1) *Meet the individualized learning needs of each student by modifying schoolwork,* and 2) *ensure that instructional procedures are culturally sensitive to each class member.*

Individualized Schoolwork In order to meet the individualized learning needs of each student, teachers will need methods to modify schoolwork so students can participate actively alongside peers in ways that are meaningful while also acquiring useful knowledge and skills. Special education and general education teachers will need to work collaboratively to modify schoolwork so it "fits" students, allowing the students to participate actively and to learn.

There are many ways to plan and modify schoolwork. *Modifying Schoolwork* (Janney & Snell, 2000), a companion booklet in this series, provides detailed information regarding methods of modifying schoolwork so that all students can actively participate in a classroom. This chapter briefly describes a less complex approach to better accommodate some class members in cooperative groups (Putnam, 1997). The modifications range from simple to extensive and can be used as general guidelines across age groups and teaching content. Although Putnam's (1997) approach is straightforward, it is not comprehensive. Using this simpler system, teachers plan modifications in the student response, the method for presentation of material, the workload, the materials, or the objective itself. As special and general educators gain more experience adapting school work for individual learners and using the following five adaptations within cooperative learning groups, they will want to use a more comprehensive process:

1. *Same objective with an alternate response:* A student may work on the same learning objective as other students but make responses in a different form. For example, instead of responding in writing, a student with a learning disability may respond orally. Likewise, a student with a physical disability may use a computer; students with visual limitations may tape-record rather than write their answers to an assignment.

2. *Same objective with an alternate presentation of the lesson:* The lesson may be presented to the student in an alternate manner. For example, a fellow student may read the material to the student, or a student may listen to an audiotape made by another student.

3. *Same objective with a reduced workload:* The learning objective remains the same, but the student is required to complete fewer assignments. A student with chronic illness and, consequently, reduced stamina may benefit from such an accommodation. (*The cooperative lesson plan for Susan and her fifth-grade class in science* [Figure 5.6] *makes use of a reduced workload for Susan and the alternate response of speaking rather than writing.*)

4. *Same objective with modified expectations or materials:* Although a student works toward the same objective as his or her peers, expec-

---

Teaching group social skills in social studies cooperative groups with fourth graders

Targeted social skills (SCORE):
- Share your ideas with others.
- Correct each other's work.
- Offer praise to each other.
- React to others, but do so calmly.
- Encourage and help other group members.

Strategies for teaching these skills:
- Students are assigned team roles (e.g., materials manager, recorder, checker, or organizer).
- Initially, children play games daily for a week to learn and practice these group social skills.
- In the second week, the skills are practiced in the context of the social studies cooperative groups.
- Reinforcements for using group social skills consist of the following:
  - Teachers and assistants rotate among groups to monitor use of skills.
  - Stickers are given contingent on performance of a SCORE skill by a group member.
  - Stickers are placed on a group chart in proper SCORE column (by skill).

Characteristics of cooperative learning groups and content:
- Focus on U.S. states and social studies (e.g., Northeast, Southeast, Great Lakes states, Great Plains states, Southwest, and mountain states).
- Present or review new material during 10-minute whole-class lecture.
- Hold 40-minute cooperative group sessions (distribute materials tubs, 10 minutes key word peer tutoring, 8 minutes fact card peer tutoring, 5 minutes team activity with a worksheet or research activity, 5 minutes of whole-class activity to wrap up).
- For each group, seat four class members at desks pulled together (one student with high academic skills, two with moderate academic skills, one with minimal academic skills).

Figure 5.5.   Strategies for teaching group social skills. (Source: Dugan et al., 1994.)

tations may be set at a lower grade or developmental level. For example, a fourth-grade group is studying Australia. A student with a difficulty in reading may be provided with reading materials at a second-grade level. (*For a cooperative group lesson on the Boston Tea Party in his tenth-grade American History class, Walter, a student with cognitive disabilities, creates comic book illustrations for the group's written lesson on the Boston Tea Party.*)

5. *Personalized objective:* Instead of working on the same academic objective as peers, a student may master an individualized functional or interpersonal objective during a cooperative activity. For example, a student could work on learning fellow students' names, one-to-one correspondence, and various mobility skills by being the group's materials manager. (When you read through the example of the cooperative learning group for teaching money

skills in Figure 5.7, note that Jessica has personalized objectives.)

Cultural Sensitivity   In addition to modifying learning objectives to meet individual student learning needs in the context of cooperative groups, a second requirement for teaching through cooperative learning groups is that teachers demonstrate *cultural sensitivity* in their teaching and in their behavior toward students. Cultural sensitivity, for some students, helps reduce the differences between familiar learning environments at home and in their community and unfamiliar environments such as school, thereby improving the likelihood that students will be motivated to attend school and, therefore, to learn. For the student's classmates who are in the "cultural majority," culturally sensitive instruction broadens their familiarity with other cultures and reduces "strangeness" by increasing knowledge. When classroom instruc-

---

Cooperative Learning Lesson Plan

Content Area: _Science_   **Date:** _November 1_

Grade: _5th_   **Teacher:** _Roberta Jones_

Lesson Goals

1. **_Group Lesson Objective(s):_** _Using a list of 20 names of human bones and a diagram of a skeleton, students will label the bones and achieve a 50% increase over their pretest score._

2. **_Cooperative Skill Objective(s):_** _Students will take turns, give positive encouragement to all, fill group roles, and give Susan encouragement and prompts only as needed_

Adaptations/Accommodations for Individual Learning Needs

Student	Adaptations/Accommodation(s)
Susan	_Shortened word list (10 words)_
	Peer reader
	Oral responses
	Self-monitoring behavioral checklist

Materials:

Skeleton model, skeleton diagrams, pencils, data sheets

Group Tasks:

1. _Group reads task description and selects individual roles_
   - _Early jobs: Cut out bones; find information on bone function, bone problems, and bone benefits; think of a way to classify the bones_
   - _Later jobs: Color bones; make color coding key; print labels; paste; add name, age, benefits, and problems to chart_

2. _Group completes task: label life-size skeleton with color-coded bones_
   - _Name your skeleton, give it an age, identify any bone benefits or problems it has_
   - _Determine name and function of each bone_
   - _Use a system to classify the bones, color code them in this way_
   - _Make bone labels (print name and function, make arrow from label to bone)_
   - _Add key to color-coding system_

3. _Group works in tutoring pairs to review the names of the bones (2 minutes per student in each role, set timer)_

Checklist of required components (check when achieved):

____ Interdependent participation to achieve common goal

____ Goal achievement requires coordination among all group members

____ Goal achievement requires contributions from all members

____ Goals include both academic and social skill development

____ Individual and group accountability

(continued)

Figure 5.6. An example cooperative learning group lesson plan for a fifth-grade science unit on the human skeleton.

Figure 5.6. *(continued)*

Group Members:	Role:	Individual Goal:	Date Attained:
Susan	Encourager	Correctly label 8/10 bones	
Max	Reader	Correctly label 19/20 bones	
Alan	Recorder	Correctly label 17/20 bones	
Sandy	Helper	Correctly label 18/20 bones	

(List of groups continues)

Comments:

Pair Sandy with Susan for the tutoring activity.
Have Susan refer to her checklist for her job options.

tion is culturally sensitive, students come to understand the similarities that exist between the various ways of saying and doing things (e.g., speaking, reacting, social amenities, food, holidays, dress, traditions, leisure interests, religions and beliefs). Putnam (1997) summarized Franklin's suggestions for fostering culturally sensitive instructional practices. These suggestions include

- Incorporating cultural practices from the learner's home and community environments
- Identifying and building on a student's strengths and interests
- Understanding the language that is used in the student's home
- Building bridges between prior learning and a variety of instructional activities

Cooperative learning classrooms can be environments where cultural diversity is recognized and respected. Recognition and respect occurs when students see diversity simply as *variations of their own ways of doing things.*

COOPERATIVE GROUPS INVOLVING MEMBERS WITH MORE EXTENSIVE DISABILITIES

Some readers might wonder *if it really is possible for all group members to achieve the group learning objectives* when one member has a more exten-

sive physical and/or cognitive disability. Others might question whether group members who have difficulty attending to and completing tasks due to short attention spans and distractibility will learn *or will let others learn.* Finally, some teachers and parents may ask "What about those students who are disruptive . . ." (perhaps as a result of their behavioral disorders) ". . . will they learn or will they just disrupt the learning of others?" These are legitimate concerns. Two studies lend clear support to the likelihood that *all students,* including students with autism and multiple disabilities, can learn in a cooperative group context when the teacher preparation and support are adequate (Dugan et al., 1995; Hunt et al., 1994); however, the success of cooperative learning strategies often depends on the teacher:

1. Teachers' *preparation* for a cooperative learning group lesson
2. Teachers' supports given *during* the ongoing cooperative group activity

Preparation

Teachers should work and plan in the following ways to prepare for cooperative learning groups that have members with more support:

- Work collaboratively with other teachers and support staff.

Teachers' preparation for a cooperative learning group lesson

Grade Level: _2nd_   **Curricular Unit:** _Math (money)_   **Focus Student:** _Jessica_

1. Prepare a cooperative learning activity on money skills with several features:
   - Require interdependent participation to achieve a common goal.
   - Require coordination among members and successful contributions from all to achieve goal.
   - Set goals that address both academic and social skills development.
   - Devise ways to track individual and group accountability.
   - Divide class randomly into groups of four; assign focus student to one group for the entire unit.
   - Schedule time and length of cooperative groups (daily for 45 minutes in the morning).

2. Specify the skills for those class members who are expected to achieve second-grade academic goals (money skills):
   - Identify coins, coin value, and purchase amount, and calculate change.
   - Administer short paper-and-pencil test to address all these skills.
   - Administer pretest before first day of instruction.

3. Specify the targeted skills and learning conditions for group members whose learning needs differ (Jessica); this involves collaboration among general education and special education teachers; parents; integration support teachers; and occupational, physical, and speech-language therapists.
   - Set objectives for active participation:

     When a peer asks her if she wants a turn, Jessica will activate a switch to play a tape-recorded message ("Yes, I want a turn") and then take her turn.
     When a peer asks Jessica to pass an item needed in the activity (e.g., coin, price card), she will take the object from the peer on her right and pass it to the person who requested it.
   - Determine how to teach Jessica these objectives (e.g., proper seating and position, which hand and how, placement of object, switch placement, recorded statement, time needed to respond, requests from peers, ways to prompt).

4. Identify where groups will meet and positioning considerations:
   - Students sit on floor, and Jessica sits in an adapted chair.

5. Identify any needed social interaction skills (but teach within the context of the groups):
   - Are peers familiar with Jessica as a classmate?
   - Are peers familiar with Jessica's ways of communicating (e.g., uses a variety of facial expressions, movements, and vocalizations to indicate likes and dislikes and to interact socially with others) and do peers know to prompt, cue, or reinforce her?
   - Are peers familiar with Jessica's ways of passing objects (i.e., ways in which peers will prompt, cue, or reinforce Jessica)?

(continued)

Figure 5.7.   An example of what teachers do to prepare for and support cooperative learning groups. (From Hunt, P., Staur, D., Alwell, M., & Goetz, L. [1994]. Achievement by all students within the context of cooperative learning groups. *Journal of the Association for Persons with Severe Handicaps, 19,* 290–301. © 1994 JASH; adapted by permission.)

Figure 5.7.   *(continued)*

Teachers' supports given during the ongoing cooperative group activity

1. Prompt group members, and, initially, practice ways they can support each other:
   - Meet with each learning group for 3–6 minutes before math lesson (review meeting).
   - Teach peers the specific natural cues ("Jessica, do you want a turn?"), prompts (used if Jessica does not respond within 3 seconds), and consequences (let Jessica take her turn).
   - During lesson, remind students to provide designated cues, prompts, and reinforcers.
   - Aim for six opportunities for Jessica to communicate desire for a turn and four opportunities to pass objects during each session.

2. Circulate among groups and provide equal attention:
   - Besides the general education teacher, support staff may include parent volunteers, a university practicum student, or a teaching assistant.

3. Provide "planned attention" to promote interdependence among group members:
   - Reduce reminders to students to cue, prompt, and reinforce Jessica.
   - Initially, provide reminders as needed and note the number. Reduce that number in successive lessons while again noting number; finally, eliminate all reminders.
   - Staff members should collaborate to determine whether to reduce or maintain reminders and whether to reduce or reinstitute reviews over time.

4. Provide ways for students to generalize support of focus student across classmates and activities:
   - At end of coin unit, rotate groups so Jessica is in a new group.
   - Repeat review meetings with new group as needed.
   - Institute new math unit.
   - Adjust Jessica's skill objectives to suit her progress and needs and to provide opportunities.

5. Take notes on issues that need problem solving and on group progress:
   - Members of groups that have a focus student with multiple disabilities, such as Jessica, learned as much as members of groups that did not have students like Jessica; learning was not hampered by having a member with extensive support needs.
   - Group members consistently and accurately provided cues, prompts, and reinforcers to focus students; during the final weeks of the eight- to ten-week unit, the peers were lending support to the focus students in their group with little or no disruption.

- Set reasonable learning objectives, individualized for as many students as necessary.
- Make the necessary adaptations in materials and content.
- Make adjustments to suit students who are not fluent in English or students who use alternative communication systems.
- Allow for any accommodations required by some students.
- If a student requires direct instruction on social interaction (e.g., staying on task, listening to others, accepting feedback, offering constructive feedback, accepting and giving praise), find ways to teach the necessary skills within cooperative groups and at other times; for example, teach and encourage other group members to provide explanations for problem solving or to give elaborations. Design behavioral support

plans with self-management features to be used unobtrusively by students who need them. (*Susan uses her self-management checklist system or is reminded to do so by her buddy; afterward, she reviews her performance by counting up the pluses on her checklist.*)

• Teach the social interaction skills needed by various class members for effective participation in cooperative groups (Cosden & Haring, 1992).

Supporting Students During the Lesson

To lend support to students during the lesson (before, during the ongoing cooperative group activity, and immediately after) teachers should take several actions:

• After some initial practice, remind group members of the specific ways they might support some of their fellow group members to enable their participation.

• Circulate among all the groups, taking care to provide equal attention to each group.

• Use "planned attention," which 1) is given only as needed, 2) reminds students to do the things they already know regarding working cooperatively and supporting one another, 3) motivates group members to be less dependent on adults and more dependent on one another, and 4) is systematically diminished from more to less to none.

• Provide ways to generalize peer support of group members with additional learning needs across other classmates and different cooperative activities.

• Take notes on issues that need problem solving and on progress made by groups; use these notes during later discussions with groups and/or among teachers.

Other sources that provide numerous examples of cooperative learning across different age groups and content areas may be consulted for more detail (Ayres, O'Brien, & Rogers, 1992; Johnson & Johnson, 1991; Nevin, Thousand, & Villa, 1994; Putnam, 1993; Villa & Thousand, 1994). The next step

is to apply these guidelines and construct a lesson that could be implemented with a group of students. Refer back to Figure 5.6 for an example of a cooperative group lesson for fifth-grade science. (A blank cooperative learning lesson form is located at the back of this booklet.)

PEER TUTORING

Peer tutoring is one-to-one instruction on a particular topic or assignment by a classmate, a peer, or an older student; it is a well-established general method to promote learning in students. This instructional arrangement is particularly effective in *incremental learning*, in which there is a single correct answer that the tutor is able to guide the tutee toward. There is no *single or correct way* to structure peer tutoring programs; instead, there are many ways. This section of the chapter introduces strategies for selecting and training tutors, describes a few examples of program designs that have varying amounts of supportive research, and presents a case application in which cross-age peer tutoring was implemented in a fifth-grade classroom.

Some Background on Peer Tutoring Programs

Peer tutoring, also referred to as *peer-mediated instructional arrangements*, has been recommended by many researchers as an alternative or supplemental method to traditional instructional approaches such as lectures and student discussions. Advocates of peer tutoring assert that it provides the following benefits: increased student opportunity to respond, lengthened practice time for skills, and improved cooperation among peers (Greenwood, Carta, & Kamps, 1990).

During the 1980s and 1990s, evidence of the instructional, social, and cost effectiveness of student-to-student tutoring has increased. Cohen, Kulik, and Kulik's (1982) meta-analysis found that structured programs that used tutors who knew the content well had better results; in 45 of the 52 studies examined, students who were tutored by older students made more gains than did those tutored by peer tutors. (See Figure 5.8 for more evidence.) Peer tutoring programs offer a promising approach for increasing academic and social outcomes for diverse groups of learners. The next sections of this chapter review the basic steps in developing a tutoring program.

Selecting Tutors

The tutor–tutee relationship must be positive in order to work well. This requires helping students accept individual differences and work cooperatively. Several authors have offered guidance for selecting tutors that is relevant to establishing positive relationships. For example, Campbell and Campbell (1995) suggested that it is important to assess and consider

1. What students know about individuals with diverse learning abilities

2. What students believe to be true about individuals with diverse learning abilities

3. How students interact with individuals who have diverse learning abilities

Based on these considerations, educators can design instruction for students to understand *real versus perceived* differences between themselves and their peers with diverse learning abilities. Careful selection of tutors is likely to prevent many difficulties in implementing a peer tutoring program. (Guidelines for selecting younger peer tutors are listed in Figure 5.9.) Strictly speaking, *peer* tutors are peers of the same age, though they may be from the same or different classrooms and of the same or different abilities. Tutors need not always, however, be the same age as tutees.

It is both our view and the view of other researchers (Van der Klift & Kunc, 1994) that one-way teaching or helping arrangements in which the tutor and tutee are classmates of the same age can sometimes work against the development of positive, reciprocal relationships. Even though the tutee may make meaningful skill gains when the interaction is weighted in one direction, it is less likely that mutual interactions will develop or that friendships might evolve.

> Clearly, there is nothing wrong with help; friends often help each other. However, it is essential to acknowledge that help is not and can never be the basis of friendship. Unless help is reciprocal, the inherent inequity between helper and helpee will contaminate the authenticity of a relationship. (Van der Klift & Kunc, 1994, p. 393)

Classwide peer tutoring has been effective in
- Improving spelling performances of elementary school students (Kohler & Greenwood, 1990) and students with mild disabilities (Harper, Mallette, & Moore, 1991)
- Producing faster oral reading rates (Greenwood, Delquadri, & Hall, 1984)
- Yielding gains in spelling accuracy and lengthened positive social interactions between peers and classmates with learning disabilities and mental retardation requiring intermittent support (Sideridis et al., 1997)
- Incorporating instructional components that match a range of learning styles, which can be valuable for many learners of differing ethnicities (Garcia, 1992)

Other methods of peer tutoring have been effective in improving reading
- In students with mental retardation (e.g., Koury & Browder, 1986)
- In integrated environments with students who have learning disabilities (Mathes, Fuchs, Fuchs, Henley, & Sanders, 1994) and autism (Kamps, Barbetta, Leonard, & Delquadri, 1994)

Evidence of cognitive and affective benefits to the tutors indicates
- That tutors have increased opportunity to practice learning activities
- That tutors may gain in social status (Franca, Kerr, Reitz, & Lambert, 1990)

Figure 5.8.   Evidence of the effectiveness of peer tutoring.

What the Research Says

Strain and Odom (1986) offered a set of guidelines that are useful for selecting peer tutors of preschool or early elementary school age:

1. Choose students who typically comply with teacher requests.
2. Choose students with strong attendance records.
3. Choose students who have age-appropriate interests.
4. Choose peer tutors who have either a positive history or no history with the focus student.
5. Choose students who display a willingness and ability to participate.

Figure 5.9.   Guidelines for selecting younger peer tutors.

Peer Tutor Training Model

Peer tutors need specific training in order to be effective. The following training components are based on guidelines outlined by Campbell and Campbell (1995):

1. *Peer tutoring directions:* Peer tutoring directions consist of an instructional sequence and a script for teaching a particular task. The sequence provides the order of teaching; the tutoring script states exactly what the tutor says to the student, the reinforcement and correction methods the tutor should use, and strategies to collect data.

2. *Session information:* The teacher determines the materials that will be needed, the length of time of the tutoring session, and the location where the session will be held.

3. Tutors are trained using five general steps

   - *Model tutoring:* The teacher models the tutoring process with the tutor.

   - *Guided practice:* The tutor practices his or her role with the teacher, who plays the tutee; the teacher then provides feedback on the tutor's performance.

   - *Supervised practice:* The tutor practices with a typical classmate who role-plays the tutee and gives the tutor additional practice time. The teacher observes and then provides feedback.

   - *Training:* The peer tutor conducts a session with his or her assigned tutee. The teacher observes and provides feedback

following the session. The teacher conducts periodic observations to support the tutor.

   - *Evaluation:* The teacher makes follow-up observations to determine whether the tutor needs additional training or if any other changes are needed (e.g., materials, teaching method, tutor–tutee pairing, schedule, or model of peer tutoring).

This approach to peer tutoring is strikingly different from the typical "pair-them-up-and-hope-it-works" approach. Because training and supervision are essential features of this peer tutoring approach, it may be useful for a team of teachers to work together to establish a peer tutoring program. Once the peer tutoring process is in place and supported by a group of teachers, it should not be overwhelming and can, therefore, be maintained for years. The Tutoring Guide form located on page 172 in Appendix B of this booklet can be used by teachers to plan a peer tutoring program.

DESIGNS FOR PEER TUTORING PROGRAMS

There are many program designs for implementing peer tutoring programs. Figure 5.10 describes several of them. Most tutoring programs contain six elements: 1) partner pairing strategies, 2) teaching roles for tutors, 3) regularly scheduled sessions, 4) materials adapted

Reciprocal peer tutoring	Fixed tutor/tutee roles
Classwide Peer Tutoring (CWPT) (Delquadri et al., 1986)	Cross-Age Tutoring (Tutee younger than tutor): 1) Tutor performs at grade level 2) Tutor performs below grade level or has an IEP but has the skills needed by Tutee
Tutoring within Cooperative Learning Groups (Dugan et al., 1995)	Peer Tutoring (Tutor and Tutee are the same age)

Figure 5.10.   Designs for peer tutoring programs. (*Note:* May yield meaningful learning by tutee, but does not promote mutual interdependence; not likely to lead to the formation of reciprocal social relationships or a mentoring relationship.)

for tutoring, 5) frequent tests to evaluate learning, and 6) teacher monitoring of tutoring activities (Greenwood & Terry, 1997).

Two program designs and specific examples of each are described next.

Reciprocal Peer Tutoring

Classwide Peer Tutoring   Juniper Gardens Children's Project first developed Classwide Peer Tutoring (CWPT) in the late 1970s as an intervention for improving children's learning in urban classrooms (Delquadri, Greenwood, Whorton, Carta, & Hall, 1986). Researched initially as a successful approach for building academic skills for all participants and, more recently, for building social interaction skills between students with disabilities and their peers without disabilities, the CWPT program involves tutor-tutee pairs who work together on competing teams. *A reciprocal approach is used with CWPT; peers alternate in their roles of tutor and tutee.* The following are key elements of the CWPT procedure:

1. The teacher introduces or reviews material to be learned.

2. The teacher prepares the content materials that will be tutored (e.g., reading passages, spelling word lists, or math fact lists).

3. New partners are assigned each week.

4. A partner pairing strategy is applied (e.g., high-performing student with low-performing student) and the class is divided into teams that are balanced in ability.

5. Reciprocal tutoring is used, during which paired students alternate roles during a session; the teacher may use a timer to indicate the end of a 10-minute period for each partner as the tutor and then as the tutee (e.g., the role of the tutor was to read a word from the week's spelling list, the role of the tutee was to spell the word out loud and write it down).

6. Teams compete for the highest team point total.

7. Individual tutees earn points contingent on their performance (e.g., two points for correct answer, one point for corrected answer).

8. Tutors provide immediate error correction to tutee.

9. Individual and team scores are posted in the classroom (e.g., individual points were added daily and logged on the team's chart, individual and team points were added at the end of the week to determine the winning team and the three best spellers of the week).

10. Social rewards are given to the winning team (Greenwood, Delquadri, & Carta, 1988).

These 10 generic steps involved in CWPT can be modified to suit individual learners and classrooms.

The materials used in CWPT are important. Reciprocal tutoring involves the random pairing of students, though one student should have higher academic ability and the other lower ability. Each member of the pair alternates between being the tutor and being tutored. Therefore, for peer tutoring to work effectively, teachers must design individualized materials (e.g., spelling word lists) and ensure that tutors are adequately trained.

1. The learning materials for the *partner with fewer skills* need to suit that student's ability level despite the fact that they will be relatively easy for the partner serving as tutor. Tutor training and classroom practices should emphasize an individualization philosophy: "Just because we are in the same class does not mean that we all learn the same things at the same time." Higher-ability tutors need to rid themselves of elitist attitudes in order to fill their tutor role effectively.

2. The materials for dyad *members with more advanced skills* must also be matched to their ability, or the tutoring will be wasted time. When their partners (with fewer skills) are in the tutor role, the materials and training must be organized so that the difficulty level of the tutoring materials does not interfere with the tutor's effectiveness.

Note that, unlike some of the cooperative approaches discussed thus far, some level of competition is encouraged with the CWPT design. Students' rewards depend not just on their own performances but also on the collective performance of their partners and team.

As with cooperative groups in which students help each other and have interdependent roles, the CWPT approach rotates the tutor-tutee roles, though in a more structured way, with timers to signal turn-taking. This feature of reciprocity (or mutual role sharing) promotes cooperative interdependence.

Combining Peer Tutoring and Cooperative Learning Groups   Adding reciprocal peer tutoring to cooperative learning groups is an effective means for providing group members with directed practice on targeted concepts or facts; in addition to working together as a whole group to achieve a specified goal, students would pair up to briefly, review the learning matter, then rotate roles (Figure 5.5). Students could start with 10 minutes of peer tutoring to review materials from the previous lesson, then add new material just prior to breaking into cooperative groups. A brief tutoring session also might be placed at the end of the cooperative group activity to review or increase students' proficiency in the major concepts that the group activity addressed.

Fixed Tutor/Tutee Roles

Cross-Age Tutoring Programs   There are two basic types of cross-age tutoring programs. The first type involves *older students, who are performing at grade level and are familiar with the subject matter, tutoring younger students who are just learning the material.* The age difference between the tutor and tutee facilitates a positive, mentoring relationship. These tutoring programs focus on meeting the learning needs of younger children who may be performing below grade level and receiving special education services. As with any approach, tutor training and careful planning between the students' teachers is essential for program success.

Susan's team decided that she would benefit from having an older student tutor her rather than one of her classmates, which they thought might interfere with the development of social relationships between Susan and her peers. Once Susan agreed to the idea, her special education teacher, Ms. Bradley, worked with the seventh-grade team to identify 10 students who wanted to fulfill the middle school service requirement by learning something about teaching.

These students worked with Ms. Bradley to learn the tutoring methods; then, in cooperation with their homeroom teachers and the fourth- and fifth-grade classroom teachers who had identified 10 students, including Susan, needing tutors, they paired tutors and tutees and selected days and times for the tutors to walk to the elementary school that adjoined the middle school and work with the fourth and fifth graders. Aside from meeting her academic goals, Susan also made friends in the school she would transition to the following year (Figure 5.11).

In addition to the tutees' learning the necessary information, a second model of cross-age tutoring focuses on having *tutors learn through their teaching role* (Gartner & Lipsky, 1990). This arrangement can be particularly useful for tutors who are performing below their grade level. These tutors are paired with younger students who are also performing at a lower grade level, allowing the tutor to benefit via the teaching process while the tutee learns the information. A variation of this procedure could institute cross-age tutoring across two entire classes, one of older students and one of

---

Tutoring Guide

Subject: _Math_   **When:** _1_ to _1:30_   _M W F_

Skill: _Additional facts_   **Where:** _reading alcove in classroom_

Performance: *When presented with single-digit addition facts on flash cards, Susan will correctly solve nine out of ten facts.*

Materials: *Flashcards*
      Data collection form
      Pencil
      Card box

Student to be Tutored/Teacher: *Susan (5th grade, Ms. Berlier's class)*
Tutor/Teacher: *Marie (7th grade, Mr. Randell's class)*

Tutor Directions:
1. *Present one flashcard at a time.*
2. *Wait 5 seconds for tutee to respond.*
3. *If response is correct, say, "good job," and record a "+" next to that fact on the data form; return the card to the card box.*
4. *If no response or an incorrect response is given, record a "0" next to the fact on the data form. Then, model the correct response (e.g. say, "6 + 7 = 13; what is 6 + 7 ?"), and allow the tutee to respond again following the correction.*
5. *If tutee makes a correct response following a correction, say, "Good job." If the tutee makes an error after a correction, model the correct response and place the card at the bottom of the stack. Present this card again at the end of the session.*
6. *Present the next item.*

Reinforcement: *Praise Susan each time she responds correctly (e.g., "Good job").*

Correction Procedure: *Model correct response, and allow Susan to respond again following the correction.*

Evaluation: *Record a "+" for correct responses on the first try and a "0" for incorrect responses.*

Figure 5.11.   Tutoring guide for Susan's seventh-grade tutor. (Adapted from Campbell & Campbell, 1995.)

younger students. Some teachers use this approach for DEAR time (Drop Everything and Read), using cross-age tutoring pairs to facilitate reading at the lower grade level.

Students with disabilities are often neglected as potential tutors because *they* are seen as the students who need help; however, providing these students with opportunities to serve in the tutoring role can be quite beneficial. With adequate planning and training, students with disabilities can fill the role of tutor by using the CWPT model or a cross-age tutoring program design. Gartner and Lipsky (1990) described an innovative program implemented through Brigham Young University in which children with disabilities tutored peers with and without disabilities in areas such as sign language and reading. This program demonstrated that students with disabilities could learn to perform effectively as tutors; both tutors and tutees improved academically, and many tutors also experienced increased social acceptance as a result of tutoring typical peers (Gartner & Lipsky, 1990).

Cooperative learning classrooms are places where heterogeneous groups of students learn to work together and accept one another while also achieving positive academic and social outcomes. Peer tutoring programs facilitate cooperation among peers and can provide both tutors and tutees with academic and social benefits. Tutor selection, tutor training, systematic tutor–tutee matching, and supervision are essential elements of effective programs. Tutoring sessions provide students with increased opportunities to practice skills. Social benefits of tutoring take the form of increased social acceptance for both the students who fill tutoring roles and the tutees who have older students as tutors.

Chapter 6

Getting Started and Keeping it Going

Student Snapshot

Jennifer has cognitive disabilities and performs academics at a first- to second-grade level. She readily speaks, though she often uses a simpler vocabulary than her fifth-grade classmates; she is social but not readily included in class networks. To assess issues they faced with each factor influencing Jennifer's social relationships, team members used the Social Relationship Worksheet (Figure 6.1). As they focused on each factor, they pooled what they knew and reached agreement; however, in some areas they sought additional information. After reviewing all areas and isolating influencing factors (left column of worksheet), they identified actions to be taken (right column). Using an Issue/Action Planning Form (Figure 6.2), they discussed possible actions they might take by reviewing and checking the actions listed in the worksheet's right column and brainstorming others. As the group made decisions about the actions they would take, they identified people responsible and set dates for when these actions would be implemented.

Jennifer's team decided to focus on several things at once. To improve her opportunities for interaction with classmates, they planned to improve her one-to-one teaching sessions by adding peers; they also decided to implement weekly cross-age tutoring for Jennifer using several eighth graders. They thought a tutor would help motivate improvement in reading skills and give Jennifer practice with more mature interactions. Second, they wanted to build peer support and motivate her to interact with peers in age-appropriate ways; to do this, they planned to start a lunch pals club. Jennifer's team identified specific actions they would take in these areas, determined who would be responsible, and set dates. For the social competence factor, the team identified issues around a general lack of cooperative skills among class members. They decided to explore classwide social skills using a skills checklist from the ACCESS program (suitable for fifth graders and familiar to the special

education teacher) and then discussed possible instruction with this program and also in using cooperative learning groups. If these seemed needed and feasible, they would seek in-service from the elementary supervisor on cooperative groups and from Merrill (the special education teacher) on ASSET (Hazel, Schumaker, Sherman, & Sheldon-Wildgen, 1981). Jennifer's mom agreed to explore strategies in the generalization component (memberships in 4-H and Scouts) and report back at the next monthly meeting.

Consistent with what is stated in previous chapters, it is suggested that schools follow some general guidelines when planning, selecting, and implementing social support plans:

1. *Use collaborative teams to make decisions and implement actions.*

2. *Examine the student's current social relationships as the yardstick for identifying needs and judging success.*

3. *Involve students in the process* of planning, problem-solving, implementing, and evaluating the social support plan.

4. *Seek team consensus, and then take the simplest, yet still effective, actions first:* This often translates into increasing social opportunities before undertaking more complex actions.

5. *Contextualize teaching* by embedding it in daily routines and natural social contexts.

6. *Don't let supports become barriers to social interaction:* Hovering adults, overzealous "helpers," stigmatizing support or instruction, and a failure to fade assistance will hinder natural peer-to-peer contact.

FACTORS INFLUENCING SOCIAL RELATIONSHIPS

Social relationships among and between children are influenced by many factors: parental resources, social preferences, and values; the family's income level; the neighborhood density, location, and safety; the child's tempera-

Social Relationship Worksheet

Classroom: _Lynn Harris, 5th grade_   **School:** _Roundhill Elementary_   **Date:** _10/4/99_

Focus Student(s): _Jennifer_   **Team Members:** _Lynn (5th grade teacher),_

Merrill (special education teacher), Boyce (Jennifer's mom), Ed (physical education teacher),

Sally (guidance counselor)

Factors influencing social participation and relationships	Actions taken by individuals in school, classroom, and home to improve social contexts and skills
Opportunity: Being physically present around typical peers on a regular basis with routine and spontaneous occasions to interact. **Issues?** (Yes) No **List priority issues:** _Too much one-to-one teaching time_	❏ Assign all students to general education classes with needed supports. ❏ Increase time in general education classes. ❏ Create during- and after-school social interaction options through friendship groups, peer support clubs, and so forth. ☑ Reduce one-to-one time with adults. ☑ Add in peers and increase small-group instruction. ☑ Integrate student seating in class, at lunch, in school activities. ❏ Identify and create integrated community options.
Atmosphere: Prevailing staff and student attitudes toward human differences and talents and related values people hold about social relationships, peer support, a competitive versus a cooperative focus, student involvement in the resolution of social concerns, regard for everyone's unique talents, and so forth. **Issues?** (Yes) No **List priority issues:** 1. _Class seems less cooperative than last year._ 2. _Respect is lacking across group; respect others' abilities, value your peer groups, listen & consider other opinions._	❏ Have staff examine values toward ability, disability, and learning. ❏ Involve staff, parents, and students in creating a school mission statement. ❏ Organize ability and disability awareness activities. ❏ Organize grade-level service activities. ☑ Hold teacher in-service on cooperative learning and support for its use in classrooms. ❏ Explore alternatives to ability grouping and competitive activities. ❏ Hold staff training on social skills and relationships and their facilitation. ☑ Adopt and use a social skills curriculum. ❏ Train staff and students in collaborative teaming and problem solving. ☑ Offer student forums on social concerns such as teasing and ridicule; engage students in problem-solving school solutions. ❏ Increase the number and range of extra-curricular opportunities for students to use and develop their unique talents. _(continued)_

Figure 6.1.   Social Relationship Worksheet for Jennifer. (Adapted from Breen, Haring, Weiner, Laitinen, & Bernstein, 1991.)

Figure 6.1.   *(continued)*

Social support and motivation: Having the needed supports and encouragement from adults and peers to interact socially and build relationships. **Issues?** (Yes) No **List priority issues:** *Jennifer seems to lack motivation for improving her interactions with peers.*	❑ Explore types of adult facilitation that can encourage appropriate social interactions (e.g., modeling, backing off). ☑ Explore types of peer support (e.g., peer groups using problem-solving & goal setting; friendship groups, natural relationships strategies). ❑ Adjust and fade adult facilitation and supports. ❑ Identify interaction problems (e.g., aggression, excess teasing, isolation); plan and use teaching and peer supports to improve student behavior. ❑ Identify and resolve barriers to social interaction (e.g., schedules, student hygiene, peer network values). ❑ Improve communication rates by addressing student motivation, communication system, or social skill performance. ☑ Involve students; examine the social contexts for interest, variety, age/ability match, cooperative features, participation, and needed modifications. ☑ Use or improve peer networks.
Academic achievement: Possessing needed academic skills (e.g., in such areas as reading, writing, math, science, social studies, vocational and community training) and the confidence that comes from having and using these skills. **Concerns:** (Yes) No **List top concerns:** *Is her reading where it should be? How to improve small-group instruction?*	❑ Add what is needed to enable students to succeed in learning needed skills (e.g., student choice and involvement in IEP and program, incentives for learning, accommodations, environmental changes, modifications in schoolwork that are only as special as necessary). ☑ Make use of reciprocal peer tutoring and cross-age tutoring. ❑ Add cooperative learning methods to science, math, social studies, and literature lessons.
Social competence and interaction skills: Being able to initiate interactions with peers, respond to peers' initiations, and elaborate on the initiations or responses of peers at a typical rate. **Issues?** (Yes) No	☑ Adopt and use a social skills curriculum. ❑ Examine skills involved in social interactions and identify acquisition and performance problems or competing behaviors. ❑ Plan and use teaching methods and peer supports to improve social skill problems. ☑ Involve students in planning.

Figure 6.1. *(continued)*

List priority issues: *social skills are lacking across class.*	❑ Identify student's communication ability; target needed skills (e.g., improve rate, expand vocabulary, improve consistency, augment with communication book/device for clarity). ❑ Check peers' skills using alternative modes of communicating. ❑ Determine nonstigmatizing ways to teach (format, methods) within routine contexts.
Maintenance and generalization of relationships: Keeping and extending social relationships as well as remembering and transferring known social skills across different people and school and nonschool settings. **Issues?** (Yes) No **List priority issues:** *Improve behavior next year in middle school for Jennifer and several classmates.*	❑ Contextualize any instruction. ❑ Use adult facilitation in natural contexts. ☑ Fade adult facilitation to self-monitoring. ❑ Teach students to problem-solve; encourage their independent use of these skills. ☑ Teach students to self-manage. ☑ Involve family. ❑ Include social support in IEP. ☑ Plan for transition across classrooms and schools and to community and employment settings.

ment and emotional self-control; the presence or absence of a disability in the child and any counterbalancing abilities, talents, and supports; and the school and classroom a child attends, the social opportunities and instruction offered, and the student's level of achievement and success. All of these factors, and certainly others, can have an influence on a child's social activities, interaction style, and numbers and types of companions. Although some of these influences originate at the individual and family levels, others may begin within the classroom or school.

"Getting started" usually requires team members to make some informal assessment of each of six factors: opportunities, atmosphere, social support and motivation, academic success, social competence and interaction skills, and maintenance and generalization of relationships. Assessment might be directed toward a whole classroom or an individual student. When a factor is found to be weak and

specific issues of concern are identified, teams need to plan ways to strengthen the conditions so that supportive social relationships can develop in their school community.

The Social Relationship Worksheet (Figure 6.1) provides the team with a format to plan school and classroom improvements. The worksheet lists the factors that influence social participation and provides a partial listing of effective strategies alongside each factor. When planning school and classroom improvements, teams first meet and use the worksheet to identify any issues they have across the six influencing factors. Then, they target several priority issues for problem-solving, taking care to address first the issues that have team consensus and a strong influence on social relationships. Finally, teams should use an Issue/Action Planning Form (Figure 6.2) as they focus on each issue to record their ideas and identify who is responsible for taking action and when the action should be taken.

Issue/Action Planning Form

Student/Team/Group: _____ *Jennifer and 5th grade class* _____ **Date:** ___ *10/11/99* ___

Team Members Present: _____ *Lynn (5th grade teacher), Merrill (special education teacher),*

Boyce (Jennifer's mom), Sally (guidance counselor) _____

Issue	Planned action	Person(s) responsible	By when
Too much one-to-one instruction	Add one to two peers to J's math and reading.	Lynn, Merrill	11/5
Little interaction with peers at lunch	Start a lunch pals club that will eat once a week in old resource room; explore during peer planning.	Merrill	10/29 10/13
Lack of motivation for improving her social skills; reading skills not progressing fast	Contact Millie Jones in middle school; draw on her cross-age peer tutoring program for 8th graders.	Merrill	10/18
Class social skills need improvement: Respect for different opinions, abilities, friends	Explore ACCESS program. Use skill assessment on whole class. Plan how to integrate 5th grade guidance objectives with ACCESS program.	Lynn, Merrill Lynn, Sally	10/18 10/25 10/15
Behavior and social group issues in middle school	Meet with middle school special education teacher to plan spring visitation; call to set date. Visit middle school and observe lunch and in-between-class routines.	Merrill Merrill & Boyce	End of October Early Nov.

Figure 6.2.   Issue/Action Planning Form for Jennifer.

Some of the actions and changes people make in schools can improve the conditions for supportive social relationships, but other actions will make conditions less conducive to social relationships. When teams can coordinate their planning with administrators and communicate their rationale to the larger group (administrators, parents, and peers), unexpected social barriers can often be prevented.

CLASS COMPOSITION: SOCIAL NETWORKS AND STUDENT DISTRIBUTION

Sometimes, things done with good intentions in schools actually are counterproductive to the formation of pos-

itive social relationships in school environments. As teams complete the Social Relationships Worksheet for students, they must also be alert to the influence of existing social networks and class distribution on their planned activities. For example, a paraprofessional could be assigned to a student who has multiple disabilities in order to address the student's extra support needs; however, in doing so, the student may be prevented from interacting with his or her classmates. Unique attendance and transportation schedules that are adopted for students with physical and cognitive disabilities could reduce interaction opportunities and complicate extracurricular activities. Other errors that are often made include a failure to recognize the ways in which kids rapidly change during their school years, the effects these changes have on their social relationships, and the failure of teachers and school staff to make the program modifications that are needed to balance the students' development.

The composition of a classroom, which can be planned by teachers and administrators to a certain extent, can help or hinder the formation of social relationships. Class composition influences a student's social position and the networks to which the individual student belongs. The work of Farmer and Farmer (1996), which studied third- and fourth-grade classrooms, and their colleagues' related work with 16 mainstream elementary classrooms suggests that students with learning disabilities and emotional disturbances are *not* outcasts in mainstream environments; these students were well integrated into their classroom's social structure, though not in random ways. Some patterns and subtleties in the studied students' relationships provide clues about classroom social structures and the social positions of students with disabilities. Each classroom had three distinct clusters (social network groups)—prosocial, antisocial, and shy; the students who filled these roles were influenced by the cluster members' characteristics and the composition of the classroom. Clusters were not randomly formed but seemed to be influenced both by the class composition and the members' characteristics; members were similar to each other with regard to personal and/or social characteristics (e.g., popular girls; shy boys; aggressive, athletic boys; antisocial boys). Some clusters had high centrality in the classroom's social structure; others had low. Both boys and girls filled prosocial clusters and held high to low positions within their cluster; however, some students were isolated and not associated with any cluster. There were no cross-gender clusters in these three third- and fourth-grade classrooms.

Farmer and Farmer's (1996) findings, along with the findings of other researchers, have clear implications for planning class composition in ways that will promote positive social relationships for many students.

- Special education classroom cultures were viewed as being "likely to severely constrain students' social development and impede rather than enhance the likelihood that they will learn positive social skills that generalize to other environments" (Farmer, Pearl, & Van Acker, 1996, p. 249).

- The behavior of mainstreamed students labeled as having emotional disturbances seemed to vary substantially depending on the availability of compatible partners, suggesting that the number of students with emotional disturbances per classroom be limited to encourage less antisocial behavior.

- Proportionally, more of the mainstreamed students with disabilities (39%) than students without disabilities (31%) held highly prominent membership in a highly prominent peer group (Farmer & Hollowell, 1994). Students with disabilities were not outcasts. Unfortunately, the students with disabilities held these positions because of, not in spite of, their problematic behavior; some teachers commented that these students were "more or less in charge of the social climate of the classroom" (Farmer et al., 1996, p. 250). Under these circumstances, general education class membership could actually hinder the social development of students with emotional disturbances. Farmer and Hollowell's research lends support to limiting the number of students with antisocial behavior in a classroom, attending to the overall composition of each class, teaching social skills on a classwide basis, and examining the social networks within a class as part of the plan for fostering positive social relationships.

- These researchers advised educators to have a critical mass of boys receiving gifted services in one general education classroom (two or three); this enabled the boys to form a core prosocial group and to support their prosocial behavior and diminish antisocial behavior.

- In these classrooms studies, the social integration of African American students in classrooms (regardless of whether they received special education services, gifted services, or neither) was less than ideal, particularly for girls. Additional study of larger groups is needed, but two things were found: Girls were not well integrated into the classroom's social structure, and boys were disproportionately members of antisocial clusters. Both race and gender, therefore, play a role in the social structure of a classroom and the social clusters that form; these aspects of classroom composition need to be sensitively considered when designing social support plans.

One clear conclusion is that "The composition of students in a classroom appeared to affect the possible positions any individual would hold within the structure" (Farmer & Farmer, 1996, p. 448) The ways in which teachers can influence class composition from year to year is not a simple issue. Grade-level teams and principals must work cooperatively to plan classes with a balance of students so that class composition is not a barrier to the development of positive social relationships. Although classroom planning is possible in the elementary grades, it is complicated in middle and high school by a variety of factors, including departmental organization, credits and requirements for graduation, class designations (e.g., general, advanced placement, honors), and course entry requirements.

Rule of Natural Proportions

The rule of natural proportions is an important guideline that can help teachers plan their class composition. This rule states that the percentage of students with disabilities in a given classroom should not exceed the percentage expected in the larger school population (e.g., in a school where approximately 10% of the students have IEPs, a classroom of 25 should not have more than two or three students with IEPs, only 1 of whom might have more extensive support needs). Furthermore, it would be wise to spread out students who are "antisocial" or who act out and provide the classes to which those students are assigned with the needed supports. This same guideline also advises teachers to avoid an imbalance in gender or racial composition. An exception to this "rule" applies to students

receiving gifted services; they should be assigned to classrooms in gender-matched groups of two or three students rather than being isolated by themselves. This exception may be more important for boys than for girls; it would allow boys to form a prosocial network and to avoid grouping themselves with antisocial boys or being isolated. Because girls' clusters more often accept the characteristic of "being good at schoolwork," girls getting gifted services appear to be less at risk for membership in antisocial groups or exclusion. Finally, existing supportive relationships and networks for students who have been isolated or socially needy should be maintained when possible.

Building Peer Support Networks within Classrooms

Teachers can use cooperative groups to build peer support within a classroom, particularly when the classroom contains a heterogeneous combination of students. This topic was covered in some detail in the previous chapter; however, Meyer and Henry (1993) suggested some additional ways for teachers to address the issues of isolated students and antisocial or noncooperative social networks that often exist in classrooms. Meyer and Henry found that some students who were socially isolated fit the description of being clinically depressed; others were aggressive, engaged in acting-out behavior, and belonged to social clusters in which other students followed their lead. Some of the students had special education labels, although many did not; most were included in general education classes. All of the students disliked school. Some of the students' peers believed that the students were treated unfairly by teachers or were treated according to a double standard; classroom rules were enforced when these students violated them but bent when more cooperative or more social students violated them. Teachers were not always aware of their differential rule enforcement.

In order to create a community for their students that was more supportive than that of most middle schools, teachers organized themselves into interdisciplinary teams of six to seven teachers, and each team made a 2-year commitment to a group of 135 seventh graders. Teams used an assessment device (School Rating Scale; Meyer & Henry, 1993; see Chapter 4, Table 4.1) to identify students who seemed to need peer support. Teams met weekly to share their ideas and impressions and to problem-solve difficulties concerning the focus students and other specific students. Cooperative groups, heterogeneous in composition, were organized in each class using the criteria in Figure 6.3. These cooperative groups functioned as peer support networks with the goal of identifying potential friends for students who were at risk for being unable to gain peer support on their own. Reconfiguring the class into cooperative groups allowed teachers to create peer support networks using criteria and information that each student reported about him- or herself after about 1 month of school; this informa-

tion included the student's name, grade, gender, race, favorite activity outside school, and preferences specific to the class content (e.g., strengths and interests relating to English class). These groups functioned both as peer support networks and as cooperative learning groups in class and remained intact for a minimum of the 10-week grading period, though sometimes changes were needed. Meyer and Henry reported positive changes in academic progress during the group activities and in social connections with peers.

Eric is a student who displays few signs of engagement during classroom instruction. During the cooperative learning structure in math class, Eric's behavior and performance changed dramatically. In other classes, Eric would slump in his seat and show all the signs of disengagement—this was most pronounced when the teacher

---

General Criteria for Groups

Each group in the class period should be heterogeneous with respect to

- Gender
- Ethnicity (e.g., African American, Native American, European American)
- Achievement levels in the subject area
- Academic ability
- Preferred in-class activities (e.g., writing versus speaking)

Specific Criteria for Peer Support Networking

With rare exceptions, each group should contain no more than one "at-risk" student per group.

If a student receiving English as a Second Language services is in the group, try to also include another student who is bilingual (same first language) but more fluent in English.

Avoid potentially explosive or otherwise negative group combinations (e.g., two volatile students who would set one another off, a "macho" boy with "victims," too many off-task students within one group).

Try to plant one "worker" and/or a "diplomat/peacekeeper" in each of the groups.

Building Specific Peer Supports

For each group, select at least one and possibly two students who might be a potential friend for the student at risk. These matches should

- Be good influences/models
- Have similar academic ability (although doing better academically and/or attending school more regularly)
- Seem to be a good personality match with the at-risk child (How to judge? Use your observations/best hunches)

Figure 6.3. Criteria for constructing peer support networks. (From Meyer, L.H., & Henry, L.A. [1993]. Cooperative classroom management: Student needs and fairness in the regular classroom. In J.W. Putnam [Ed.], *Cooperative learning and strategies for inclusion: Celebrating diversity in the classroom* [pp. 93–121]. Baltimore: Paul H. Brookes Publishing Co.; reprinted by permission.)

was presenting material in a traditional lecture format. In contrast, during cooperative learning group time, he voluntarily participated and actually led his group through the assignments. He became a group leader, helping those who did not understand, encouraging peers, and keeping the group on task.

 The change was particularly evident during shop period. For a month, Eric entered the shop class at the bell and talked to no one during the entire period. A student from the special education class was then placed in the shop class during this period, and the teacher paired him with Eric, using the buddy system to provide the exceptional student with a natural support. Eric took the student under his wing, answering questions, instructing, and guiding him through the individual projects. Once the other student had the opportunity to see how well Eric worked with his assigned buddy, they began asking him questions and for help on their projects. By the end of the 10-week marking period, Eric had become a major source of support and assistance for peers, who either voluntarily sought his assistance or were guided to him by the teacher. (Meyer & Henry, 1993, p. 117)

Class composition can have positive or negative effects on social relationships and interactions. For this reason, teachers need to be constantly aware of the interplay between social networks and of the distribution of students by gender, race, ability level, and disability. Planning can help promote the positive effects of diversity; assigning students to cooperative learning groups can help reconfigure peer networks and create the opportunity for isolated students to be included.

SUSTAINING RELATIONSHIPS AND INTEGRATING THEM INTO STUDENTS' LIVES AFTER SCHOOL

Thus far, this booklet has primarily focused on the school environment for building social rela-

tionships among peers. However, for every school day, there is time after school; for every school week, there is a weekend; and for every school year, there is a summer. The manner in which peer supports and relationships survive vacations depends heavily on the student's family and the student; however, they can be positively influenced by team planning as well. When a team is successful in fostering strong social networks for students with or without disabilities, the positive forces of the relationships act to sustain them. Typically, classmates who are friends will talk about one another at home, ask their parents for permission to get together, call each other on the telephone, and invite each other to participate in activities. When a student's friend is fairly different than his or her typical peer with regard to ability, means of communicating, or mobility, parents of the typical student may not be as open to sustaining the relationship; this is often due to fear, a lack of knowledge of and experience with children with disabilities, worry about liability or equipment, and even prejudice. There are several approaches schools can take to help sustain friendships during nonschool hours; however, these approaches vary according to the students' ages, social/cultural protocol in the community and within the students' families, and the schools' comfort in being involved.

Familiarizing the Parents of Classmates with Each Other and with Peer Support Efforts

For students in elementary and middle school, parents typically like to know the peers with whom their children participate in after-school activities. Neighborhood schools provide greater proximity among classmates than do systems that bus students with disabilities. Proximity may mean that kids actually live in the same neighborhood, which makes after-school visiting easier. Despite proximity, many parents will be unfamiliar with the parents of their child's classmates.

 Teachers can promote cross-classroom familiarity among parents in several ways. *First, teachers can share, through PTA meetings and class newsletters, information* about the peer support programs (name, purpose, and activities performed) or friendship programs they initiate in their classrooms. Because parental permission will be required for students to participate in these activities, parents will receive some information beforehand. Teachers can send home newsletters and use parent–teacher conferences to update parents on the progress of these groups and to keep parents informed.

Second, teachers can put together class "telephone books," though parental permission will be necessary. Even having a list of each child's name (with or without his or her address, parents' names, and telephone) can be helpful to parents of class members.

Third, family activities might be planned on a classwide, grade-level, or schoolwide basis to bring parents and classmates together more often; activities might include class plays or concerts, potluck dinners, field day events, or class trips with family support. In middle school and high school, school orientations; parent-teacher conferences; PTA-sponsored events (e.g., spaghetti dinner, spring fling, craft fair); and sports, school plays, and musical activities (e.g., band, chorus) are the primary ways families socialize with other families at school. These various activities can familiarize parents with their child's classmates and family members and may facilitate out-of-school efforts to maintain friendships.

Setting Goals to Sustain Relationships Outside School

When building peer support into a student's IEP, teams should focus not only on the school day but also on the student's free time after school and during summer vacations. Many school systems or communities have summer recreation programs or educational or library reading programs. Teams might encourage members from peer networks to enroll in such activities together. Clubs such as Scouts or 4-H and recreational sports teams such as soccer or baseball leagues for adolescents provide other opportunities for children to get together after school and during the summer. Teachers can also organize classwide or grade-level summer activities (e.g., service

activities, community cleanup, school improvement efforts, reading programs) to bring students together during the summer. In some classrooms, especially in elementary schools, teachers assist parents in setting up telephone trees and car pools to facilitate student participation in class activities; if these organizational efforts are useful to families, they are often naturally maintained by parents over the summer or for weekend activities.

Addressing Physical Disabilities Outside School

If a child has special needs with regard to transportation (e.g., assistance in getting in and out of a wheelchair, adaptive equipment storage, special seating) or health or feeding concerns, the student's family members will often need to become actively involved in group activities before other parents will become comfortable with transportation or supervision of the child. When children are young, it is not unusual for their parents to accompany them to activities and take care of their needs; however, hovering parents or grandparents can be just as damaging to peer interactions as hovering teaching assistants. Finding solutions to these kinds of after-school barriers will be up to the student's team and the student him- or herself; but when approved by the focus student, the student's classmates or peers can also become involved in problem-solving.

Some older students who have restricted voluntary movement will not want to share their personal needs for support (e.g., assistance with using the bathroom, getting into pajamas before a slumber party) but will want to attend the entire activity without having a parent there to help. Other students will be less aware of or concerned with receiving the physical help they need (e.g., eating, dressing, toileting) to enable their participation in an activity. The solutions to these situations will be highly individualized, although problem-solvers will all focus on a common goal: to include the focus student in a way that is non-stigmatizing, allows active participation, and provides enjoyment.

Making Peer Support Programs Permanent

Much of the work that goes into developing peer facilitation programs occurs during the planning and initial implementation phases. Because of their broad investment and use, peer facilitation programs are more likely to be maintained year after year when schools work together as a community to plan, pilot, and extend them. If the task is left up to several special education teachers or to an isolated classroom teacher who happens to be "good at that sort of thing," it is much more difficult to keep social relationship support efforts active. When principals lend their support to efforts to implement a peer facilitation program and when staff identify such an effort as a school goal, the task is legitimized and shared.

Once a program geared toward improving peer social relationships has been piloted, school staff members may want to informally evaluate its outcomes and seek ways to improve it, expand it, and make it more efficient to maintain. For example, when high school students were given credit for participating in a regular friendship activity with a student who had extensive disabilities, less effort was needed to recruit additional participants and schedule their interactions; therefore, staff members were able to spend more time preparing the participating general education student and guiding the interaction, allowing for more substantive relationships (Helmstetter, Peck, & Giangreco, 1994; Keachie, 1997a). When a cross-age tutoring program was judged a success for tutors and tutees, it became a regular cooperative program between the eighth and fifth graders in two adjoining schools (a middle and an elementary school); school resources were assigned to support the effort and consequently the program recurred every year.

References

Achenbach, T.M. (1991). *The Child Behavior Checklist: Manual for the Teacher's Report Form.* Burlington: University of Vermont, Department of Psychiatry.

Americans with Disabilities Act (ADA) of 1990, PL 101-336, 42 U.S.C. §§ 12101 *et seq.*

Aronson, E. (1978). *The jigsaw classroom.* Thousand Oaks, CA: Sage Publications.

Ayres, B., O'Brien, L., & Rogers, T. (1992). *Working together, sharing and helping each other: Cooperative learning in a first grade classroom that includes students with disabilities.* Syracuse, NY: Syracuse University, The Inclusive Education Project.

Bak, J.J., Cooper, E.M., Dobroth, K.M., & Siperstein, G. (1987). Special class placements as labels: Effects on children's attitudes toward learning handicapped peers. *Exceptional Children, 54,* 151–155.

Barton, E. (1986). Modification of children's prosocial behavior. In P.S. Strain, M.J. Guralnick, & H.M. Walker (Eds.), *Children's social behavior: Development, assessment, and modification* (pp. 331–372). Orlando, FL: Academic Press, Inc.

Baumeister, R.F., & Leary, M.R. (1995). The need to belong: Desire for interpersonal attachments as a fundamental human motivation. *Psychological Bulletin, 117,* 497–529.

Beckman, P.J., & Kohl, F.L. (1987). Interactions of preschoolers with and without handicaps in integrated and segregated settings: A longitudinal study. *Mental Retardation, 25,* 5–11.

Berliner, D.C. (1988). The half-full glass: A review of research on teaching. In E.L. Meyen, G.A. Vergason, & R.J. Whelan (Eds.), *Effective instructional strategies for exceptional children* (pp. 7–31). Denver, CO: Love Publishing.

Berman, S. (1990). The real ropes course: The development of social consciousness. *Educating for Social Responsibility, 1,* 1–18.

Berndt, T. (1989). Obtaining support from friends during childhood and adolescence. In D. Belle (Ed.), *Children's social networks and social supports* (pp. 308–331). New York: John Wiley & Sons, Inc.

Biklen, D., Corrigan, C., & Quick, D. (1989). Beyond obligation: Students' relations with each other in integrated classes. In D. Lipsky & A. Gartner (Eds.), *Beyond separate education: Quality education for all* (pp. 207–221). Baltimore: Paul H. Brookes Publishing Co.

Brady, M.P., & McEvoy, M.A. (1989). Social skills training as an integration strategy. In R. Gaylord-Ross (Ed.), *Integration strategies for students with handicaps* (pp. 213–231). Baltimore: Paul H. Brookes Publishing Co.

Breen, C.G. (1991). Setting up and managing peer support networks. In C.G. Breen, C.H. Kennedy, & T.G. Haring (Eds.), *Social context research project: Methods for facilitating the inclusion of students with disabilities in integrated school and community contexts* (pp. 54–104). Santa Barbara: University of California.

Breen, C.G., Haring, T.G., Weiner, J., Laitinen, R.E., & Bernstein, D.D. (1991). Evaluating the inclusion and social competence of students with severe disabilities in community and school environments. In C.G. Breen, C.H. Kennedy, & T.G. Haring (Eds.), *Social context research project: Methods for facilitating the inclusion of students with disabilities in integrated school and community contexts* (pp. 23–53). Santa Barbara: University of California.

Breen, C.G., & Lovinger, L. (1991). PAL (Partners at Lunch) Club: Evaluation of a program to support social relationships in a junior high school. In C.G. Breen, C.H. Kennedy, & T.G. Haring (Eds.), *Social context research project: Methods for facilitating the inclusion of students with disabilities in integrated school and community contexts* (pp. 106–128). Santa Barbara: University of California.

Bromfield, R., Weisz, J.R., & Messer, T. (1986). Children's judgments and attributions in response to the "mentally retarded" label: A developmental approach. *Journal of Abnormal Psychology, 95,* 81–87.

Brotherson, M.J., & Goldstein, B.L. (1992). Time as a resource and constraint for parents of young children with disabilities: Implications for early intervention services. *Topics in Early Childhood Special Education, 12,* 508–527.

Browder, D.M., Bambara, L.M., & Belifore, P.J. (1997). Using a person-centered approach in community-based instruction for adults with developmental disabilities. *Journal of Behavioral Education, 7,* 519–528.

Brown, B.B. (1990). Peer groups and peer cultures. In S.S. Feldman & G.R. Elliott (Eds.), *At the threshold: The developing adolescent* (pp. 171–196). Cambridge, MA: Harvard University Press.

Brown, B.B., & Lohr, M.J. (1987). Peer-group affiliation and adolescent self-esteem: An integration of ego-identity and symbolic-interaction theories. *Journal of Personality and Social Psychology, 52,* 47–55.

Brown, W.H., & Odom, S.L. (1994). Strategies and tactics for promoting generalization and maintenance of young children's social behavior. *Research in Developmental Disabilities, 15,* 99–118.

Bukowski, W.M., & Newcomb, A.F. (1984). Stability and determinants of sociometric status and friendship choice: A longitudinal perspective. *Developmental Psychology, 20,* 941–952.

Buysse, V., & Bailey, D.B., Jr. (1993). Behavioral and developmental outcomes in young children with disabilities in integrated and segregated settings: A review of comparative settings. *Journal of Special Education, 26,* 434–461.

Campbell, P.C., & Campbell, C.R. (1995). Peer involvement: Skills for involving nondisabled peers in the inclusive education school. In *Building inclusive schools: Innovative practices that support students with diverse learning abilities in neighborhood schools* (pp. 10–18). Lawrence: University of Kansas.

Carr, E.G., Levin, L., McConnachie, G., Carlson, J.I., Kemp, D.C., & Smith, C.E. (1994). *Communication-based intervention for problem behavior: A user's guide for producing positive change.* Baltimore: Paul H. Brookes Publishing Co.

Chadsey-Rusch, J. (1992). Toward defining and measuring social skills in employment settings. *American Journal on Mental Retardation, 96,* 405–418.

Chandler, L.K. (1992). Promoting children's social/survival skills as a strategy for transition to mainstreamed kindergarten programs. In S.L. Odom, S.R. McConnell, & M.A. McEvoy (Eds.), *Social competence of young children with disabilities* (pp. 245–276). Baltimore: Paul H. Brookes Publishing Co.

Clegg, J.A., & Standen, P.J. (1991). Friendship among adults who have developmental disabilities. *American Journal on Mental Retardation, 95,* 663–667.

Cochran, M., & Riley, D. (1988). Mothers' reports of children's personal networks: Antecedents, concomitants, and consequences. In S. Salzinger, J. Antrobus, & M. Hammer (Eds.), *Social networks of children, adolescents, and college students* (pp. 113–147). Mahwah, NJ: Lawrence Erlbaum Associates.

Cohen, P.A., Kulik, J.A., & Kulik, C. (1982). Educational outcomes of tutoring: A meta-analysis of findings. *American Educational Research Journal, 191,* 237–248.

Coie, J.D., Dodge, K.A., & Coppotelli, H. (1982). Dimensions of types of social status: A cross-age perspective. *Developmental Psychology, 18,* 557–560.

Cole, D.A., & Meyer, L.H. (1991). Social integration and severe disabilities: A longitudinal analysis of child outcomes. *Journal of Special Education, 25,* 340–351.

Corsaro, W.A. (1985). *Friendship and peer culture in the early years.* Norwood, NJ: Ablex Publishing Corp.

Cosden, M.A., & Haring, T.G. (1992). Cooperative learning in the classroom: Contingencies, group interactions, and students with special needs. *Journal of Behavioral Education, 2,* 53–71.

Davern, L., Ford, A., Erwin, E., Schnorr, R., & Rogan. P. (1993). *Working toward inclusive schools: Guidelines for developing a building-based process to create change.* Syracuse, NY: Syracuse University, The Inclusive Education Project.

Davidson, N. (1985). Small-group learning and teaching in mathematics: A selective review of the research. In R. Slavin, S. Sharan, S. Kagan, R. Hertz-Lazarowitz, C. Webb, & R. Schmuch (Eds.), *Learning to cooperate, cooperating to learn* (pp. 211–229). New York: Praeger.

Delquadri, J., Greenwood, C.R., Whorton, D., Carta, J.J., & Hall, R.V. (1986). Classwide peer tutoring. *Exceptional Children, 52,* 535–542.

Dodge, K.A. (1986). A social information processing model of social competence in childhood. In M. Perlmutter (Ed.), *Cognitive perspectives on children's social and behavioral development* (pp. 77–125). Mahwah, NJ: Lawrence Erlbaum Associates.

Drummond, T. (1993). *The Student Risk Screening Scale (SRSS).* Grants Pass, OR: Josephine County Mental Health Program.

Dugan, E., Kamps, D., Leonard, B., Watkins, N., Rheinberger, A., & Stackhaus, J. (1995). Effects of cooperative learning groups during social studies for students with autism and fourth-grade peers. *Journal of Applied Behavior Analysis, 28,* 175–188.

Durand, V.M. (1988). The Motivation Assessment Scale. In M. Hersen & A. Bellack (Eds.), *Dictionary of behavioral assessment techniques* (pp. 309–310). Tarrytown, NY: Pergamon.

Durand. V.M., & Crimmins, D.B. (1988). *The Motivation Assessment Scale, An administration manual.* Albany: State University of New York Press, Department of Psychology.

Elam, J.J., & Siegelman, C.K. (1983). Developmental differences in reactions to children labeled mentally retarded. *Journal of Applied Developmental Psychology, 4,* 303–315.

Elliott, S., & Gresham, F. (1991). *Social skills intervention guide.* Circle Pines, MN: American Guidance.

Epstein, J. (1986). Friendship selection: Developmental and environmental influences. In E. Mueller & C.R. Cooper (Eds.), *Process and outcome in peer relationship* (pp. 129–160). New York: Academic Press.

Evans, C., & Eder, D. (1993). "No exit": Processes of social isolation in the middle school. *Journal of Contemporary Ethnography, 22,* 139–170.

Evans, I.M., Salisbury, C.L., Palombaro, M.M., Berryman, J., & Hollowood, T. (1992). Peer interactions and social acceptance of elementary-age children with severe disabilities in an inclusive school. *Journal of The Association for Persons with Severe Handicaps, 17,* 205–212.

Falvey, M.A., Forest, M., Pearpoint, J., & Rosenberg, R.L. (1992). *All my life's a circle: Using the tools: Circles, MAPS & PATHS.* Toronto: Inclusion Press.

Farmer, T.W., & Farmer, E.M.Z. (1996). Social relationships of students with exceptionalities in mainstream classrooms: Social networks and homophily. *Exceptional Children, 62,* 431–450.

Farmer, T.W., & Hollowell, J.H. (1994). Social networks in mainstream classrooms: Social affiliations and behavioral characteristics of students with emotional and behavioral disorders. *Journal of Emotional and Behavioral Disorders, 2,* 143–155, 163.

Farmer, T.W., Pearl, R., & Van Acker, R.M. (1996). Expanding the social skills deficit framework: A developmental synthesis perspective, classroom social networks, and implications for the social growth of students with disabilities. *The Journal of Special Education, 30,* 232–256.

Farrington, K. (1992, May). *Practicum improvement plan: Disability awareness week at a middle school.* Unpublished manuscript, University of Virginia, Department of Curriculum, Instruction, and Special Education, Charlottesville.

Favazza, P.C., & Odom, S.L. (1996). Use of the Acceptance Scale to measure attitudes of kindergarten-age children. *Journal of Early Intervention, 20,* 232–249.

Fisher, M.M., & Snell, M.E. (1999). *The use of MAPS peer support groups and teacher support in middle schools to facilitate the inclusion of students with moderate and severe disabilities.* Unpublished manuscript, Purdue University, Department of Special Education.

Ford, A., & Davern, L. (1989). Moving forward with school integration: Strategies for involving students with severe handicaps in the life of the school. In R. Gaylord-Ross (Ed.), *Integration strategies for students with handicaps* (pp. 11–31). Baltimore: Paul H. Brookes Publishing Co.

Forest, M., & Lusthaus, E. (1989). Promoting educational equality for all students: Circles and maps. In S. Stainback, W. Stainback, & M. Forest (Eds.), *Educating all students in the mainstream of regular education* (pp. 43–57). Baltimore: Paul H. Brookes Publishing Co.

Forest, M. (Producer and Director). (1986). *MAPS: McGill Action Planning System* [Videotape]. Downsview, Ontario, Canada: The G. Allan Roeher Institute.

Forness, S.R., & Kavale, K.A. (1996). Treating social skill deficits in children with learning disabilities: A meta-analysis of the research. *Learning Disabilities Quarterly, 19,* 2–13.

Franca, V.M., Kerr, M.M., Reitz, A.L., & Lambert, D. (1990). Peer tutoring among behaviorally disordered students: Academic and social benefits to tutor and tutee. *Education and Treatment of Children, 13,* 109–128.

Franklin, M.E. (1992). Culturally sensitive instructional practices for African-American learners with disabilities. *Exceptional Children, 59,* 115–122.

Fritz, M.F. (1990). A comparison of social interactions using a friendship awareness activity. *Education and Training in Mental Retardation, 25,* 352–359.

Fryxell, D., & Kennedy, C.H. (1995). Placement along the continuum of services and its impact on students' social relationships. *Journal of The Association for Persons with Severe Handicaps, 20,* 259–269.

Furman, W., & Buhrmester, D. (1992). Age and sex differences in perceptions of networks of personal relationships. *Child Development, 63,* 103–115.

Furman, W., & Robbins, P. (1985). What's the point? Issues in the selection of treatment objectives. In B.H. Schneider, K.H. Rubin, & J.E. Ledingham (Eds.), *Children's peer relations: Issues in assessment and intervention* (pp. 41–54). New York: Springer-Verlag.

Furnham, A., & Gibbs, M. (1984). School children's attitudes towards the handicapped. *Journal of Adolescence, 7,* 99–116.

Garcia, E.E. (1992). Linguistically and culturally diverse children: Effective instructional practices and related policy issues. In H.C. Waxman, J.W. deFelix, J.E., Anderson, & H.P. Baptiste, Jr. (Eds.), *Students at risk in at-risk schools: Improving environments for learning* (pp. 65–86). Thousand Oaks, CA: Sage Publications.

Garrison-Harrell, L., Kamps, D., & Kravits, T. (1997). The effects of peer networks on social-communicative behaviors for students with autism. *Focus on Autism and Other Developmental Disabilities, 12,* 241–254.

Gartner, A., & Lipsky, D. (1990). Students as instructional agents. In W. Stainback & S. Stainback (Eds.), *Support networks for inclusive schooling: Interdependent integrated education.* Baltimore: Paul H. Brookes Publishing Co.

Giangreco, M.F., Cloninger, C.J., Dennis, R.E., & Edelman, S.W. (1994). Problem-solving methods to facilitate inclusive education. In J.S. Thousand, R.A. Villa, & A.I. Nevin (Eds.), *Creativity and collaborative learning* (pp. 321–346). Baltimore: Paul H. Brookes Publishing Co.

Giangreco, M.F., Dennis, R., Cloninger, C., Edelman, S., & Schattman, R. (1993). "I've counted Jon:" Transformational experiences of teachers educating students with disabilities. *Exceptional Children, 59*, 359–372.

Giangreco, M.F., Edelman, S.W., Luiselli, T.E., & MacFarland, S.Z.C. (1997). Helping or hovering? Effects of instructional assistant proximity on students with disabilities. *Exceptional Children, 64*, 7–18.

Goldstein, A. (1988). *The Prepare Curriculum: Teaching prosocial competencies.* Champaign, IL: Research Press.

Goldstein, H., English, K., Shafer, K., & Kaczmarek, L. (1997). Interaction among preschoolers with and without disabilities: Effects of across-the-day peer intervention. *Journal of Speech, Language, and Hearing Disorders, 40*, 33–48.

Goodman, G. (1994). *Inclusive classrooms from A to Z: A handbook for educators.* Columbus, OH: Teacher's Publishing Group.

Goodman, J. (1989). Does retardation mean dumb? Children's perceptions of the nature, cause, and course of mental retardation. *Journal of Special Education, 23*, 313–329.

Grabowski, S. (1997). *Manual for the faculty advisor, Best Buddies Colleges, Eastern Region.* Washington, DC: Best Buddies, Eastern Regional Office.

Graetz, B., & Shute, R. (1995). Assessment of peer relationships in children with asthma. *Journal of Pediatric Psychology, 20*, 205–216.

Graffi, S., & Minnes, P.M. (1988). Attitudes of primary school children toward the physical appearance and labels associated with Down syndrome. *American Journal on Mental Retardation, 93*, 28–35.

Green, S.K., & Shinn, M.R. (1994). Parent attitudes about special education and reintegration: What is the role of student outcomes? *Exceptional Children, 61*, 269–281.

Greenspan, S. (1981). Defining childhood social competence: A proposed working model. In B.K. Keogh (Ed.), *Advances in special education* (Vol. 3, pp. 1–39). Greenwich, CT: JAI Press.

Greenwood, C.R., Carta, J., & Kamps, D. (1990). Teacher-mediated versus peer-mediated instruction: A review of educational advantages and disadvantages. In H. Foot, M. Morgan, & R. Shute (Eds.), *Children helping children* (pp. 177–205). New York: John Wiley and Sons.

Greenwood, C.R., Delquadri, J., & Carta, J.J. (1988). *Classwide peer tutoring.* Seattle: Educational Achievement Systems.

Greenwood, C.R., Delquadri, J., & Hall, R.V. (1984). Opportunity to respond and student academic performance. In W.L. Heward, T.E.

Heron, J. Trap-Porter, & D.S. Hill (Eds.), *Focus on behavior analysis in education* (pp. 55–88). Columbus, OH: Merrill.

Greenwood, C.R. & Terry, B. (1997, June). *Classwide peer tutoring.* Paper presented at 20th Annual Intervention Procedures Conference for At-Risk Children and Youth, Utah State University, Logan.

Gresham, F.M. (1997). Social competence and students with behavior disorders: Where we've been, where we are, and where we should go. *Education and Treatment of Children, 20*, 233–249.

Gresham, F.M., & Elliott, S. (1990). *The Social Skills Rating System (SSRS).* Circle Pines, MN: American Guidance.

Gresham, F.M. (1981). Conceptual issues in the assessment of social competence in children. In P. Strain, M. Gurlanick, & H. Walker (Eds.), *Children's social behavior: Development, assessment, and modifications* (pp. 143–179). New York: Academic Press.

Groden, J., & LeVassuer, P. (1994). Cognitive picture rehearsal: A system to teach self-control. In K.A. Quill (Ed.), *Teaching children with autism: Strategies to enhance communication and socialization* (pp. 287–306). Albany, NY: Delmar Publishers, Inc.

Guralnick, M., & Groom, J.M. (1987). The peer relations of mildly delayed and nonhandicapped preschool children in mainstreamed play groups. *Child Development, 58*, 1556–1572.

Guralnick, M.J. (1986). The peer relations of young handicapped and nonhandicapped children. In P.S. Strain, M.J. Guralnick, & H.M. Walker (Eds.), *Children's social behavior: Development, assessment, and modification* (pp. 93–140). Orlando, FL: Academic Press.

Guralnick, M.J. (1990). Social competence and early intervention. *Journal of Early Intervention, 14*, 3–14.

Guralnick, M.J., Connor, R.T., & Hammond, M. (1995). Parent perspectives of peer relationships and friendships in integrated and specialized programs. *American Journal on Mental Retardation, 99*, 457–476.

Gustafson, R.N., & Haring, N.G. (1992). Social competence issues in the integration of students with handicaps. In K.A. Haring, D.L. Lovett, & N.G. Haring (Eds.), *Integrated lifestyle services for persons with disabilities* (pp. 20–58). New York: Springer-Verlag.

Hamre-Nietupski, S., Ayres, B., Nietupski, J., Savage, M., Mitchell, B., & Bramman, H. (1989). Enhancing integration of students with severe disabilities through curricular infusion: A general/special educator partnership. *Education and Training of the Mentally Retarded, 24*, 78–88.

Hanline, M.F., & Halvorsen, A. (1989). Parent perceptions of the integration transition process: Overcoming artificial barriers. *Exceptional Children, 55*, 487–492.

Haring, T.G. (1991). Social relationships. In L.H. Meyer, C.A. Peck, & L. Brown (Eds.), *Critical issues in the lives of people with severe disabilities* (pp. 195–217). Baltimore: Paul H. Brookes Publishing Co.

Haring, T.G. (1992). The context of social competence: Relations, relationships, and generalization. In S.L. Odom, S.R. McConnell, & M.A. McEvoy (Eds.), *Social competence of young children with disabilities* (pp. 307–320). Baltimore: Paul H. Brookes Publishing Co.

Haring, T.G., & Breen, C.G. (1992). A peer-mediated social network intervention to enhance the social integration of persons with moderate and severe disabilities. *Journal of Applied Behavior Analysis, 25,* 319–333.

Harper, G.F., Mallette, B., & Moore, J. (1991). Peer-mediated instruction: Teaching spelling to primary school children with mild disabilities. *Journal of Reading, Writing, and Learning Disabilities International, 7*(3), 137–151.

Hartup, W.W. (1996). The company they keep: Friendships and their developmental significance. *Child Development, 67,* 1–13.

Hartup, W.W., & Laursen, B. (1993). Conflict and context in peer relations. In C. Hart (Ed.), *Children on playgrounds: Research perspective and applications* (pp. 44–84). Albany: State University of New York Press.

Hawkins, X. (1991). Is social validity what we are interested in? Argument for a functional approach. *Journal of Applied Behavior Analysis, 24,* 205–213.

Hazel, J., Schumaker, J., Sherman, J., & Sheldon-Wildgen, J. (1981). *ASSET: A social skills program for adolescents.* Champaign, IL: Research Press.

Helmstetter, E., Peck, C.A., & Giangreco, M. (1994). Outcomes of interactions with peers with moderate or severe disabilities: A statewide survey of high school students. *Journal of The Association for Persons with Severe Handicaps, 19,* 263–276.

Hendrickson, J.M., Shokoohi-Yekta, M., Hamre-Neitupski, S., & Gable, R.A. (1996). Middle and high school students' perceptions on being friends with peers with severe disabilities. *Exceptional Children, 63,* 19–28.

Hirsche, B., & Rapkin, B.D. (1987). The transition to junior high school: A longitudinal study of self-esteem, psychological symptomatology, school life and social support. *Child Development, 58,* 1235–1243.

Hodgdon, L.Q. (1994). Solving social-behavioral problems through the use of visually supported communication. In K.A. Quill (Ed.), *Teaching children with autism: Strategies to enhance communication and socialization* (pp. 265–286). Albany, NY: Delmar Publishers, Inc.

Hops, H., & Walker, H.M. (1988). *CLASS: Contingencies for learning academic and social skills.* Seattle: Educational Achievement System.

Horner, R.H., & Carr, E.G. (1997). Behavioral support for students with severe disabilities: Functional assessment and comprehensive intervention. *Journal of Special Education, 31,* 84–104.

Horner, R.H., O'Neil, R.E., & Flannery, K.B. (1993). Building effective behavior support plans from functional assessment information. In M.E. Snell (Ed.), *Instruction of students with severe disabilities* (4th ed., pp. 184–214). Columbus, OH: Merrill.

Howes, C. (1988). Peer interaction of young children. *Monographs of the Society for Research in Child Development, 53* (1, Series No. 217).

Hubbard, J.A., & Coie, J.D. (1994). Emotional correlates of social competence in children's peer relationships. *Merrill-Palmer Quarterly, 40,* 1–20.

Hughes, C., Harmer, M.L., Killian, D.J., & Niarhos, F. (1995). The effects of multiple-exemplar self-instructional training on high school students' generalized conversational interactions. *Journal of Applied Behavior Analysis, 28,* 201–218.

Hunt, P., Alwell, M., Farron-Davis, F., & Goetz, L. (1996). Creating socially supportive environments for fully included students who experience multiple disabilities. *Journal of The Association for Persons with Severe Handicaps, 21,* 53–71.

Hunt, P., Alwell, M., & Goetz, L. (1991a). Establishing conversational exchanges with family and friends: Moving from training to meaningful communication. *The Journal of Special Education, 25,* 305–319.

Hunt, P., Alwell, M., & Goetz, L. (1991b). Interaction with peers through conversation turntaking with a communication book adaptation. *Augmentative and Alternative Communication, 7,* 117–126.

Hunt, P., Alwell, M., Goetz, L., & Sailor, W. (1990). Generalized effects of conversation skill training. *Journal of The Association for Persons with Severe Handicaps, 15,* 250–260.

Hunt, P., Staub, D., Alwell, M., & Goetz, L. (1994). Achievement by all students within the context of cooperative learning groups. *Journal of The Association for Persons with Severe Handicaps, 19,* 290–301.

Hymel, S., Rubin, K., Rowden, L., & LeMare, L. (1990). Children's peer relationships: Longitudinal prediction of internalizing and externalizing problems from middle to late childhood. *Child Development, 61,* 2004–2021.

Hymel, S., Wagner, E., & Butler, L.J. (1990). Reputational bias: View from the peer group. In S.R. Asher & J.D. Coie (Eds.), *Peer rejection in childhood* (pp. 156–186). New York: Cambridge University Press.

Inderbitzen-Pisaruk, H.M., & Foster, S.L. (1990). Adolescents friendships and peer acceptance: Implications for social skills training. *Clinical Psychology Review, 10,* 425–439.

Integrator Checklist: A guide to full inclusion of students with disabilities. (1989). Minneapolis: University of Minnesota Institute on Community Integration.

Janney, R.E., & Snell, M.E. (1996). How teachers use peer interactions to include students with moderate and severe disabilities in elementary general education classes. *Journal of The Association for Persons with Severe Handicaps, 21,* 72–80.

Janney, R.E., & Snell, M.E. (1997). How teachers include students with moderate and severe disabilities in elementary classes: The means and meaning of inclusion. *Journal of the Association for Persons with Severe Handicaps, 22,* 159–169.

Janney, R.E., & Snell, M.E. (2000). *Teachers' guides to inclusive practices: Behavioral support.* Baltimore: Paul H. Brookes Publishing Co.

Janney, R.E., & Snell, M.E. (2000). *Teachers' guides to inclusive practices: Modifying schoolwork.* Baltimore: Paul H. Brookes Publishing Co.

Jenkins, J.R., Odom, S.L., & Speltz, M.L. (1989). Effects of social integration on preschool children with handicaps. *Exceptional Children, 55,* 420–428.

Johnson, D.W., & Johnson, R.T. (1989). *Cooperation and competition: Theory and research.* Edina, MN: Interaction Books.

Johnson, D.W., & Johnson, R.T. (1991). *Learning together and alone: Cooperation, competition, and individualization* (3rd ed.). Englewood Cliffs, NJ: Prentice-Hall.

Johnson, D.W., Johnson, R., & Holubec, E. (1993). *Circles of learning: Cooperation in the classroom* (4th ed.). Edina, MN: Interaction Book Co.

Johnson, D.W., Johnson, R.T., Holubec, E.J., & Roy, P. (1984). Circles of learning: cooperation in the classroom. Alexandria, VA: Association for Supervision and Curriculum Development.

Jorgensen, C. (1992). Natural supports in inclusive schools: Curricular and teaching strategies. In J. Nisbet (Ed.), *Natural supports in school, at work, and in the community for people with severe disabilities* (pp. 179–215). Baltimore: Paul H. Brookes Publishing Co.

Kamps, D., Barbetta, P.M., Leonard, B.R., & Delquadri, J. (1994). Classwide peer tutoring: An integration strategy to improve reading skills and promote peer interactions among students with autism and general education peers. *Journal of Applied Behavior Analysis, 27,* 49–61.

Kamps, D.M., Potucek, J., Lopez, A.G., Kravits, T., & Kemmerer, K. (1997). The use of peer networks across multiple settings to improve social interaction for students with autism. *Journal of Behavioral Education, 7,* 335–357.

Kazak, A. (1987). Families with disabled children: Stress and social networks in three samples. *Journal of Abnormal Psychology, 15,* 137–146.

Kazak, A., & Marvin, R. (1984). Differences, difficulties, and adaptation: Stress and social networks in families with a handicapped child. *Family Relations, 33,* 67–77.

Keachie, J. (1997a, Fall). Pals, parties, and proms. *Impact 10*(3), 19.

Keachie, J. (1997b, Fall). Social inclusion in a high school: The Peer Connections Program. *Impact, 10*(3), 18–19.

Kennedy, C.H., Cushing, L.S., & Itkonen, T. (1997). General education participation improves the social contacts and friendship networks of students with severe disabilities. *Journal of Behavioral Education, 7,* 167–189.

Kennedy, C.H., & Itkonen, T. (1994). Some effects of regular class participation on the social contacts and social networks of high school students with severe disabilities. *Journal of The Association for Persons with Severe Handicaps, 19,* 1–13.

Kennedy, C.H., Shukla, S., & Fryxell, D. (1997). Comparing the effects of educational placement on the social relationships of intermediate school students with severe disabilities. *Exceptional Children, 64,* 31–47.

Koegel, R.L., Koegel, L.K., & Parks, D.R. (1995). Autonomy through self-management. In R.L. Koegel & L.K. Koegel (Eds.), *Teaching children with autism* (pp. 67–77). Baltimore: Paul H. Brookes Publishing Co.

Kincaid, D. (1996). Person-centered planning. In L.K. Koegel, R.L. Koegel, & G. Dunlap (Eds.), *Positive behavioral support* (pp. 439–465). Baltimore: Paul H. Brookes Publishing Co.

Kinney, D.A. (1993). From nerds to normals: The recovery of identity among adolescents from middle school to high school. *Sociology of Education, 66,* 21–40.

Kishi, G.S., & Meyer, L.H. (1994). What children report and remember: A six-year follow-up of the effects of social contact between peers with and without severe disabilities. *Journal of The Association for Persons with Severe Handicaps, 19,* 277–289.

Kohler, F., & Greenwood, C.R. (1990). Effects of collateral peer supportive behaviors with the classwide peer tutoring program. *Journal of Applied Behavior Analysis, 23,* 307–322.

Koury, M., & Browder, D. (1986). The use of delay to teach sight words by peer tutors classified as moderately mentally retarded. *Education and Training of the Mentally Retarded, 17,* 93–102.

Ladd, G.W. (1990). Having friends, keeping friends, making friends and being liked by peers in the classroom: Predictors of children's early school adjustment? *Child Development, 61,* 1081–1100.

Ladd, G.W., & Emerson, E.S. (1984). Shared knowledge in children's friendships. *Developmental Psychology, 20,* 932–940.

Ladd, G.W., & Golter, B.S. (1988). Parents' management of preschooler's peer relations: Is it related to children's social competence? *Developmental Psychology, 24,* 109–117.

Lazzari, A.M., & Wood, J.W. (1997). Mental retardation. In J.W. Wood & A.M. Lazzari (Eds.), *Exceeding the boundaries: Understanding exceptional lives* (pp. 424–461). Fort Worth, TX: Harcourt, Brace & Co.

Lewis, M., Fiering, C., & Kotsonis, M. (1984). The social network of the young child. In M. Lewis (Ed.), *Beyond the dyad* (pp. 129–160). New York: Plenum Press.

Lloyd, J.W., Crowley, E.P., Kohler, F., & Strain, P. (1988). Redefining the applied research agenda: Cooperative learning, pre-referral, teacher consultation, and peer mediated interventions. *Journal of Learning Disabilities, 21*, 43–52.

Lloyd, J.W., Kauffman, J.M., Landrum, T.J., & Roe, D.L. (1991). Why do teachers refer pupils for special education? An analysis of referral records. *Exceptionality, 2*, 113–126.

Lowenbraum, S., Madge, S., & Affleck, J. (1990). Parental satisfaction with integrated class placements of special education and general education students. *Remedial and Special Education, 11*, 37–36.

Luftig, R.L. (1989). Estimated ease of making friends, perceived social competency, and loneliness among mentally retarded and nonretarded students. *Education, 109*, 200–211.

Maccoby, E.E. (1990). Gender and relationships. *American Psychologist, 45*, 513–520.

Mathes, P.G., Fuchs, D., Fuchs, L.S., Henley, A.M., & Sanders, A. (1994). Increasing strategic reading practice with Peabody classwide peer tutoring. *Learning Disabilities Research and Practice, 9*, 44–48.

McConnell, S.R., Sisson, L.A., Cort, C.A., & Strain, P.S. (1991). Effects of social skills training and contingency management on reciprocal interaction of preschool children with behavioral handicaps. *Journal of Special Education, 24*, 473–495.

McGee, G.G., Almeida, M.C., Sulzer-Azaroff, B., & Feldman, R.S. (1992). Promoting reciprocal interactions via peer incidental teaching. *Journal of Applied Behavior Analysis, 25*, 117–126.

McGinnis, E., & Goldstein, A. (1990). *Skillstreaming in early childhood: Teaching prosocial skills to the preschool and kindergarten child*. Champaign, IL: Research Press.

McGinnis, E., & Goldstein, A. (1997a). *Skillstreaming the adolescent: New strategies and perspectives for teaching prosocial skills*. Champaign, IL: Research Press.

McGinnis, E., & Goldstein, A. (1997b). *Skillstreaming the elementary school child: New strategies and perspectives for teaching prosocial skills*. Champaign, IL: Research Press.

McGregor, G., & Vogelsberg, R.T. (1998). *Inclusive schooling practices: Pedagogical and research foundations*. Pittsburgh, PA: Allegheny University of the Health Sciences.

McIntosh, R., Baughn, S., & Zaragoza, N. (1991). A review of social interventions for students with learning disabilities. *Journal of Learning Disabilities, 24*, 451–458.

Meyer, L.H., & Henry, L.A. (1993). Cooperative classroom management: Student needs and fairness in the regular classroom. In J.W. Putnam (Ed.), *Cooperative learning and strategies for inclusion* (pp. 93–121). Baltimore: Paul H. Brookes Publishing Co.

Meyer, L.H., Harootunian, B., & Williams, D. (1991, April). *Identifying at-risk status and preventing school dropout*. Paper presented at the annual meeting of the American Educational Research Association, Chicago.

Meyer, L.H., Minondo, S., Fisher, M., Larson, M.J., Dunmore, S., Black, J.W., & D'Aquanni, M. (1998). Frames of friendship: Social relationships among adolescents with diverse abilities. In L.H. Meyer, H. Park, M. Grenot-Scheyer, I.S. Schwartz, & B. Harry (Eds.), *Making friends: The influences of culture and development* (pp. 189–218). Baltimore: Paul H. Brookes Publishing Co.

Meyer, L.H., Park, H., Grenot-Scheyer, M., Schwartz, I.S., & Harry, B. (Eds.). (1998). *Making friends: The influences of culture and development*. Baltimore: Paul H. Brookes Publishing Co.

Morris, D. (1997, Fall). *Invented and adapted games that allow active participation by students with severe disabilities and their peers*. Unpublished manuscript.

Mount, B., & Zwernick, K. (1988). *It's never too early, it's never too late*. (Publication No. 421-88-109). St. Paul, MN: Metropolitan Council.

Murray-Seegert, C. (1989). *Nasty girls, thugs, and humans like us: Social relations between severely disabled and nondisabled students in high school*. Baltimore: Paul H. Brookes Publishing Co.

National Center for Children and Youth with Disabilities (NICHCY) (1995, July). Planning for inclusion. *NICHCY News Digest, 5*(1), 1–31.

Neary, T., Halvorsen, A., Kronberg, R., & Kelly, D. (1992, December) *Curriculum adaptations for inclusive classrooms*. San Francisco: San Francisco State University, California Research Institute. (ERIC Document Reproduction Service No. ED 358 637)

Nelson, J. (1987). *Positive discipline*. New York: Ballantine Books.

Nevin, A.I., Thousand, J.S., & Villa, R.A. (1994). Creative cooperative groups lesson plans. In J.S. Thousand, R.A. Villa, & A.I. Nevin (Eds.), *Creativity and collaborative learning: A practical guide to empowering students and teachers* (pp. 129–225). Baltimore: Paul H. Brookes Publishing Co.

Newcomb, A., & Bukowski, W.M. (1983). Social impact and social preference as determinants of children's peer group status. *Developmental Psychology, 19*, 856–867.

Newcomb, A.F., & Bagwell, C.L. (1995). Children's friendship relations: A meta-analytic review. *Psychological Bulletin, 117*, 306–347.

O'Brien, J. (1987). A guide to lifestyle planning: Using *The Activities Catalog* to integrate services and natural support systems. In B. Wilcox &

G.T. Bellamy (Eds.), *A comprehensive guide to* The Activities Catalog: *An alternative curriculum for youth and adults with severe disabilities* (pp. 175–189). Baltimore: Paul H. Brookes Publishing Co.

Odom, S.L., McConnell, S.R., & Chandler, L.K. (1993). Acceptability and feasibility of classroom-based social interaction interventions for young children with disabilities. *Exceptional Children, 60,* 226–236.

Odom, S.L., McConnell, S.R., & McEvoy, M.A. (1992). Peer-related social competence and its significance for young children with disabilities. In S.L. Odom, S.R. McConnell, & M.A. McEvoy (Eds.), *Social competence of young children with disabilities* (pp. 3–36). Baltimore: Paul H. Brookes Publishing Co.

O'Neill, R.E. (1997). Autism. In J.W. Wood & A.M. Lazzari (Eds.), *Exceeding the boundaries: Understanding exceptional lives* (pp. 424–461). Fort Worth, TX: Harcourt & Brace Co.

O'Neill, R.E., Horner, R.H., Albin, R.W., Sprague, J.R., Storey, K., & Newton, J.S. (1997). *Functional assessment and program development for problem behavior: A practical handbook.* Pacific Grove, CA: Brooks/Cole.

PACER Center (1989, September). It's the "person first"—then the disability. *Pacesetter,* p. 12.

Parke, R.D., & Bhavnagri, N.P. (1989). Parents as managers of children's peer relationships. In D. Belle (Ed.), *Children's social networks and social supports* (pp. 241–259). New York: John Wiley & Sons.

Parke, R.D., MacDonald, K.B., Beitel, A., & Bhavnagri, N.P. (1988). The role of the family in the development of peer relationships. In R.D. Peter & R.J. McMahon (Eds.), *Social learning and system approaches to marriage and the family* (pp. 17–44). New York: Brunner/Mazel.

Parker, H.G., & Gottman, J.M. (1989). Social and emotional development in a relational context. In T.J. Berndt & G. Ladd (Eds.), *Peer relationships in child development* (pp. 95–131). New York: John Wiley & Sons.

Parker, J.G., & Asher, S.R. (1987). Peer relations and later personal adjustment: Are low-accepted children at risk? *Psychological Bulletin, 102,* 357–389.

Parker, J.G., & Asher, S.R. (1993). Friendship and friendship quality in middle childhood: Links with peer group acceptance and feelings of loneliness and social dissatisfaction. *Developmental Psychology, 29,* 611–621.

Peck, C.A., Donaldson, J., & Pezzoli, M. (1990). Some benefits nonhandicapped adolescents perceive for themselves from their social relationships with peers who have severe handicaps. *Journal of The Association for Persons with Severe Handicaps, 15,* 241–249.

Perske, R. (1988) *Circles of friends: People with disabilities and their friends enrich the lives of one another.* Nashville, TN: Abingdon Press.

Putnam, J.W. (1993). *Cooperative learning and strategies for inclusion: Celebrating diversity in the classroom.* Baltimore: Paul H. Brookes Publishing Co.

Putnam. J.W. (1997). *Cooperative learning in diverse classrooms.* Upper Saddle River, NJ: Merrill.

Reichart, D.C., Lynch, E.C., Anderson, B.C., Svobodny, L.A., Di Cola, J.M., & Mercury, M.G. (1989). Parental perspectives on integrated preschool opportunities for children with handicaps and children without handicaps. *Journal of Early Intervention, 13,* 6–13.

Ridlehoover, H.M. (1996). *Occupational therapy use of peer-mediated intervention in a preschool setting.* Unpublished master's thesis, University of Alabama, Birmingham.

Rizzo, T.A. (1989). *Friendship development among children in school.* Norwood, NJ: Ablex Publishing Corp.

Roach, V. (1995, May). *Winning ways: Creating inclusive schools, classrooms, and communities.* Alexandria, VA: National Association of State Boards of Education.

Rosenbaum, P., Armstrong, R.W., & King, S.M. (1986). Improving attitudes toward the disabled: A randomized controlled trial of direct contact versus Kids-on-the-Block. *Journal of Developmental and Behavioral Pediatrics, 7,* 302–307.

Rubin, Z. (1980). *Children's friendships.* Cambridge, MA: Harvard University Press.

Rubin, Z., & Sloman, J. (1984). How parents influence their children's friendships. In M. Lewis (Ed.), *Beyond the dyad* (pp. 223–250). New York: Plenum Press.

Rusch, F.R., Chadsey-Rusch, J., & Johnson, J.R. (1990). Supported employment: Emerging opportunities for employment integration. In L. Meyer, C. Peck, & L. Brown (Eds.), *Critical issues in the lives of people with severe disabilities* (pp. 145–169). Baltimore: Paul H. Brookes Publishing Co.

Sale, P., & Carey, D. (1995). The sociometric status of students with disabilities in a full-inclusion school. *Exceptional Children, 62,* 6–19.

Salisbury, C.L., & Palombaro, M.M. (Eds.). (1993). *No problem: Working things out our way.* Pittsburgh, PA: Allegheny Singer Research Institute, Child and Family Studies Program.

Salisbury, C.L., Evans, I.M., & Palombaro, M.M. (1997). Collaborative problem-solving to promote the inclusion of young children with significant disabilities in primary grades. *Exceptional Children, 63,* 195–209.

Salisbury, C.L., Gallucci, C., Palombaro, M.M., & Peck, C.A. (1995). Strategies that promote social relations among elementary students with and without severe disabilities in inclusive schools. *Exceptional Children, 62,* 125–137.

Salisbury, C.L., Palombaro, M.M., & Evans, I.M. (Eds.). (1993). *Collaborative problem solving: Instructor's manual.* Pittsburgh, PA: Allegheny Singer

Research Institute, Child and Family Studies Program.

Salisbury, C.L., Palombaro, M.M., & Hollowood, T. (1993). On the nature and change of an inclusive elementary school. *Journal of The Association for Persons with Severe Handicaps, 18,* 75–84.

Sapon-Shevin, M., & Schniedewind, N. (1992). If cooperative learning is the answer, what are the questions? *Journal of Education, 174*(2), 11–37.

Schaffner, B., & Buswell, B.E. (1992). *Connecting students: A guide to thoughtful friendship facilitation for educators and families.* Colorado Springs, CO: PEAK Parent Center, Inc.

Schaffner, B., Buswell, B., Summerfield, A., & Kovar, G. (1988). *Discover the possibilities: A curriculum for teaching parents about integration.* Colorado Springs, CO: PEAK Parent Center.

Schneider, B.H. (1992). Didactic methods for enhancing children's peer relations: A qualitative review. *Clinical Psychology Review, 12,* 362–382.

Schnorr, R.F. (1997). From enrollment to membership: "Belonging" in middle and high school classes. *Journal of The Association for Persons with Severe Handicaps, 22,* 1–15.

Schrumpf, F., Crawford, D., & Usadel, H. (1991). *Peer mediation: Conflict resolution in schools.* Champaign, IL: Research Press.

Shantz, C.U., & Hobart, C.J. (1989). Social conflict and development. In T.J. Berndt & G.W. Ladd (Eds.), *Peer relationships in child development* (pp. 71–94). New York: John Wiley & Sons, Inc.

Sharan, S. (1994). *Handbook of cooperative learning methods.* Westport, CT: Greenwood Press.

Sideridis, G.D., Utley, C., Greenwood, C.R., Delquadri, J., Dawson, H., Palmer, P., & Reddy, S. (1997). Classwide peer tutoring: Effects on the spelling performance and social interactions of students with mild disabilities and their typical peers in an integrated instructional setting. *Journal of Behavioral Education, 7,* 435–462.

Siperstein, G.N., & Bak, J.J. (1989). Social relationships of adolescents with moderate mental retardation. *Mental Retardation, 27,* 5–10.

Siperstein, G.N., & Leffert, J.S. (1997). Comparison of socially accepted and rejected children with mental retardation. *American Journal on Mental Retardation, 101,* 339–351.

Siperstein, G.N., Leffert, J.S., & Wenz-Gross, M. (1997). Quality of friendships between children with and without learning problems. *American Journal on Mental Retardation, 102,* 111–125.

Slavin, R.E. (1990). *Cooperative learning: Theory, research and practice.* Englewood Cliffs, NJ: Prentice-Hall.

Slavin, R.E. (1991). Synthesis of research on cooperative learning. *Educational Leadership, 48*(5), 71–82.

Slavin, R.E. (1995). *Cooperative learning: Theory, research and practice* (2nd ed.). Needham Heights, MA: Allyn & Bacon.

Snell, M.E., & Raynes, M., with Byrd, J.O., Colley, K.M., Gilley, C., Pityonak, C., Stallings, M.A., Van Dyke, R., Williams, P.S., & Willis, C.J. (1995). Changing roles in inclusive schools: Staff perspectives at Gilbert Linkous Elementary. *Kappa Delta Pi Record, 31,* 104–109.

Snell, M.E., & Janney, R.E. (2000). *Teachers' guides to inclusive practices: Collaborative teaming.* Baltimore: Paul H. Brookes Publishing Co.

Social Integration Project. (1989). *Let's be social.* Tucson, AZ: Communication Skill Builders.

Staub, D., Schwartz, I.S., Gallucci, C., & Peck, C. (1994). Four portraits of friendship at an inclusive school. *Journal of The Association for Persons with Severe Disabilities, 19,* 314–325.

Staub, D., Spaulding, M., Peck, C.A., Gallucci, C., & Schwartz, I.S. (1996). Using nondisabled peers to support the inclusion of students with disabilities. *Journal of The Association for Persons with Severe Handicaps, 21,* 194–205.

Strain, P.S., & Odom, S.L. (1986). Peer social initiations: Effective intervention for social skills development of exceptional children. *Exceptional Children, 52,* 543–551.

Strain, P.S. (1985). Social and nonsocial determinants of acceptability in handicapped preschool children. *Topics in Early Childhood Special Education, 4,* 47–58.

Taylor, A. (1989). Predictors of peer rejection in early elementary grades: Roles of problem behavior, academic achievement, and teacher preference. *Journal of Clinical Child Psychology, 18,* 360–365.

Tharinger, D., Horton, C.B., & Millea, S. (1990). Sexual abuse and exploitation of children and adults with mental retardation and other handicaps. *Child Abuse and Neglect, 14,* 301–312.

Utah State Office of Education (1994). *Peer power* [Videotape]. (Available from the Utah State Office of Education, Salt Lake City, UT.)

Van der Klift, E., & Kunc, N. (1994). Beyond benevolence: Friendship and the politics of help. In J.S. Thousand, R.A. Villa, & A.I. Nevin (Eds.), *Creativity and collaborative learning: A practical guide to empowering students and teachers* (pp. 391–401). Baltimore: Paul H. Brookes Publishing Co.

Vandell, D.L., & Hembree, S.E. (1994). Peer social status and friendship: Independent contributors to children's social and academic adjustment. *Merrill-Palmer Quarterly, 40,* 461–477.

Vanderbilt/Minnesota Social Interaction Project. (1993). *Play time/social time: Organizing your classroom to build social interactions.* Tucson, AZ: Communication Skill Builders.

Vandercook, T. (1991). Leisure instruction outcomes: Criterion performance positive interactions, and acceptance by typical high school peers. *Journal of Special Education, 25,* 320–339.

Vandercook, T., York, J., & Forest, M. (1989). The McGill Action Planning System (MAPS): A strategy for building the vision. *Journal of The Association for Persons with Severe Handicaps, 14*, 205–215.

Vaughn, S., Levine, L., & Ridley, C.A. (1986). *PALS: Problem-solving and affective learning strategies.* Chicago: Science Research Associates.

Villa, R.A., & Thousand, J.S. (1994). One divided by two or more. In J.S. Thousand, R.A. Villa, & A.I. Nevin (Eds.), *Creativity and collaborative learning* (pp. 79–101). Baltimore: Paul H. Brookes Publishing Co.

Vogtle, L.K. (1996). Friendship between children with and without disabilities. *Dissertation Abstracts International, 57/01,* AAC9421262.

Vygotsky, L.S. (1978). *Mind in society.* Cambridge, MA: Harvard University Press.

Walker, H., Todis, B., Holmes, D., & Horton, G. (1988). *The Walker Social Skills Curriculum: The ACCESS program* (adolescent curriculum for communication and effective social skills). Austin, TX: PRO-ED.

Walker, H.M., Colvin, G., & Ramsey, E. (1995). *Antisocial behavior in school: Strategies and best practices.* Pacific Grove, CA: Brooks/Cole.

Walker, H.M., Hops, H., & Greenwood, C.R. (1993). *RECESS: A program for reducing negative-aggressive behavior.* Seattle, WA: Educational Achievement Systems.

Walker, H.M., & McConnell, S.R. (1988). *The Walker-McConnell Scale of Social Competence and School Adjustment* (Rev. ed.). Eugene: University of Oregon, Center of Human Development.

Walker, H.M., & Severson, H.H. (1990). *Systematic Screening for Behavior Disorders (SSBD): User's guide and technical manual.* Longmont, CO: Sopris West.

Walker, H.M., McConnell, S.R., Holmes, D., Todis, B., Walker, J., & Golden, N. (1983). *The Walker Social Skills Curriculum: The ACCEPTS program (a curriculum for children's effective peer and teacher skills).* Austin, TX: PRO-ED.

Walker, H.M., McConnell, S.R., Walker, J.L., Clarke, J.Y., Todis, B., Cohen, G., & Rankin, R. (1983). Initial analysis of the SBS curriculum: Efficacy of instructional and behavior management procedures for improving the social competence of handicapped children. *Analysis and Intervention in Developmental Disabilities, 3,* 105–127.

Walker, H.M., Schwarz, I.E., Nippold, M., Irwin, L.K., & Noell, J. (1994). Social skills in school-age children and youth: Issues and best practices in assessment and intervention. In M. Nippold (Ed.), *Topics in Language Disorders: Pragmatics and Social Skills in School-Age Children and Adolescents, 14*(3), 70–82.

Walker, H.M., Severson, H.H., & Feil, E.G. (1994). *The Early Screening Project: A Proven Child-Find Process.* Longmont, CO: Sopris West.

Weinberg, N. (1978). Preschool children's perceptions of orthopedic disability. *Rehabilitation Counseling Bulletin, 7,* 183–189.

Weiserbs, B., & Gottlieb, J. (1992). Perceived risk as a factor influencing attitudes toward physically disabled children. *Journal of Developmental and Physical Disabilities, 4,* 341–352.

Wilcox., B., & Nicholson, N. (1990). *The complete elementary school: Including all students with disabilities—Guidelines for principals.* Bloomington: Institute for the Study of Developmental Disabilities, Indiana University.

Wilcox, B., Nicholson, N., & Farlow, L. (1990). *The complete middle school: Including all students with disabilities: Guidelines for principals.* Bloomington: Institute for the Study of Developmental Disabilities, Indiana University.

Williams, G.A., & Asher, S.R. (1992). Assessment of loneliness at school among children with mild mental retardation. *American Journal on Mental Retardation, 96,* 373–385.

Wittmer, D., Doll, B., & Strain, P. (1996). Social and emotional development in early childhood: The identification of competence and disabilities. *Journal of Early Intervention, 20,* 299–318.

York-Barr, J. (Ed.). (1996). *Creating inclusive school communities.* Baltimore: Paul H. Brookes Publishing Co.

Youniss, J., & Smoller, J. (1985). *Adolescent relations with mothers, fathers, and friends.* Chicago: University of Chicago Press.

Zaragoza, N., Vaughn, S., & McIntosh, R. (1991). Social skills interventions and children with behavior problems: A review. *Behavioral Disorders, 16*(4), 260–275.

Zetlin, A.G., & Murtaugh, M. (1988). Friendship patterns in mildly learning handicapped and nonhandicapped high school students. *American Journal on Mental Retardation, 92,* 447–454.

Zola, I.K. (1982). *Missing pieces: A chronicle of living with a disability.* Philadelphia: Temple University Press.

Appendix A

Blank Forms

A Rating Scale to Assess a Student's Social Relationships

School: _____   **Date:** _____

Classroom: _____   **Focus Student(s):** _____

Ratings: Frequently   Sometimes   Never   No Opportunity to Observe (NO)

Assessment Question	Rating	Ideas for Improvement
Ghost/Guest: Does the focus child frequently get "passed over" as if he or she were not there (ghost)? Do staff members talk about another placement as soon as there is a problem (guest)?	Frequently Sometimes Never NO	
Inclusion child: Does the teacher say "I have 27 students plus 2 included students?"	Frequently Sometimes Never NO	
I'll help: Do classmates use the words "work with" or "help" whenever they refer to times spent with the focus child?	Frequently Sometimes Never NO	
Just another child: Is the child expected to participate in class activities along with everyone else?	Frequently Sometimes Never NO	
Regular friend: Has the child ever been invited to a party by a classmate?	Frequently Sometimes Never NO	
Best friend: Does the focus child have one or more friends who call him or her on the telephone at home and/or who visit him or her after school or on weekends?	Frequently Sometimes Never NO	

(From Meyer, L.H., Minondo, S., Fisher, M., Larson, M.J., Dunmore, S., Black, J.W., & D'Aquanni, M. [1998]. Frames of friendship: Social relationships among adolescents with diverse abilities. In L.H. Meyer, H. Park, M. Grenot-Scheyer, I.S. Schwartz, & B. Harry [Eds.], *Making friends: The influences of culture and development* [pp. 189–218]. Baltimore: Paul H. Brookes Publishing Co.; adapted by permission.)

Social Relationships and Peer Support, Snell & Janney, © 2000 Paul H. Brookes Publishing Co.

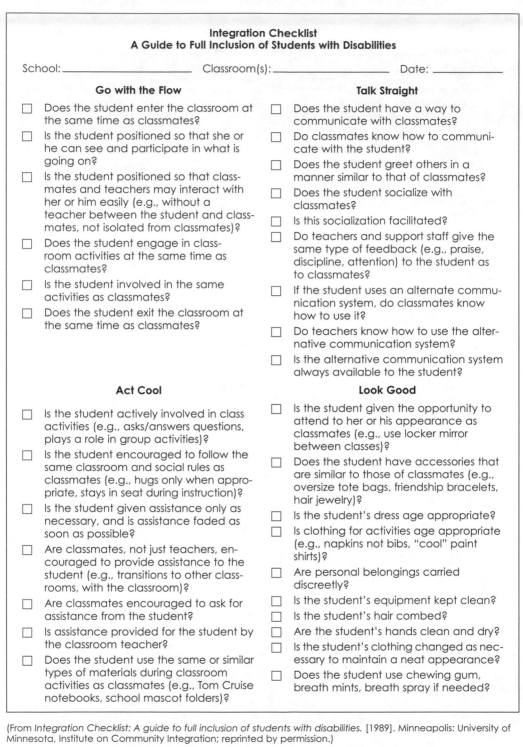

Integration Checklist
A Guide to Full Inclusion of Students with Disabilities

School: _____ Classroom(s): _____ Date: _____

Go with the Flow

☐ Does the student enter the classroom at the same time as classmates?

☐ Is the student positioned so that she or he can see and participate in what is going on?

☐ Is the student positioned so that classmates and teachers may interact with her or him easily (e.g., without a teacher between the student and classmates, not isolated from classmates)?

☐ Does the student engage in classroom activities at the same time as classmates?

☐ Is the student involved in the same activities as classmates?

☐ Does the student exit the classroom at the same time as classmates?

Talk Straight

☐ Does the student have a way to communicate with classmates?

☐ Do classmates know how to communicate with the student?

☐ Does the student greet others in a manner similar to that of classmates?

☐ Does the student socialize with classmates?

☐ Is this socialization facilitated?

☐ Do teachers and support staff give the same type of feedback (e.g., praise, discipline, attention) to the student as to classmates?

☐ If the student uses an alternate communication system, do classmates know how to use it?

☐ Do teachers know how to use the alternative communication system?

☐ Is the alternative communication system always available to the student?

Act Cool

☐ Is the student actively involved in class activities (e.g., asks/answers questions, plays a role in group activities)?

☐ Is the student encouraged to follow the same classroom and social rules as classmates (e.g., hugs only when appropriate, stays in seat during instruction)?

☐ Is the student given assistance only as necessary, and is assistance faded as soon as possible?

☐ Are classmates, not just teachers, encouraged to provide assistance to the student (e.g., transitions to other classrooms, with the classroom)?

☐ Are classmates encouraged to ask for assistance from the student?

☐ Is assistance provided for the student by the classroom teacher?

☐ Does the student use the same or similar types of materials during classroom activities as classmates (e.g., Tom Cruise notebooks, school mascot folders)?

Look Good

☐ Is the student given the opportunity to attend to her or his appearance as classmates (e.g., use locker mirror between classes)?

☐ Does the student have accessories that are similar to those of classmates (e.g., oversize tote bags, friendship bracelets, hair jewelry)?

☐ Is the student's dress age appropriate?

☐ Is clothing for activities age appropriate (e.g., napkins not bibs, "cool" paint shirts)?

☐ Are personal belongings carried discreetly?

☐ Is the student's equipment kept clean?

☐ Is the student's hair combed?

☐ Are the student's hands clean and dry?

☐ Is the student's clothing changed as necessary to maintain a neat appearance?

☐ Does the student use chewing gum, breath mints, breath spray if needed?

(From *Integration Checklist: A guide to full inclusion of students with disabilities.* [1989]. Minneapolis: University of Minnesota, Institute on Community Integration; reprinted by permission.)

Social Relationships and Peer Support, Snell & Janney, © 2000 Paul H. Brookes Publishing Co.

Directions: Think about the people you spend time with in your life. Put their names or the group's names in circles that best describe their relationship with you.

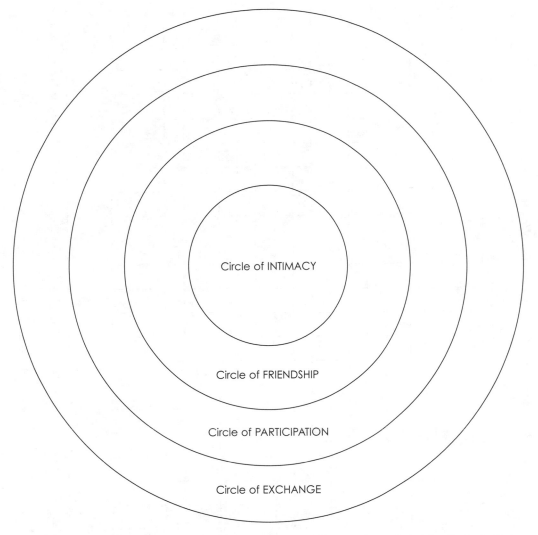

(From Falvey, M.A., Forest, M., Pearpoint, J., & Rosenberg, R.L. [1992]. *All my life's a circle: Using the tools: Circles, MAPS & PATHS.* Toronto: Inclusion Press; reprinted by permission.)

Social Relationships and Peer Support, Snell & Janney, © 2000 Paul H. Brookes Publishing Co.

Form for Determining Social Skills Target Across Whole Class

Student Names

Social Skills																					Average social-skill score
1. Listening																					
2. Greeting others																					
*3. Joining in																					
*4. Complimenting																					
*5. Expressing anger																					
6. Keeping friends																					
7. Doing quality work																					
8. Following rules																					
9. Using self-control																					
10. Offering assistance																					
*11. Disagreeing with others																					
12. Being organized																					
13. Having conversations																					
Average Student Score																					

*Low average social-skill score.
†Low average student score.

(From *Antisocial Behavior in School: Strategies and Best Practices, 1st edition*, by H.M. Walker, G. Colvin, and E. Ramsey. © 1995. Reprinted with permission of Wadsworth Publishing, a division of Thomson Learning. Fax 800 730-2215.)

Social Relationships and Peer Support, Snell & Janney, © 2000 Paul H. Brookes Publishing Co.

ABC Assessment

Student: _____ Observer: _____ Date: _____

From: _____ To: _____ Class/Routine: _____ Location: _____

Behavior(s): _____ Possible Setting Event: _____

Antecedents	Behavior	Consequences
What happened before?	**What problem behavior?**	**What happened afterward?**

Social Relationships and Peer Support, Snell & Janney, © 2000 Paul H. Brookes Publishing Co.

Cooperative Learning Lesson Plan

Content Area: _____ Date: _____

Grade: _____   Teacher: _____

Lesson Goals

1.

2.

Adaptations/Accommodations for Individual Learning Needs

Student   Adaptations/Accommodation(s)

Materials:

Group Tasks:

Checklist of required components (check when achieved):

____ Interdependent participation to achieve common goal

____ Goal achievement requires coordination among all group members

____ Goal achievement requires contributions from all members

____ Goals include both academic and social skill development

____ Individual and group accountability

(continued)

Social Relationships and Peer Support, Snell & Janney, © 2000 Paul H. Brookes Publishing Co.

(continued)

Group Members: **Role:** **Individual Goal:** **Date Attained:**

Comments:

Social Relationships and Peer Support, Snell & Janney, © 2000 Paul H. Brookes Publishing Co.

Tutoring Guide

Subject: _____ **When: from** ____ **to** _____

Skill: _____ **Where:** _____

Performance:

Materials:

Student to be Tutored/Teacher:

Tutor/Teacher:

Tutor Directions:

Reinforcement:

Correction Procedure:

Evaluation:

(Adapted from Campbell & Campbell, 1995.)

Social Relationships and Peer Support, Snell & Janney, © 2000 Paul H. Brookes Publishing Co.

The Social Relationship Worksheet

Classroom: _____ School: _____ Date: _____

Focus Student(s): _____ Team Members: _____

_____

_____

Factors influencing social participation and relationships	Actions taken by individuals in school, classroom, and home to improve social contexts and skills
Opportunity: Being physically present around typical peers on a regular basis with routine and spontaneous occasions to interact. **Issues? Yes No** **List priority issues:**	❏ Assign all students to general education classes with needed supports. ❏ Increase time in general education classes. ❏ Create during and after-school social inter-action options through friendship groups, peer support clubs, and so forth. ❏ Reduce one-to-one time with adults. ❏ Add in peers and increase small-group instruction. ❏ Integrate student seating in class, at lunch, in school activities. ❏ Identify and create integrated community options.
Atmosphere: Prevailing staff and student attitude toward human differences and talents and related values people hold about social relationships, peer support, a competitive versus a cooperative focus, student involvement in the resolution of social concerns, regard for everyone's unique talents and so forth. **Issues? Yes No** **List priority issues:**	❏ Have staff examine values toward ability, disability, and learning. ❏ Involve staff, parents, and students in creating a school mission statement. ❏ Organize ability and disability awareness activities. ❏ Organize grade-level service activities. ❏ Hold teacher in-service on cooperative learning and support for its use in classrooms. ❏ Explore alternatives to ability grouping and competitive activities. ❏ Hold staff training on social skills and relationships and their facilitation. ❏ Adopt and use a social skills curriculum. ❏ Train staff and students in collaborative teaming and problem solving. ❏ Offer student forums on social concerns such as teasing and ridicule; engage students in problem-solving school solutions. ❏ Increase the number and range of extra-curricular opportunities for students to use and develop their unique talents. *(continued)*

(Adapted from Breen, Haring, Weiner, Laitinen, & Bernstein, 1991.)

Social Relationships and Peer Support, Snell & Janney, © 2000 Paul H. Brookes Publishing Co.

(continued)

Social support and motivation: Having the needed supports and encouragement from adults and peers to interact socially and build relationships. **Issues? Yes No** **List priority issues:**	❑ Explore types of adult facilitation that can encourage appropriate social interactions (e.g., modeling, backing off). ❑ Explore types of peer support (e.g., peer groups using problem-solving & goal setting; friendship groups, natural relationships strategies). ❑ Adjust and fade adult facilitation and supports. ❑ Identify interaction problems (e.g., aggression, excess teasing, isolation); plan and use teaching and peer supports to improve student behavior. ❑ Identify and resolve barriers to social interaction (e.g., schedules, student hygiene, network values). ❑ Improve communication rates by addressing student motivation, communication system, or social skill performance. ❑ Involve students; examine the social contexts for interest, variety, age/ability match, cooperative features, participation, and needed modifications. ❑ Use or improve peer networks.
Academic achievement: Possessing needed academic skills (e.g., in such areas as reading, writing, math, science, social studies, vocational and community training) and the confidence that comes from having and using these skills. **Concerns: Yes No** **List top concerns:**	❑ Add what is needed to enable students to succeed in learning needed skills (e.g., student choice and involvement in IEP and program, incentives for learning, accommodations, environmental changes, modifications in schoolwork that are only as special as necessary). ❑ Make use of reciprocal peer tutoring and cross-age tutoring. ❑ Add cooperative learning methods to science, math, social studies, and literature lessons.
Social competence and interaction skills: Being able to initiate interactions with peers, respond to peers' initiations, and elaborate on the initiations or responses of peers at a typical rate. **Issues? Yes No**	❑ Adopt and use a social skills curriculum. ❑ Examine skills involved in social interactions and identify acquisition and performance problems or competing behaviors. ❑ Plan and use teaching methods and peer supports to improve social skill problems. ❑ Involve students in planning. *(continued)*

Social Relationships and Peer Support, Snell & Janney, © 2000 Paul H. Brookes Publishing Co.

(continued)

List priority issues:	❏ Identify student's communication ability; target needed skills (e.g., improve rate, expand vocabulary, improve consistency, augment with communication book/device for clarity). ❏ Check peers' skills using alternative modes of communicating. ❏ Determine nonstigmatizing ways to teach (format, methods) within routine contexts.
Maintenance and generalization of relationships: Keeping and extending social relationships as well as remembering and transferring known social skills across different people and school and nonschool settings. **Issues? Yes No** **List priority issues:**	❏ Contextualize any instruction. ❏ Use adult facilitation in natural contexts. ❏ Fade adult facilitation to self-monitoring. ❏ Teach students to problem-solve; encourage their independent use of these skills. ❏ Teach students to self-manage. ❏ Involve family. ❏ Include social support on IEP. ❏ Plan for transition across classrooms and schools and to community and employment settings.

Social Relationships and Peer Support, Snell & Janney, © 2000 Paul H. Brookes Publishing Co.

Issue/Action Planning Form

Student/Team/Group: _____ **Date:** _____

Team Members Present: _____

_____

Issue	Planned action	Person(s) responsible	By when?

Social Relationships and Peer Support, Snell & Janney, © 2000 Paul H. Brookes Publishing Co.

Appendix B

Resources on
Social Relationships and Peer Support

COOPERATIVE GROUPS

Cosden, M.A., & Haring, T.G. (1992). Cooperative learning in the classroom: Contingencies, group interactions, and students with special needs. *Journal of Behavioral Education, 2,* 53–71.

Dugan, E., Kamps, D., Leonard, B., Watkins, N., Rheinberger, A., & Stackhaus, J. (1995). Effects of cooperative learning groups during social studies for students with autism and fourth-grade peers. *Journal of Applied Behavior Analysis, 28,* 175–188.

Hunt, P., Staub, D., Alwell, M., & Goetz, L. (1994). Achievement by all students within the context of cooperative learning groups. *Journal of The Association for Persons with Severe Handicaps, 19,* 290–301.

Nevin, A.I., Thousand, J.S., & Villa, R.A. (1994). Creative cooperative groups lesson plans. In J.S. Thousand, R.A. Villa, & A.I. Nevin (Eds.), *Creativity and collaborative learning: A practical guide to empowering students and teachers* (pp. 131–225). Baltimore: Paul H. Brookes Publishing Co.

Putnam, J.W. (1997). *Cooperative learning in diverse classrooms.* Upper Saddle River, NJ: Merrill.

Sharan, S. (1994). *Handbook of cooperative learning methods.* Westport, CT: Greenwood Press.

Slavin, R.E. (1995). *Cooperative learning: Theory, research and practice* (2nd ed.). Needham Heights, MA: Allyn & Bacon.

INCLUSIVE SCHOOLS

Fryxell, D., & Kennedy, C.H. (1995). Placement along the continuum of services and its impact on students' social relationships. *Journal of The Association for Persons with Severe Handicaps, 20,* 259–269.

McGregor, G., & Vogelsberg, R.T. (1998). *Inclusive schooling practices: Pedagogical and research foundations.* Baltimore: Paul H. Brookes Publishing Co.

National Center for Children and Youth with Disabilities (NICHCY). (1995, July). Planning for inclusion. *NICHCY News Digest, 5*(1), 1–31.

Roach, V. (1995, May). *Winning ways: Creating inclusive schools, classrooms, and communities.* Alexandria, VA: National Association of State Boards of Education.

Schaffner, B., Buswell, B., Summerfield, A., & Kovar, G. (1988). *Discover the possibilities: A curriculum for teaching parents about integration.* Colorado Springs, CO: PEAK Parent Center.

York-Barr, J. (Series Ed.). (1996). *Creating inclusive school communities: A staff development series for general and special educators.* Baltimore: Paul H. Brookes Publishing Co.

FRIENDSHIPS

Meyer, L.H., Park, H.-S., Grenot-Scheyer, M., Schwartz, I.S., & Harry, B. (1998). *Making friends: The influences of culture and development.* Baltimore: Paul H. Brookes Publishing Co.

Rubin, Z. (1980). *Children's friendships.* Cambridge, MA: Harvard University Press.

PEER/CROSS-AGE TUTORING

Gartner, A., & Kerzner Lipsky, D. (1990). Students as instructional agents. In W. Stainback & S. Stainback (Eds.), *Support networks for inclusive schooling: Interdependent integrated education* (pp. 81–94). Baltimore: Paul H. Brookes Publishing Co..

Greenwood, C.R., Delquadri, J., & Carta, J.J. (1988). *Classwide peer tutoring.* Seattle: Educational Achievement Systems.

Kamps, D., Barbetta, P.M., Leonard, B.R., & Delquadri, J. (1994). Classwide peer tutoring: An integration strategy to improve reading skills and promote peer interactions among students with autism and general education peers. *Journal of Applied Behavior Analysis, 27,* 49–61.

Sideridis, G.D., Utley, C., Greenwood, C.R., Delquadri, J., Dawson, H., Palmer, P., & Reddy, S. (1997). Classwide peer tutoring: Effects on the spelling performance and social interactions of students with mild disabilities and their typical peers in an integrated instructional setting. *Journal of Behavioral Education, 7,* 435–462.

PEER PROBLEM-SOLVING

Giangreco, M.F., Cloninger, C.J., Dennis, R.E., & Edelman, S.W. (1994). Problem-solving methods to facilitate inclusive education. In J.S. Thousand, R.A., Villa, & A.I. Nevin (Eds.), *Creativity and collaborative learning: A practical guide to empowering students and teachers* (pp. 321–346). Baltimore: Paul H. Brookes Publishing Co.

Salisbury, C.L., & Palombaro, M.M. (Eds.). (1993). *No problem: Working things out our way.* Pittsburgh, PA: Allegheny Singer Research Institute, Child and Family Studies Program.

Salisbury, C.L., Palombaro, M.M., & Evans, I.M. (Eds.). (1993). *Collaborative problem solving: Instructor's manual.* Pittsburgh, PA: Allegheny Singer Research Institute, Child and Family Studies Program.

PEER RELATIONSHIPS THROUGH PEER SUPPORT

Garrison-Harrell, L., Kamps, D., & Kravits, T. (1997). The effects of peer networks on social-communicative behaviors for students with autism. *Focus on Autism and Other Developmental Disabilities, 12,* 241–254.

Haring, T.G., & Breen, C.G. (1992). A peer-mediated social network intervention to enhance the social integration of persons with moderate and severe disabilities. *Journal of Applied Behavior Analysis, 25,* 319–333.

Hendrickson, J.M., Shokoohi-Yekta, M., Hamre-Nietupski, S., & Gable, R.A. (1996). Middle and high school students' perceptions on being friends with peers with severe disabilities. *Exceptional Children, 63,* 19–28.

Hunt, P., Alwell, M., Farron-Davis, F., & Goetz, L. (1996). Creating socially supportive environments for fully included students who experience multiple disabilities. *Journal of The Association for Persons with Severe Handicaps, 21,* 53–71.

Janney, R.E., & Snell, M.E. (1996). How teachers use peer interactions to include students with moderate and severe disabilities in elementary general education classes. *Journal of The Association for Persons with Severe Handicaps, 21,* 72–80.

Kamps, D.M., Potucek, J., Lopez, A.G., Kravits, T., & Kemmerer, K. (1997). The use of peer networks across multiple settings to improve social interaction for students with autism. *Journal of Behavioral Education, 7,* 335–357.

Perske, R. (1988) *Circles of friends: People with disabilities and their friends enrich the lives of one another.* Nashville, TN: Abingdon Press.

Salisbury, C.L., Gallucci, C., Palombaro, M.M., & Peck, C.A. (1995). Strategies that promote social relations among elementary students with and without severe disabilities in inclusive schools. *Exceptional Children, 62,* 125–137.

Schaffner, B., & Buswell, B.E. (1992). *Connecting students: A guide to thoughtful friendship facilitation for educators and families.* Colorado Springs, CO: PEAK Parent Center, Inc.

Schneider, B.H. (1992). Didactic methods for enhancing children's peer relations: A qualitative review. *Clinical Psychology Review, 12,* 362–382.

Staub, D., Spaulding, M., Peck, C.A., Gallucci, C., & Schwatz, I.S. (1996). Using nondisabled peers to support the inclusion of students with disabilities. *Journal of The Association for Persons with Severe Handicaps, 21,* 194–205.

Utah State Office of Education. (1994). *Peer power* [videotape]. (Available from the Utah State Office of Education, Salt Lake City, UT)

PROBLEM BEHAVIOR

Carr, E.G., Levin, L., McConnachie, G., Carlson, J.I., Kemp, D.C., & Smith, C.E. (1994). *Communication-based intervention for problem behavior: A user's guide for producing positive change.* Baltimore: Paul H. Brookes Publishing Co.

Janney, R.E., & Snell, M.E. (2000). *Teachers' guides to inclusive practices: Behavioral support.* Baltimore: Paul H. Brookes Publishing Co.

Keogel, R.L., Koegel, L.K., & Parks, D.R. (1995). "Teach the individual" model of generalization: Autonomy through self-management. In R.L. Koegel & L.K. Koegel (Eds.), *Teaching children with autism: Strategies for initiating positive interactions and improving learning opportunities* (pp. 67–77). Baltimore: Paul H. Brookes Publishing Co.

O'Neill, R.E., Horner, R.H., Albin, R.W., Storey, K., & Sprague, J.R. (1990). *Functional analysis of problem behavior: A practical assessment guide.* Pacific Grove, CA: Brooks/Cole.

Walker, H.M., Colvin, G., & Ramsey, E. (1995). *Antisocial behavior in school: Strategies and best practices.* Pacific Grove, CA: Brooks/Cole.

SOCIAL COMPETENCE

Gresham, F.M. (1997). Social competence and students with behavior disorders: Where we've been, where we are, and where we should go. *Education and Treatment of Children, 20,* 233–249.

Gustafson, R.N., & Haring, N.G. (1992). Social competence issues in the integration of students with handicaps. In K.A. Haring, D.L. Lovett, & N.G. Haring (Eds.), *Integrated lifestyle services for persons with disabilities* (pp. 20–58). New York: Springer-Verlag.

SOCIAL RELATIONSHIPS

Haring, T.G. (1991). Social relationships. In L.H. Meyer, C.A. Peck, & L. Brown (Eds.), *Critical issues in the lives of people with severe disabilities* (pp. 195–217). Baltimore: Paul H. Brookes Publishing Co.

Meyer, L.H., Park, H.-S., Grenot-Scheyer, M., Schwartz, I.S., & Harry, B. (1998). *Making friends: The influences of culture and development.* Baltimore: Paul H. Brookes Publishing Co.

Odom, S.L., McConnell, S.R., McEvoy, M.A. (1992). Peer-related social competence and its significance for young children with disabilities. In S.L. Odom, S.R. McConnell, & M.A. McEvoy (Eds.), *Social competence of young children with disabilities: Issues and strategies for intervention* (pp. 3–36). Baltimore: Paul H. Brookes Publishing Co.

Pianta, R.C., & Walsh, D.J. (1996). *High-risk children in schools: Constructing sustaining relationships.* New York: Routledge.

Snell, M.E., & Vogtle, L.K. (1996). Interpersonal relationships of school-aged children and adolescents with mental retardation. In R.L. Schalock (Ed.), *Quality of life: Its application to persons with disabilities* (Vol. 2, pp. 43–61). Washington, DC: American Association on Mental Retardation.

TEACHING SOCIAL SKILLS

Brown, W.H., & Odom, S.L. (1994). Strategies and tactics for promoting generalization and maintenance of young children's social behavior. *Research in Developmental Disabilities, 15*, 99–118.

Chandler, L.K. (1992). Promoting children's social/survival skills as a strategy for transition to mainstreamed kindergarten programs. In S.L. Odom, S.R. McConnell, & M.A. McEvoy (Eds.), *Social competence of young children with disabilities* (pp. 245–276). Baltimore: Paul H. Brookes Publishing Co.

English, K., Shafer, K., Goldstein, H., & Kaczmarek, L. (1997). *Teaching buddy skills to preschoolers.* Washington DC: American Association on Mental Retardation.

Forness, S.R., & Kavale, K.A. (1996). Treating social skill deficits in children with learning disabilities: A meta-analysis of the research. *Learning Disabilities Quarterly, 19*, 2–13.

Hodgdon, L.Q. (1994). Solving social-behavioral problems through the use of visually supported communication. In K.A. Quill (Ed.), *Teaching children with autism: Strategies to enhance communication and socialization* (pp. 265–286). New York: Delmar Publishers, Inc.

McGee, G.G., Almeida, M.C., Sulzer-Azaroff, B., & Feldman, R.S. (1992). Promoting reciprocal interactions via peer incidental teaching. *Journal of Applied Behavior Analysis, 25*, 117–126.

McIntosh, R., Baughn, S., & Zaragoza, N. (1991). A review of social interventions for students with learning disabilities. *Journal of Learning Disabilities, 24*, 451–458.

Odom, S.L., McConnell, S.R., & Chandler, L.K. (1995). Acceptability and feasibility of classroom-based social interaction interventions for young children with disabilities. *Exceptional Children, 60*, 226–236.

Walker, H.M., Colvin, G., & Ramsey, E. (1995). *Antisocial behavior in school: Strategies and best practices.* Pacific Grove, CA: Brooks/Cole.

Walker, H.M., Schwarz, I.E., Nippold, M., Irwin, L.K., & Noell, J. (1994). Social skills in school-age children and youth: Issues and best practices in assessment and intervention. In M. Nippold (Ed.), *Topics in Language Disorders: Pragmatics and Social Skills in School age Children and Adolescents, 14* (3), 70–82.

TEAM PLANNING

Giangreco, M.F., Cloninger, C.J., Dennis, R.E., & Edelman, S.W. (1994). Problem-solving methods to facilitate inclusive education. In J.S. Thousand, R.A., Villa, & A.I. Nevin (Eds.), *Creativity and collaborative learning: A practical guide to empowering students and teachers* (pp. 321–346). Baltimore: Paul H. Brookes Publishing Co.

Snell, M.E., & Janney, R.E. (2000). *Teachers' guides to inclusive practices: Collaborative teaming.* Baltimore: Paul H. Brookes Publishing Co.

Index

Page numbers followed by "f" indicate figures; numbers followed by "t" indicate tables.

Teachers' Guides to Inclusive Practices!

Following the same friendly format as **Social Relationships and Peer Support,** the three other books in this series provide general and special educators with current research and field tested techniques on

Modifying Schoolwork
Full of proven strategies, this guidebook shows educators ways to adapt schoolwork to provide individualized attention to students with a broad range of learning and developmental disabilities.
Stock #3548 • $25.00 • 2000 • 112 pages • 7 x 10 • paperback • ISBN 1-55766-354-8

Collaborative Teaming
This resource explains how to create successful education teams by building teamwork skills, developing problem-solving methods, implementing action plans, teaching collaboratively, and improving communication skills.
Stock #353X • $25.00 • 2000 • 176 pages • 7 x 10 • paperback • ISBN 1-55766-353-X

Behavioral Support
Educators will discover fresh, proactive ideas for helping students develop appropriate behavior skills, form positive relationships, and communicate effectively with peers and adults.
Stock #3556 • $25.00 • 2000 • 120 pages • 7 x 10 • paperback • ISBN 1-55766-355-6

PLACE YOUR ORDER NOW! — · — · — · — · — · — · — · — · —

___ *Modifying Schoolwork* / Stock #3548 / $25.00
___ *Collaborative Teaming* / Stock #353X / $25.00
___ *Social Relationships and Peer Support* / Stock #3564 / $25.00
___ *Behavioral Support* / Stock #3556 / $25.00
___ **Buy the four-book set and SAVE!** / Stock #3572 / $90.00

___ Check enclosed (payable to Brookes Publishing Co.)
___ Purchase Order attached (bill my institution)
___ Please charge my credit card: ○ American Express   ○ MasterCard   ○ Visa

Photocopy this form and mail it to
Brookes Publishing Co., P.O. Box 10624,
Baltimore, MD 21285-0624, U.S.A.; FAX **410-337-8539;**
call **1-800-638-3775** (8 A.M. 5 P.M. ET U.S.A. and
Canada) or **410-337-9580** (worldwide);
or order online at **www.brookespublishing.com**

Credit Card #: _____ Exp. Date: _____

Signature (required with credit card use): _____

Name: _____ Daytime phone: _____

Street Address: _____ ❑ residential ❑ commercial
Complete street address required.

City/State/ZIP: _____ Country: _____

E-mail Address: _____
❑ Yes! I want to receive special web site discount offers! My e-mail address will not be shared with any other party.

Shipping rates for orders within the
continental U.S.A. sent via UPS Ground delivery*
If your product total (before tax) is:
$0.00 to $49.99, add $5.00
$50.00 to $399.99, add 10% of product total
$400.00 and over, add 8% of product total
*For other shipping options and rates,
call **1-800-638-3775** (in the U.S.A. and Canada)
and **410-337-9580** (worldwide).

Policies and prices subject to change
without notice. Prices may be higher
outside the U.S.A.

You may return books within 30 days
for a full credit of the product price.
Refunds will be issued for prepaid
orders. Items must be returned in resal-
able condition.

Product Total $_____
Shipping Rate (see chart) $_____
Maryland Orders add 5%
sales tax (to product total only) $_____

Grand Total U.S.A.$_____
Your source code is **BA 79**